IT'S A CAT'S LIFE

IT'S A CAT'S LIFE

CARTOONS BY DAVID SIPRESS

Author of *IT'S A MOM'S LIFE*

A PLUME BOOK

PLUME
Published by the Penguin Group
Penguin Books USA Inc., 375 Hudson Street, New York, New York 10014, U.S.A.
Penguin Books Ltd, 27 Wrights Lane, London W8 5TZ, England
Penguin Books Australia Ltd, Ringwood, Victoria, Australia
Penguin Books Canada Ltd, 10 Alcorn Avenue, Toronto, Ontario, Canada M4V 3B2
Penguin Books (N.Z.) Ltd, 182-190 Wairau Road, Auckland 10, New Zealand

Penguin Books Ltd, Registered Offices: Harmondsworth, Middlesex, England

First published by Plume, an imprint of New American Library,
a division of Penguin Books USA Inc.

First Printing, February, 1992
10 9 8 7 6 5 4 3 2 1

 REGISTERED TRADEMARK—MARCA REGISTRADA

LIBRARY OF CONGRESS CATALOGING-IN-PUBLICATION DATA:

Sipress, David.
    It's a cat's life / David Sipress.
        p.   cm.
    ISBN 0-452-26758-7
    1. Cats—Caricatures and cartoons.   2. American wit and humor,
Pictorial.   I. Title.
NC1429.S532A4   1992
741.5'973—dc20
                                                                91-25244
                                                                      CIP

Printed in the United States of America

BOOKS ARE AVAILABLE AT QUANTITY DISCOUNTS WHEN USED TO PROMOTE PRODUCTS OR SERVICES.
FOR INFORMATION PLEASE WRITE TO PREMIUM MARKETING DIVISION, PENGUIN BOOKS USA INC.,
375 HUDSON STREET, NEW YORK, NEW YORK 10014.

Let's discuss your options, Carlo:
You can continue to act like a
total maniac, upsetting everybody, or you can give us all
a break and have the operation, with added benefit of
freeing yourself from frustration
for the rest of your life.

SIPRESS

Before we talk about anything else, Carol, I think we need to examine your decision to come to couples' therapy in the first place.

"A large object is dropped by someone 300 miles away."

SIPRESS

How did it become "her" chair when I'm the one who bought and paid for it?

Flossie is like a member of the family

SIPRESS

We're always getting them mixed up.

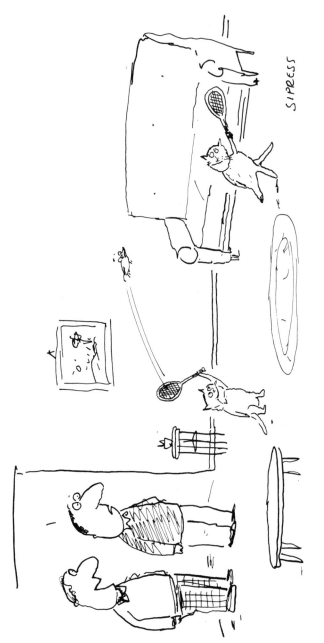

SIPRESS

They like to play with it a little before they finish it off.

What your cat's body language really means.

Rubbing of the head against your body is:
1. A display of great affection.
2. A plea for food.

Relentless purring and nuzzling is:
1. An indication your cat is happy and secure.
2. A plea for food.

Lying on back with paws raised is:
1. A seductive expression of submission.
2. A plea for food.

Licking of your face is:
1. A sign of cats love for you.
2. A plea for food.

Grabbing on and biting is:
1. A primitive expression of sexual feelings and/or hunting instincts.
2. A plea for food.

SIPRESS

All I did was mention going to the vet.

SIPRESS

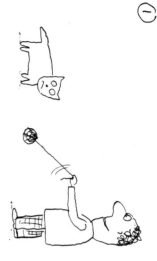

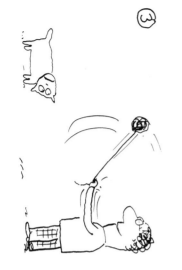

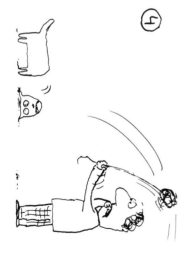

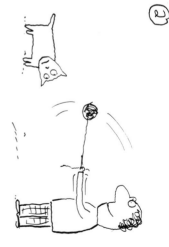

SIPRESS

"ALLERGY POWER!"

Perhaps she knows you ate those two little shrimp I was saving for her.

SIPRESS

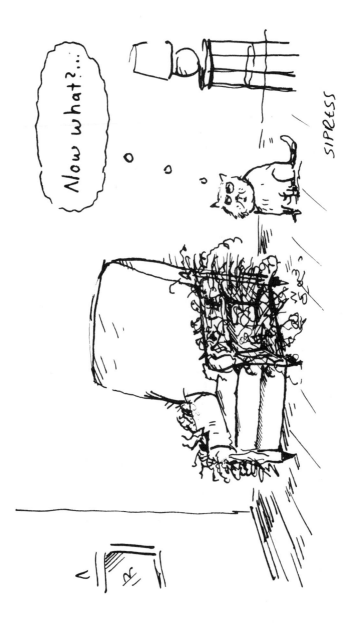

I've had to hire these two gentlemen to get you into the cat carrier.

SIPRESS

THE FOUR SEASONS.

Window open, birds fly by.

Window open, leaves fly by.

Window shut, airconditioner on.

Window shut, radiator on.

SIPRESS

Obviously they put that little vase all the way up there because it's really valuable, so let's concentrate on knocking that particular one down.

THE REALITY.

THE DREAM.

SIPRESS

She wants a guarantee you'll give her wet food for breakfast _and_ for dinner before she'll come down.

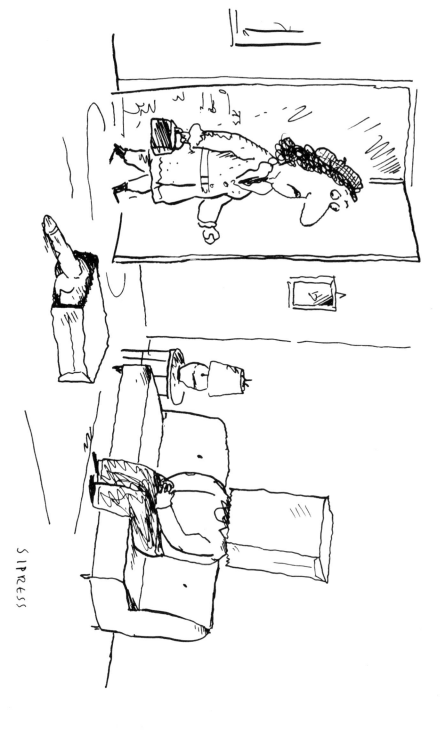

SIPRESS

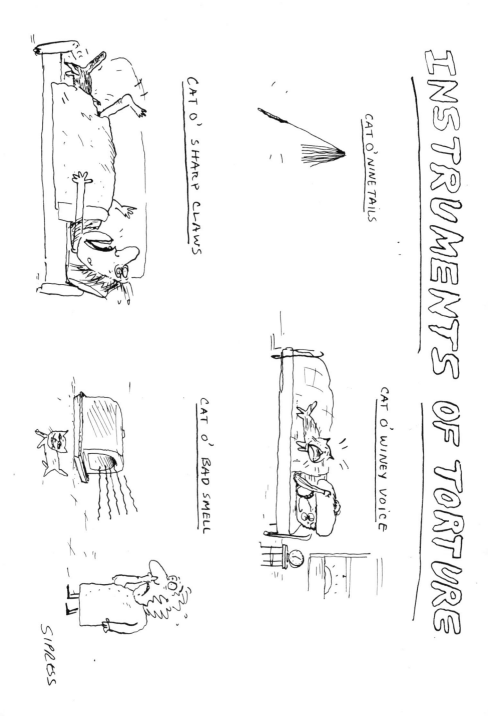

SIPRESS

The operative word here is 'empathy,' Carlo.

It must be rough being on your own. Have you ever thought about getting a person?

SIPRESS

SIPRESS

And remember, treat them with utter disdain now and then. They love that!

SIPRESS

SIPRESS

SIPRESS

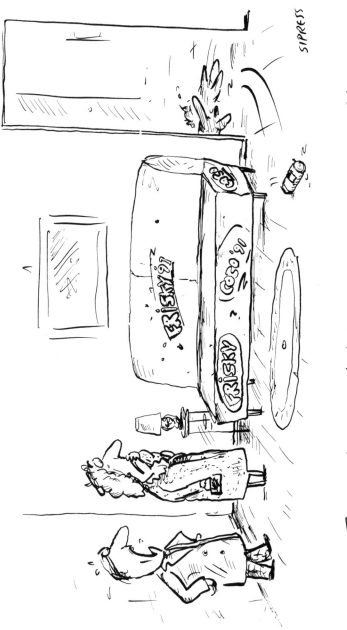

First the scratching, and now, this !!

1
WHAT CAROL HEARS
MEEEYOWW!
2
WHAT PUSSY HEARS
But soft! What light through yonder window breaks..."
SIPRESS

Kitty Group Therapy

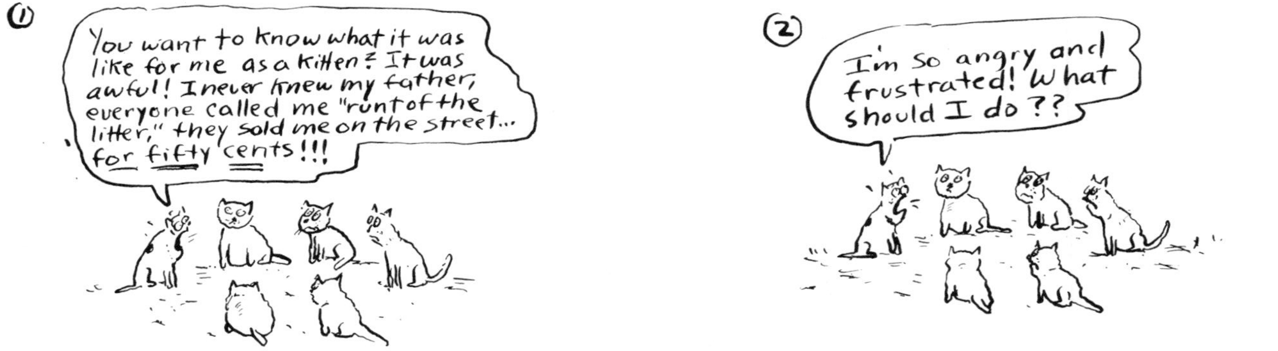

They're such clean animals!

SIPRESS

Cats are so dark and mysterious. Who knows what they're thinking about?

I just wish I knew if she's purring because I'm petting her, or if she's purring just because she's _being petted_? I mean, does it matter to her that it's me, Jane Morris who is doing the petting, or would she purr just as much no matter _who_ was petting her? Do you know what I'm saying??

SIPRESS

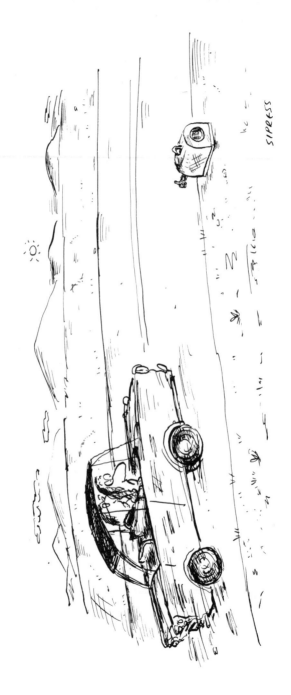

SIPRESS

The adventures of FAT CAT.
WIDE LOAD
Frisky was a lithe and svelte creature until she had her operation.
Since I got her fixed, all she thinks about is food.
I wonder what you'd think about if I got you fixed?
Yeah, she doesn't look so good.
Who cares how I look now?? It's not like I'll be dating anyone any-more!

Carol en-
couraged
Frisky to
get more
exercise:

Jump! Frisky,
Jump!

Whoops.

A strict diet was imposed:

Just ¼ of a
can per day!

I will whine, I will
scratch, I will knock
over glasses of water.
I will do everything
in my power to drive
you insane until you
forget about this
stupid diet!

Finally,
Carol had
just
to accept
Frisky for
who she
is : a
FAT
CAT.

I love you
just the
way you
are, sweet-
heart.

Yeah, yeah,
when's
dinner?

SIPRESS

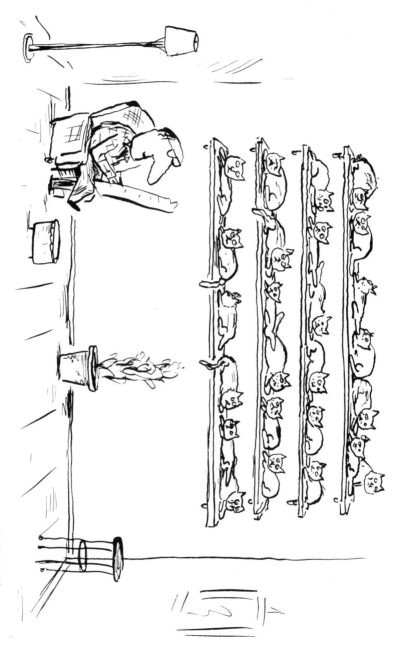

SIPRESS

Mom, Dad, this *is* Claudio!

SIPRESS

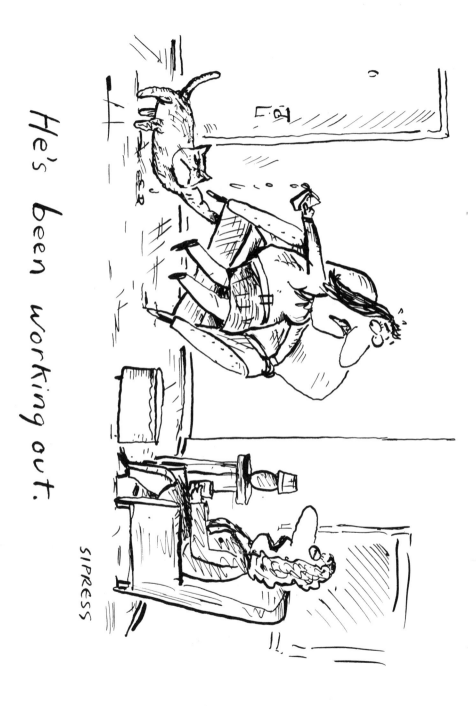

He's been working out.

SIPRESS

SIPRESS

How 'bout a nice kitten with that lemonade?

SIPRESS

That's correct, extra large with tuna and anchovies. Just leave it on the stoop and I'll pass the money under the door.

SIPRESS

SIPRESS

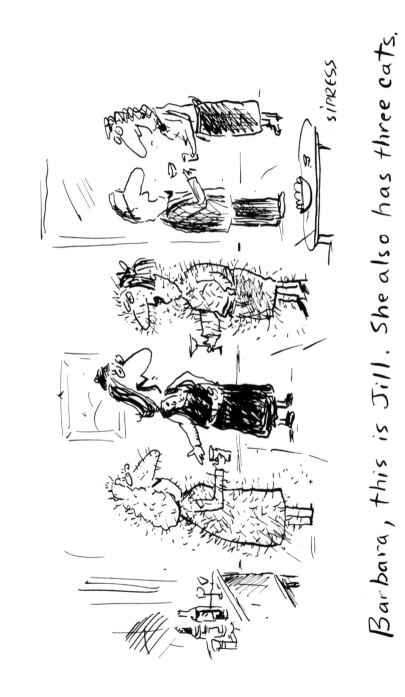

Barbara, this is Jill. She also has three cats.

SIPRESS

Do you have other interests, Marjorie?

SIPRESS

SIPRESS

We can't call Fluffy just to make sure she's O.K.,
Fluffy is a cat!

SIPRESS

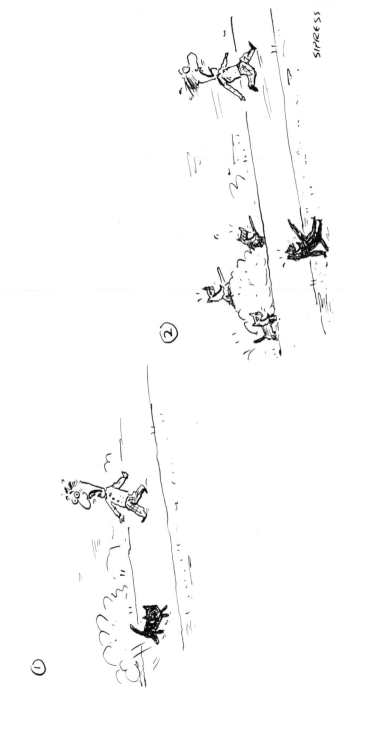

①

②

③

④

SIPRESS

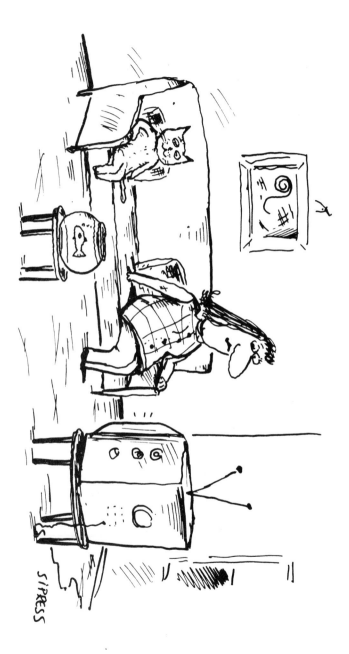

SOPHIE'S OTHER CHOICE.
Sophie was a single woman who lived by herself. She often was lonely, but she did have a companion: her be-loved Bitsy!
Sophie dated many men, but she just couldn't seem to meet Mr. Right.
I know this one is smart, Bitsy, and he's rich, and he's nice. But don't you think he's too short?
And then, just as she was about to give up hope, Sophie met Bob!!
Bob was perfect! It was love at last!

Everything was great until, one evening, Sophie got some very bad news:

Oh, did I mention that I'm horribly allergic to cats?

Sophie freaked! Just when it was all going so well, she was faced with a terrible choice:

Bitsy?

Bob

WHAT SHOULD SOPHIE DO??

The cat! The cat!! Take the cat!! Take the cat!!

The man! The man! Take the man!

As of right now, Sophie still has been unable to make a decision. But she is working hard on the issue in therapy.

Please, doctor, tell me what to do!

I'm sorry, we're out of time.

SIPRESS

I hope you've told him about the operation.

SIPRESS

PRAISE FOR

PARK AVENUE SUMMER

"A breezy, delightful novel that celebrates female friendship and ambition. With *Park Avenue Summer*, Renée Rosen brings legendary magazine editrix Helen Gurley Brown back to life and captures a beloved bygone era with acuity, wisdom and heart."

—Jamie Brenner, *USA Today* bestselling author of
The Forever Summer and *The Husband Hour*

"A smart and sexy homage to Helen Gurley Brown and her 'girls'—a generation of women taking New York City by storm and inspiring those who came after them. Filled with wit, heart and verve, Rosen's novel dazzles and empowers. Simply wonderful!"

—Chanel Cleeton, *USA Today* bestselling author of *Next Year in Havana*

"Renée Rosen's delightfully clever novel is full of heart and hope with a perfect dash of sass. Through the wonderfully depicted Helen Gurley Brown, struggling in her appointment as editor of *Cosmopolitan* magazine, and Alice Weiss, Gurley Brown's loyal secretary, Rosen delivers a cast of complex and ambitious female protagonists to truly root for. *The Devil Wears Prada* meets *Mad Men*, *Park Avenue Summer* is pure joy from cover to cover. I loved it."

—Hazel Gaynor, *New York Times* bestselling author of
The Girl Who Came Home

"*Park Avenue Summer* is both a breezy girl-takes-Manhattan fairy tale and a crackling account of how a brazen editor—against her bosses' better judgment—invented iconic *Cosmopolitan* magazine. This novel perfectly captures the zeitgeist of 1965."

—Sally Koslow, bestselling author of
Another Side of Paradise and *The Late, Lamented Molly Marx*

"Renée Rosen combines meticulous research with a true affection for her characters to bring this heady time movingly to life."

—Elizabeth Letts, #1 *New York Times* bestselling author of
The Eighty-Dollar Champion

"Renée Rosen is my go-to for whip-smart heroines who love their work. . . . *Park Avenue Summer* is a delightful summer cocktail of a read!"

—Kate Quinn, *New York Times* bestselling author of
The Alice Network

"Once again Renée Rosen works her magic, transporting us to the offices of Helen Gurley Brown's *Cosmopolitan* in 1960s New York, and the result is a delight. . . . Rosen's command of historical detail is masterful; so, too, is her ability to create fictional characters, among them her heroine Alice, who are as fully realized and compelling as the beguiling Brown herself."

—Jennifer Robson, international bestselling author of
Somewhere in France

"Part historical fiction, part coming-of-age story, this is a novel for our keeper shelves, to read and reread when we begin to doubt that there is still time to become the best version of ourselves. Lovely prose, a unique story line and a heroine who will stay with you for a long time make this a book I highly recommend."

—Karen White, *New York Times* bestselling author of
Dreams of Falling

PARK AVENUE SUMMER

RENÉE ROSEN

BERKLEY
NEW YORK

BERKLEY
An imprint of Penguin Random House LLC
1745 Broadway, New York, New York 10019

Copyright © 2019 by Renée Rosen
Readers guide copyright © 2019 by Renée Rosen
Penguin Random House supports copyright. Copyright fuels creativity, encourages
diverse voices, promotes free speech, and creates a vibrant culture. Thank you for
buying an authorized edition of this book and for complying with copyright laws by
not reproducing, scanning, or distributing any part of it in any form without
permission. You are supporting writers and allowing Penguin Random House to
continue to publish books for every reader.

BERKLEY and the BERKLEY & B colophon are registered trademarks of
Penguin Random House LLC.

Library of Congress Cataloging-in-Publication Data

Names: Rosen, Renée, author.
Title: Park Avenue Summer / Renée Rosen.
Description: First edition. | New York: Berkley, 2019.
Identifiers: LCCN 2018029367 | ISBN 9781101991145 (trade pbk.) |
ISBN 9781101991152 (ebook)
Classification: LCC PS3618.O83156 P37 2019 | DDC 813/.6—dc23
LC record available at https://lccn.loc.gov/2018029367

First Edition: April 2019

Printed in the United States of America
3 5 7 9 10 8 6 4 2

Cover art: Photo of Plaza Hotel by Granger; Frame by bomg/Shutterstock; Photo of
Woman by Keystone-France / Gamma-Keystone / Getty Images
Book design by Kristin del Rosario
Interior art: frame corner element by bomg / Shutterstock.com

To my girls:
Sara Gruen, Brenda Klem,
Mindy Mailman and Pam Rosen.
I love you all!

PROLOGUE

○——————○

2012

The breeze blows through the open windows, curtains swaying slow and lazy. It's August and already balmy first thing in the morning. As I sit at the kitchen table, a band of sunlight streaks across the newspaper and warms the backs of my hands even as my coffee turns cold. Suddenly it's too much to cross the room for a fresh cup because all I can do is stare at the headline while something catches again and again inside my chest. There it is in the *New York Times*: *Helen Gurley Brown, Cosmopolitan's Iconic Editor, Dies at 90.*

The obituary tries to paint her portrait, a tribute to the woman who gave single girls everywhere a license to join the sexual revolution, who resurrected a dying magazine and introduced the world to a new sensation, the *Cosmo* Girl. A few paragraphs down they mention other feminists like Betty Friedan and Gloria Steinem and get into Helen Gurley Brown's controversial role in the women's movement. It's all there, and this being the *Times*, I'm sure Margalit Fox got the facts right, but still, there's more to Helen's story. More than anyone but a select few will ever know.

I glance again at the obituary and one line jumps out at me: "Helen

Gurley Brown was 90, though parts of her were considerably younger." I can't help but smile at that as I run my fingers over the accompanying photograph. It's a black-and-white shot, taken in her office. The year was 1965, shortly after she started at *Cosmopolitan*. Helen, in a leopard print dress, is seated at her desk, pencil in hand, papers spread out before her. Standing to the side, bleeding off the page, I see a sliver of a young woman. Half of her has been cropped out of the image, left on the editing room floor. Still, I recognize the geometric pattern of her dress and a hint of her face: the eye, the nose and the corner of her mouth, the subtle wisps of hair brushing her collar. I know the dress well and the woman even better.

She is me, some forty-seven years ago.

CHAPTER ONE

○———○

I had creased and folded my subway map so many times over the past few days that it was on the verge of tearing in two. Somehow I had boarded the wrong train. Again. I'd ended up at Times Square instead of 57th Street. *Now what?*

I exited the train, took a few tentative steps and froze on the platform, people weaving around me, bumping up against my portfolio, jostling the photographs inside. A young woman in a pink and gold sari called to a little boy running on ahead of her, past a man playing bongos. The Times Square station was a maze of tiled corridors and tunnels, stairwells that led from one frenzied level to another. A blur of signs pointed me in all directions: **Uptown, Downtown, The Bronx, Brooklyn, 8th Avenue, 40th Street** . . .

I didn't have time to risk getting on the wrong train, so I folded my tattered map, tucked it inside my pocketbook and made my way to the 42nd Street exit where I was met with a blast of horns, a gust of exhaust. I stood at the curb feeling as bewildered as I'd been inside the station, and yet, it was exhilarating. I'd arrived in New York about a week ago, and like the city, I was alive, filled with possibility and adventure. Anything could happen now. My life was about to begin.

I'd never hailed a taxicab before and was momentarily paralyzed. All I could do was observe other people's techniques, like the businessman who raised his hand ever so slightly, accomplishing the task with just two fingers. Another man with bags under his eyes, big and full as cheeks, yelled out a commanding "Taxi," making a driver swerve across two lanes before bringing his cab to a screeching halt. Job done. The woman beside me waved her hand like a magic wand and a taxicab appeared. I mimicked her approach, my fingers flapping amateurishly. Two taxicabs barreled past me as if I wasn't there before one pulled up alongside me. I gave the driver the address while he laid on his horn, inching forward, leaving barely a whisper of air between his bumper and the taxicab in front of us. We were one in a chain of yellow cabs going nowhere fast.

I checked the clock on the dashboard. "I have an appointment in twenty minutes," I said to the driver through the cloudy Plexiglas window separating us. "Do you think we can make it in time?"

He shot me an impatient look through his rearview mirror. "You coulda walked it, lady," he said in a thick Brooklyn accent.

I sat back, trying to relax, clutching my portfolio: a homemade case that protected my photographs, mounted to sheets of construction paper and held between two cardboard covers. I used a black ribbon to tie it shut.

It was a bright, unseasonably warm day, and the driver had all the windows rolled down. I drew a deep breath, unable to place the scent until I realized that it was everything I was *not* smelling: the absence of grass, trees and those easy, open-space breezes. The flow of air, obstructed by the buildings, seemed stagnant, almost stale, yet the city was in constant motion, all vigor and energy.

At the corner of 47th and Eighth Avenue, I spotted a man and a woman waiting for the light. They reminded me of couples I'd seen in the movies. He was in a dark suit, his fedora worn with a Sinatra tilt. She was impeccably dressed in a skirt and matching jacket, belted at the waist. He pulled a cigarette from his breast pocket, offering her one before he suavely lit them both. As puffs of smoke gathered above their heads, the streetlight changed and off they went. I watched until they disappeared into the throng of New Yorkers, wishing I had my camera with me. You didn't see people like that back in Ohio.

My cab cleared the intersection and I grew giddy thinking that soon I'd be taking my place among the locals, walking with a purpose, each step bringing me closer to the very things I'd come here for. And with that, I couldn't help but think about my mother. She was supposed to have been by my side when I came to New York, and I wasn't one of those people comforted by the ethereal; *she's still with you, watching over you.*

As we continued on, I craned my neck, not wanting to miss a thing. There was more to see here in just two blocks than in all of Youngstown. I leaned forward to get a better look at the giant Camel billboard of a man smoking a cigarette, blowing actual smoke rings. All of Times Square was flashing with Canadian Club, Coca-Cola, Chevrolet and a sign for Admiral Television Appliances. Even in the middle of the day, the theater marquees were lit and winking, some reputable while others advertised peep shows starring *raw naked women.* Again, I itched for my camera. Even when I didn't have it with me, I was still taking pictures in my head.

I had moved to New York to become a photographer despite my father and everyone else, including the editor at the *Youngstown Vindicator,* telling me a woman couldn't do that kind of work. Taking personal snapshots like my mother did was one thing, but professional photographs for newspapers and magazines? Never. Maybe not in a small town, but surely New York City would be different. And just knowing they said I couldn't do it made me all the more determined to prove them wrong. Stubbornness, something I'd inherited from my mother.

My father and Faye, his new wife, said they weren't financing my *pipe dream*, so after graduating from secretarial school and working as a typist in a steel foundry for three months, I'd saved $375. I knew that wouldn't go very far, seeing as the taxicab meter had already hit 90 cents. My most immediate need was a job—*any job*. I'd already interviewed with an accounting firm, followed by a scaffolding manufacturer and an insurance agency. They were jobs I didn't want and thankfully didn't get.

That was why I finally pulled out the number I'd been carrying since I'd arrived but had been too shy or proud to use. I called Elaine Sloan. Elaine and my mother had been roommates in New York, living at the Barbizon Hotel, both of them aspiring models. My mother, beautiful as she was, had fallen short of the dream, becoming a Midwestern housewife. Elaine ended up as a book editor at Bernard Geis Associates. I'd met Elaine once, at my mother's funeral, and had exchanged a few cards and letters with her since. She said to contact her if ever I needed anything. I thought maybe she could help me land a photography job, or at the very least, something in publishing.

When I arrived at Bernard Geis Associates on East 56th Street, I found myself on the forty-second floor, in a colorful lobby filled with pop art and Eero Aarnio pod chairs suitable for a moon landing. In the middle of it all was a pole you'd expect to see in a fire station. It extended all the way through a circular cutout in the ceiling of the floor above. While I gave the receptionist my name, a woman slid down that pole, her skirt bunched up, revealing her blue garter, before landing with a respectable dismount.

Moments later Elaine Sloan made a more dignified entrance through a side door. The first thing I—or probably anyone—noticed about Elaine was her hair. She was prematurely gray, each strand a luminous shade of silvery white that caught the light and accentuated her blue eyes. Eyes that looked as though they'd seen more than most women her age. I told myself she resembled my mother, though they looked nothing alike. My mind was playing tricks on me and I knew why. Yes, I was a grown woman of twenty-one, but I still wanted my mother. Elaine Sloan—her most devoted and dearest friend—was the closest I could get to her now.

She greeted me with a warm smile and showed me into her office, which had a spectacular view of the Manhattan skyline. "Tell me how I can help you," she asked, gesturing for me to sit in the chair opposite her desk.

After sharing tidbits of my disheartening job search, I set my portfolio on her desk. "But what I'm really looking for is something in photography."

"I see." She leaned forward, reaching for my case. "May I?"

"Please . . ." I untied the ribbon for her and sat silently while she leafed through my photographs, pausing here and there but saying nothing. She closed the cover before she reached the end.

It was a blow, but I would not be ungrateful and let my disappointment show.

She smiled and sat back, inching my portfolio toward me with her fingertips. "You have an eye," she said, just to be kind.

"Thank you." I tied my portfolio shut and set it in my lap, thinking how much more competitive everything was here. Back home people appreciated my photographs, selecting them for the school newspaper and yearbook. But in New York my pictures were barely enough to hold anyone's attention.

"Well, it's not photography," she said, "but I do have something in mind." Elaine pressed the intercom on her desk and said, "Get David Brown on the line for me, will you?" She released the talk button and reached behind her for a book on her credenza. "Are you familiar with this?" She held up a copy of *Sex and the Single Girl*.

That blue cover instantly took me back to my senior year of high school, to a slumber party in Esther Feinberg's basement. Four of us had stayed up half the night, taking turns reading aloud from Helen Gurley Brown's *Sex and the Single Girl*. I remembered certain passages made us squeal and roll onto our sides, pillows pressed to our faces to smother our giggles and shock. At the time, I didn't think the book applied to me because I had Michael Segal. My future was set. At least it was until I gave him back his grandmother's ring after he said he wasn't ready to marry me. The next day I went out and bought my own copy of *Sex and the Single Girl* and read it cover to cover. More than once.

A moment later the secretary's voice squawked back on the intercom. "I have Mr. Brown on line one for you."

"The best way to get to Helen is through her husband," Elaine said as she picked up the phone and swiveled around in her chair, facing the window. "Hello, David." She leaned back and laughed at something he said. I watched her reflection in the glass as she propped her feet on the windowsill and crossed her ankles. She was wearing a pair of Gucci loafers. I recognized the interlocked gold G's on top. "Is Helen still looking for a secretary?" she asked. "Oh, good. I have someone I think she should meet." She looked back at me and winked. "Her name's Alice Weiss. Shall I send her over? Okay, let me know. Thank you, David."

She hung up, dropped her feet to the ground and swiveled back around, facing me with a smile. "I know it's a secretarial position. It's not photography, but you have an interview with her tomorrow."

"With who? Helen Gurley Brown?" I was in disbelief. Helen Gurley Brown was a celebrity. A famous author who'd been a regular on radio and television shows even though hosts like Merv Griffin and Jack Paar couldn't say the title of her book on the air.

"David's going to call back with the time. I'll let you know as soon as I hear from him. Meanwhile . . ." She scribbled an address down on a monogrammed notepad, tore the page free and slid it across the desk to me.

"Is she writing another book?"

"Actually, no. The Hearst Corporation just hired her to be the new editor in chief at *Cosmopolitan* magazine." Elaine shook her head, bewildered. "Last I heard, Hearst was folding *Cosmopolitan*. Then all of a sudden, they bring in Helen. Must be some sort of a last-ditch effort to save the magazine. Hearst isn't in the habit of hiring women for positions like that, and frankly, we're all scratching our heads, wondering how she landed the job. I'm sure David had something to do with it, seeing as Helen's never edited a magazine before. My lord, she's never even worked at a magazine." Elaine laughed at the absurdity of it all. "But I *have* worked with Helen. I was one of her editors for this." She tapped *Sex and the Single Girl* resting on her desk. "And while I don't agree with everything she says in here, I do think she's smart. And God knows she's got chutzpah."

The following morning, I arrived at 224 West 57th. I was in the lobby, waiting for the elevator, when two girls walked up beside me. They were about my age and the one, with white-blond hair teased and backcombed into a magnificent bouffant, pressed the call button a second time, as if that would make it come faster. The Bouffant was wearing a chartreuse triangle shift dress. The other girl, a brunette with a pixie and chandelier earrings that touched her shoulders, wore a short red and white checkered skirt with knee-high boots. Compared to them, I had a big *Ohio* stamped on my forehead, even in my best houndstooth sheath dress.

The elevator landed with a ding, and after the doors opened, in we went. The two girls chattered on the way up, oblivious when I exited behind them on the fourth floor and followed them into *Cosmopolitan*'s lobby. Before they disappeared down a hallway, the Pixie noticed me, glancing back with a neutral expression before she turned again, leaving me behind. There was no one at the receptionist's desk, so I waited.

The office was not what I'd been expecting. It suffered from neglect. The carpet was worn to its frayed backing. The seat cushions of the leather chairs were cracked, veins of white stuffing poking through. Even the dust clinging to the leaves on the plastic plants in the entranceway said to all who passed through those doors that the reading public had lost faith in the old gal.

Still no sign of the receptionist. To pass the time, I studied the covers from past issues strewn across the wall, hanging in cockeyed frames. I was surprised by what I saw. The *Cosmopolitan* magazine I knew was filled with casserole recipes and housekeeping tips, but the lobby walls told a different story. There was a plaque with a list of authors who'd written for the magazine going as far back as the 1800s, including Mark Twain, Edith Wharton, Kipling and others. Among the covers hanging up was the April 1939 issue featuring Somerset Maugham's *The Facts of Life*. Pearl S. Buck had a novella published in March 1935. O. Henry's *The Gift of the Magi* was also published by *Cosmopolitan*.

I was studying a 1906 cover with an Indian chief on horseback when a woman appeared from around the corner with a banker's box hoisted up on one hip, a Rolodex and a picture frame jutting out the top. Her pocketbook was hanging off her wrist.

"Excuse me," I said. "I'm looking for Mrs. Brown. I have an appointment with her."

"Straight back. Corner office." She gestured with her chin as she backed up, pushing the lobby door open with her behind.

I ventured down a long hallway that opened into a larger space with several desks near the private offices. As I approached the new editor in chief's office, I noticed the desk just outside was vacant, not a pencil or paperclip resting on top. The ashtray was spotless and the typewriter sat hooded beneath its plastic cover.

I inched closer still. The door was open and there I got my first glimpse of Helen Gurley Brown. She was perched on the edge of a mahogany desk that looked too big for her slight frame. She was on the telephone; one of her gold clip earrings—which I would later learn was a David Webb worth more than $1,000—was lying in the ashtray, where I presumed it had landed after she tossed it off to answer the phone. She was wearing a pink mullet chiffon dress with a scooped neckline. I thought she was far more attractive in person than in the photo on her book jacket. She'd been so self-deprecating in *Sex and the Single Girl*, referring to herself as a mouseburger, but the woman in front of me was no frumpy girl from the Ozarks. A rich heap of dark brown hair accentuated her dainty features, including the nose, which, according to her book, was the work of a good plastic surgeon. Her makeup, albeit heavy and dramatic, was flawless. I'd never seen anyone with eyebrows so perfectly arched, and even if they were drawn on, they called attention to her eyes, dark and mysterious and a little sad. A bouquet of red roses was stationed at her side, their soft scent mixing with her perfume.

I imagined the decor, the orange and brown striped drapes, the heavy wooden chairs, the credenza and shag carpeting, reflected her predecessor's tastes. Aside from the bulky furniture, the room was empty, right down to the bulletin board with its rivet-headed thumbtacks waiting once again to be put to use.

Mrs. Brown was still on the telephone, twisting the cord about her slender wrist. "But, David, the woman never even gave me a chance. I've only been here two days—how horrible of a boss can I be? I offered to take her to lunch my first day—and at Delmonico's like you suggested—but she said she was too busy. Apparently, she was too busy looking for another job."

Not wanting to eavesdrop, I backed away from her door but still I heard tidbits. Though she spoke softly, Helen Gurley Brown's voice carried and it was distinctive. No one sounded like her; velvety and animated, flirty and breathy like Marilyn Monroe but with a touch of lockjaw. She barely opened her mouth, and yet when she spoke, everyone heard her. Everywhere. Across the country and around the world.

While still on the phone, she walked herself around the desk and I saw that she had a faint run in her stockings, right along the back of her calf. She dropped down into her chair, leaning in on her elbows as if some tremendous burden were bearing down on her. With her back teeth clenched, she said. "What am I going to do without a managing editor, David? Who's going to fill that position? I've already lost two other editors. They're dropping like flies around here."

After she'd finished her call, she reached for her appointment book, unaware of my presence, as she drummed a pencil on the desk in time with her foot tapping the plastic floor mat. When I knocked on the doorjamb, she looked up startled and I could see that she was crying.

With an open hand splayed across her chest, the first thing she said was, "Oh dear, are you going to quit, too?"

I'd mentally rehearsed my opening lines, beginning with, *It's such an honor to meet you*, but her tears had thrown me off script.

"Actually, I'm here to interview for a job. To be your secretary. Elaine Sloan sent me. I'm Alice. Alice Weiss."

"Oh, thank God." She blinked, letting another tear escape as she rose from her desk and scampered to my side. "Alice Weiss, am I ever glad to see you." She couldn't have weighed more than a hundred pounds, but I felt the strength of a woman twice her size when she grabbed hold of my arm and pulled me into her office. Still holding tight, she looked at me with her big brown eyes. "My goodness, you're so . . . *young*. I was expecting someone older." She sounded congested from crying.

I reached into my pocketbook and handed her a tissue along with my résumé.

She thanked me, dabbed her eyes and invited me to have a seat, composing herself on the spot. "Why, you're a darling girl," she said, perking up. "Beautiful hair. Mine is so thin, you can see my scalp in places. This is a wig, you know." She tugged on a tress, shifting her mane, as if offering proof.

I didn't know what to say after that, so I sat quietly, waiting while she glanced at my credentials, making comments here and there: "Ohio, huh? I'm from Arkansas originally."

"I know. I read your book."

She smiled, her eyes still on the résumé. "I see you're a fast typist. Seventy-five words a minute. That's good. You know, I used to be a secretary, too. Oh, I was terrible," she said with an impish chuckle as she plucked her earring from the ashtray, blew the ashes away and clipped it back on her lobe. "I couldn't hold down a job for the life of me. I had seventeen secretarial positions over five years. Seventeen—can you imagine!"

She turned my résumé over, as if expecting more on the other side. "Oh dear." She looked up and frowned. "Why, you haven't got any magazine experience at all, have you?" She tilted her head and turned out her bottom lip: *Poor little lamb.*

"But I'm smart," I told her. "And I'm a hard worker."

"Oh, I'm sure you are, dear." She pressed her palms together as if in prayer, her many bracelets ringing the communion bell. "But you see, when Elaine told David about you, we were expecting someone with more credentials. I need a secretary who *knows* this business. I'm sorry you came all this way for nothing." She stood up and extended her hand. "Lovely to meet you, though."

We shook hands and I thanked her, but as I was about to leave, something stopped me. This was a once-in-a-lifetime chance to be face-to-face with Helen Gurley Brown. My job interview was over and I had nothing to lose. "Mrs. Brown?"

She looked up from her desk. "Yes?"

"In your book you encouraged single girls to find a job that could be—and I might be paraphrasing here, but—'your love, your happy pill, your means of finding out who you are and what you can do.'"

I watched her lips curve upward. "I'd say that's pretty much a direct quote."

"I guess I was hoping that working for you could become my happy pill."

She set her pencil down, her eyes on me, holding my gaze. I sensed that she saw into me, knew my secrets, my fears. She was the gypsy woman, and I, her crystal ball. After a moment I saw the shift in her posture, the way her shoulders went slack and her face softened. "Come back in here, pussycat. Have a seat."

I did as she said, my knees pressed together, my hands clutching my pocketbook.

"There's more to this job than typing and answering the phones. I'll need someone who can lock arms with me. You need to know how to deal with the public. And sometimes that means keeping them at bay and saying 'bye-bye.'" She gestured with a flirty open-and-close hand gesture. "I'll need help with everything." She began counting off her fingers. "There's my schedule, travel arrangements, meetings where I'll need you to sit in and take notes. There's my fan mail, my personal affairs, too. I need someone who can plan a gala at the drop of a hat."

I nodded, letting her know she hadn't scared me off, though in truth it sounded overwhelming.

"I've inherited a real muck of a mess here," she went on. "It's going to take a lot of hard work and long hours to turn this ship around. They're expecting me to transform *Cosmopolitan* and I have a feeling the Hearst Corporation isn't going to be very happy with what I'm planning to do. It's going to be a battle every step of the way. Are you up for this sort of challenge?"

"I am," I said, not even sure why I was petitioning so hard for this job. Yes, I needed the money, which we hadn't even discussed yet. And yes, I'd been on some dreadful interviews, but more than anything, I was caught up in the excitement—a woman in the corner office, calling the shots. I decided in that moment that if given the chance, I would do whatever I could to help her. I would see to it that Helen Gurley Brown never wanted for anything, not a cup of coffee, a sharp pencil or an impossible-to-get dinner reservation. I would be there to serve her.

"Well," she said, "you do realize that we'd be learning this business together."

"Does this mean I have the job?"

A staticky voice broke in over the intercom. "Mrs. Brown? I have Mr. Deems on the phone for you."

Helen raised a finger, putting my fate on hold. Her brow furrowed, showing her age for the first time, and I could see that she really was every bit of forty-three. Just as she had softened for me moments before, now I saw the shoulders go back, the chin rise up as she removed her earring again, jostling it in her hand like dice.

"Why, hello, Dick," she said, forcing a smile in her voice. "Yes, I know Betty quit. She gave me her letter of resignation this morning." She propped the phone between her ear and shoulder, dropped the earring and reached for a pencil, gripping either end with both hands. "Oh, I know. The timing just couldn't be worse."

I could hear Deems's muffled voice over the phone and figured he must have been with Hearst. She shifted in her chair, clutching the pencil so tightly, the color was draining from her fingertips.

"Now, Dick," she cooed, "no point in getting all worked up. We have time. The April issue just hit the stands and . . ." She drew a deep breath, the pencil beginning to bow, her voice perfectly serene. "We're going to be fine, Dick. Really. As a matter of fact, I already have someone in mind for the new managing editor." I heard him speaking again, a little louder this time. "Well," she laughed softly, brightly, "of course I'm going to review the flatplan today." She snapped the pencil in two. "That's at the top of my list."

Mrs. Brown picked up another pencil. I thought she was going to break that one, too, but instead she jotted something down on a pad of paper and turned it my way: *Can you start tomorrow?*

As soon as she hung up with Dick Deems, she turned to me, her hand still on the receiver. "Do you have any idea what a flatplan is?"

CHAPTER TWO

◦———————◦

No one would ever have accused me of leading a charmed life, but just then it seemed like I did. One week in New York City and already I had a job, working for Helen Gurley Brown no less, with a starting salary of $55 a week. Plus, I had a place to live.

I walked down the street, my pocketbook swinging at my side while I jangled the key to my new apartment, ridiculously proud that I'd made it back to 75th and Second Avenue without getting lost. I took it as a small victory after days of being disoriented, scrambling from one wrong train to another, bumbling from the East Side to the West. Sometimes it seemed like the longer I was here, the bigger the city was becoming.

Ah, but I'd made it back to my apartment. There was a butcher shop on the ground floor of my four-story walk-up. Signs in the window advertised **Pork Chops 55¢, Ground Chuck 39¢, Roast Beef 65¢**. A black cast-iron fire escape zigzagged down the brick facade.

I had found the apartment listed on a bulletin board in a coffee shop the second day I arrived. **Semi-furnished. $110 a month.** The landlord explained that Rhonda, the girl who'd been living there, had left town unexpectedly, leaving behind her bed and other furniture along with some clothes. I found a few dresses, some shoes and a pair of denim jeans in the closet. There were sweaters and other items stuffed inside one of the drawers of her abandoned bureau.

When I reached the second floor, I bumped into my neighbor across the way in 2R. Trudy Lewis was a button of a girl, petite with strawberry blond hair and a face full of freckles. She even had them on her pale lips.

"How's the job hunting going?" she asked, keying into her apartment.

When I said I'd just landed a job as Helen Gurley Brown's secretary, Trudy's hand paused on the doorknob. "This is fantastic. We have to celebrate. Stay right there. Don't you move."

I stood in the hallway while she darted through her door and came back out with a bottle of Great Western Champagne. "I've been saving this for a special occasion," she said as we entered my apartment.

My tiny unit, 2F, was what they called an efficiency, though there was nothing efficient about it. The front door was warped, the windows didn't seal and the floor was slanted, which explained why random items sometimes rolled off the table and nightstand. The tiles in the bathroom were loose and a few of them did a swan dive into the tub while I was bathing that morning.

"Now tell me everything," she said as her thumb sent the cork soaring across the room. "What's she like? Is she beautiful? What was she wearing? How tall is she?"

I fielded Trudy's questions as she filled our glasses and toasted to my new job. I was grateful for her enthusiasm. Were it not for Trudy, who had knocked on my door and introduced herself the day I moved in, I would have been completely alone in the city. Like me, Trudy was from the Midwest, a suburb outside of St. Louis, but unlike me, she seemed so settled, like an oak tree rooted in New York for a hundred years. She made me envious. I craved a routine, some stability. I was impatient, wanting to call Manhattan home already.

"Are there a lot of handsome men in the office?" she asked as she slumped down beside me on the lumpy sofa, sipping her champagne.

"I didn't see too many eligible men, but the women were dressed to the nines. They looked like they should be working for *Vogue* or *Mademoiselle*." I paused while Trudy refilled our glasses. "I'm going to need a whole new wardrobe to work there." I took a sip, the bubbles fizzing and washing over my tongue. "I already wore my best dress on the interview," I said, gesturing to my sheath. "I have no idea what to wear tomorrow."

"Oh, we can fix that," said Trudy, springing off the sofa, going to the closet and screeching hangers back and forth over the metal bar. "Ah, what about this?" She pirouetted, holding a blue shift with a white bow beneath her chin.

"That must have been Rhonda's dress," I said.

"Well, it's yours now."

I went into the bathroom and slipped it on. "What do you think?" I opened the door and stood with my arms to my sides.

"It's a little long," she said, reaching for the hem. "But we can tack it up with tape and safety pins. Oh, and I have a pocket-book you can borrow. It'd be perfect with that. What size shoes do you wear?" she asked, reaching for a box in the back of the closet.

"Seven. Sometimes, seven and a half."

"Bingo!" She handed me a pair of stylish T-straps. "Try these on."

I stepped into Rhonda's three-inch heels using my index finger as a shoehorn.

When Trudy went to refill my glass for the third time, I placed my hand over the rim. "I better not."

"Yeah, I guess you're right. We can't have you hungover on your first day, now can we? Oh well," she said, pouring her glass to the top, "more for me."

By the time Trudy left, it was going on ten o'clock, and there I was, alone in a strange place, in a city I'd been hearing about and dreaming of all my life. Nothing, though, was quite as glamorous as I'd envisioned it would be. I wasn't living in a beautiful apartment on Park Avenue with a terrace overlooking the city. And no, I hadn't landed a high-paying photography job. But despite the trade-offs, here I was in New York, carving out a new life. The allure and sophistication of the city had been instilled in me from as far back as I could remember, making my unrefined Ohio roots a source of inferiority, a deficiency to be overcome. It was time to abandon my small-town ways and wide-eyed wonder, only I found that shedding my old self and leaving her behind made me inexplicably sad. I felt hollow and surprisingly sentimental.

I thought about calling my father but realized he'd probably be asleep, and I didn't want his wife answering the phone. I knew my father thought she was the reason I left home, but Faye had nothing to do with it. Michael definitely played a role in my decision, but really, I left because of my mother.

Eight years earlier, right before she died, my mother had convinced my father that it was time to start over in New York. My father had been offered a job that would have doubled his salary at the steel foundry. A lease had been signed for a prewar Classic Five on the Upper West Side and a **For Sale** sign was nailed to a stake in our front yard. It was June. School was out for the summer and I was planning to attend junior high in Manhattan that fall. I'd been sitting on the front porch, braiding a friendship bracelet made of yarn, a good-bye present for my best friend, Esther, when the telephone rang. That was the call that changed everything. Forever.

There'd been an accident. A car ran a red light at McGuffey and Jacobs Road. My mother's DeSoto was overturned, totaled. My father needed to identify the body.

The move to New York, which had been my mother's dream, ended there. The Classic Five was sublet to another family, the house in Youngstown was taken off the market, my father's letter reneging on the job offer was in the mail and Esther's friendship bracelet, left on the front porch, had either been carried off by the wind or absentmindedly knocked into the flower bed, never to be seen again.

My father hadn't wanted to live in New York in the first place, but I had clung to my mother's dream. I always knew that some-day I would end up in Manhattan. It was innate, like knowing you're left-handed. I was infatuated with the city, and like most infatuations, my affection was largely the product of my imagina-tion. Really, the only things I knew about New York before I got here had come from books, movies and the endless stories my mother told me. I remembered her perched on the side of my bed, or standing behind me at the mirror brushing my hair, telling me about Coney Island and how she'd fallen in love with my father there. She talked about the luxurious apartments and how her neighbor at the Barbizon was a Katie Gibbs girl who'd grown up on Park Avenue and 59th Street. My mother had been invited to the girl's home, mesmerized by everything from the white-gloved doorman who called her *Miss*, to the gilt-trimmed elevator and the marbled hallways. She vowed that one day she'd live on Park Avenue, too. She told me about skyscrapers that reached the clouds, carriage rides through the park, museums and stores filled with everything you could ever imagine. The best food, the best shows, the best of everything. She'd been born and raised just outside of New York City, in Stamford, Connecticut, but she'd gone into Manhattan every chance she had. When she turned nineteen, she moved to the city, much to her parents' dismay. My mother adored New York and had been trying to make her way back there up until her dying day.

I moved to New York for her. And for me. If I'd stayed in Youngstown, what would have become of me? Esther and I had drifted apart and I realized too late that I was to blame for that. I didn't call as much, didn't make plans with her like I used to, because Michael, my hope, my hero, had become the center of everything. And then he was gone. None of the other Jewish boys in town even came close to him. I didn't want to settle. Not in love. Not in anything.

It was getting late and I had a big day tomorrow, but I knew I wouldn't be able to sleep. I still hadn't gotten around to buying drapes or shades for the windows so the streetlights poured in through the panes, along with the hum of traffic and occasional sirens going by on Second Avenue.

I decided to make myself a cup of tea in the tiny kitchenette. My mother always made tea whenever she couldn't sleep. It seemed like the thing to do. I filled the kettle from the tap and struck a match, lighting the gas burner. I supposed I knew that being in New York, in my mother's city, would have accentuated my missing her, but I hadn't anticipated just how much it would affect me. I was filled with nostalgia and longing for her that night.

Aside from my portfolio, I'd brought only two items of any value with me from home. One was my camera, which had belonged to my mother, a Leica IIIc MOOLY. It was resting on top of the bookcase in a brown leather case, worn and cracked along the edges, the Leica name embossed where it protruded to holster the lens. I picked up the camera, cradling it in my lap for a moment before I set it back on the bookcase and reached for the second valuable I'd brought from home, my tattered photo album. It had gotten banged up in my journey from Youngstown; some of the pictures had come loose from the glued photo corners. It was old to begin with, the crinkly pages starting to yellow along the outer edges.

My mother had started the album for me when I was a baby. She was an amateur with a camera but a firm believer in documenting each milestone, which she had done up until the year she left me when I turned thirteen. After she died, I found her camera and picked up where she left off, taking photos everywhere I went.

The teapot whistled and I got up, fixed myself a cup and brought it back to the sofa, where I began leafing through the album. On the first page, there was a black-and-white photo of me on a blanket with a caption: *Alice's first day home Feb 2, 1944.* It was always jarring to see my mother's handwriting, like seeing a ghost. The next photo, me in the sink, my soapy dark hair swirled up like a troll's. *Ali's first bath Feb. 3, 1944.* There was a photograph of *Ali's first steps, first birthday, first haircut, first day of school* and on and on. I was so lost in the photographs that my tea had turned cold before I'd even taken a sip.

As I turned the last page and closed the cover, I ran my fingers over the *Alice* lettering that my mother had embroidered. And she was not the type of woman who sat home and did needlepoint. Far from it. Nothing about her was conventional. I'd heard her described as *a man's kind of woman,* the sort who got on better with the husbands than the wives. Always athletic, she played tennis and swam. She golfed, too, and was better at it than my father, who'd only taken up the sport so he could entertain clients on the course. Ultimately, she took my father's place in his foursome, which raised an eyebrow or two among the suburban housewives. My mother shot pool and loved to play poker—both of which were done with a hustler's skill. She was a terrible singer, not that *that* ever stopped her. She couldn't resist singing along with the radio. Especially in the car, the windows rolled down, her dark hair blowing back. Whether she knew the lyrics or was out of key, it didn't matter, she'd sing out unapologetically. I'd always wondered what song had been playing on the radio at the time of her accident. Had she been singing along at that very moment, oblivious to the car running the red light?

I was homesick for her and for things that no longer existed. When my mother passed away, she took so much with her, so much that I could never get back. I knew I would never find those bits and pieces of myself again, and yet there I was in New York City, searching for them anyway.

CHAPTER THREE

○────────○

Working for Helen Gurley Brown was like stepping into oncoming traffic. The next morning as I came down the hallway and rounded the corner, I saw the telephone lines on my desk flashing. Mrs. Brown was already in her office, perched on the edge of her desk, bands of sunlight coming through the window behind her. Though tiny in stature, she was still an imposing figure. My eye was drawn to the fishnet stockings on her slender legs and the short leopard print skirt, hiked up, exposing a good six inches of thigh.

I thought she was alone until I realized she had a photographer with her. She smiled while he snapped off a series of pictures. With one camera on a tripod, a second one in his hand, he moved like a dancer, gracefully and fluidly, crouching for one shot, standing upright for the next.

The aspiring photographer in me was fascinated, but the telephone lines were ringing, demanding my attention. My first day had begun. I answered two successive calls before I even sat down. I still had the receiver in one hand, my pocketbook in the other, when a third call came in. It was a reporter with *News-*

week wanting an interview with the new editor in chief. I explained that Mrs. Brown was unavailable and took a message just as another line flashed. It was Norman Mailer's literary agent checking the status of an article Helen's predecessor had requested. After that I fielded another inquiry from someone calling on behalf of Lauren "Betty" Bacall. It was all happening so fast, I didn't have time to be nervous or starstruck, but my goodness, it was exciting. I'd go home that day pinching myself. But for now I placed the receiver down, reluctant to take my hand away. I stood, waiting, expecting another line to light up. Ten, fifteen, twenty seconds passed. Nothing. A respite. I shoved my pocketbook into the empty bottom drawer and went off in search of coffee.

As I ventured down the hall, three young women, presumably also secretaries, were huddled together, deep in conversation, until a young man came by, capturing their attention. They stopped talking to smile, throw their shoulders back and thrust their chests out.

"Good morning, Mr. Masterson," I overheard them say in unison.

Mr. Masterson offered a "Good day, ladies," as he lifted his fedora, exposing a full head of dark hair. He was exactly the sort of young enterprising man you'd expect to find in a bustling Manhattan office: a dark suit and tie, pocket square handkerchief, leather attaché case in hand and trench coat, probably a Burberry, slung over his forearm. I'd passed a hundred men just like him on my way into work that day, but you'd think he was something special judging by the reaction he elicited. The girls didn't resume their conversation until he had disappeared around a corner. Later that day I checked the company roster and saw that Mr. Masterson's first name was Erik.

Farther down the hall I heard the sounds of IBM Selectrics humming and *click-clacking* from behind closed doors, along with the steady ding from the elevator bank, depositing more employees. The air was scented with cigarette and pipe smoke mixed with the smell of coffee brewing. Like a bloodhound, I followed the trail until I came upon a group of women gathered in the galley kitchen. The two girls I'd seen the day before—the Pixie and the Bouffant, her hair poofed high and Aqua-Netted in place— were in there, along with two brunettes who had identical bobs. There was another girl, too, with jet-black hair worn in a flip, her complexion so pale, her skin seemed tinged with blue.

The Pixie was reading from that week's issue of *Time* magazine. "Oh *Gawd*," she groaned. "Listen to this: 'The magazine is bubbling with enthusiasm over its new editor even though she has no editing experience.'"

"'Bubbling with enthusiasm,'" said one of the brunettes. "What a load of crap. And would you look at that picture of her."

"I bet she flips her wig when she sees this," said the Pixie. "Literally." She and the Bouffant laughed as if it were the funniest thing they'd ever heard.

The Pixie turned out to be Margot Henley, and the Bouffant was Bridget Grayson. Later that day, they, along with a few other girls, took me to lunch. We went to a luncheonette on 56th between Broadway and Eighth Avenue with a torn green and white striped awning. A gumball machine and the smell of grease and onions greeted us as we stepped inside. The place was packed and noisy. We took a table in the back that had a wobble, and we all did our part to keep it steady with our elbows. I ordered a club sandwich, cut into triangles and held together by fancy toothpicks with red cellophane curlicues.

"So," said Margot, turning toward me, "has she said anything yet about who she wants to hire for the new managing editor position? She's having one hell of a time filling that *jawb*." She spoke with a thick Bronx accent.

"I know Harriet La Barre already turned it down," said Bridget with a frown. "So did Bill Guy."

"Well, what was she thinking asking the two of them anyway?" said Margot, poking her straw around in her Tab. "Bill Guy edits fiction and Harriet's a fashion editor."

"She's running out of options," said Penny, one of the brunettes with the bobbed hair and frosted lipstick. "She's practically offered that position to everyone but the janitor."

I dabbed my napkin to my mouth and said, "I don't understand why they both turned down the job. You'd think they'd want a promotion like that."

"Oh, c'mon now," Margot said, finishing off her Tab with a gurgling sound coming up through her straw. "Why would they want to be *her* managing editor? They don't want to promote her idea of a modern woman."

"Hell, I'd take the job," said Bridget. "Just imagine what *that* salary is."

Margot ignored Bridget and continued, "Helen Gurley Brown is completely missing the point. She never talks about equal pay for women. Or discrimination in the workplace."

"If you ask me," said Leslie, the raven-haired girl, "*Sex and the Single Girl* was demeaning. A how-to for catching a man."

"Exactly," said Penny.

"Wait—what's wrong with catching a man?" asked Bridget. "I didn't think her book was demeaning."

"Oh, please." Margot shot Bridget a disapproving glance. "The whole book was about how to please a man. What about a man pleasing a woman for a change? According to her, we're all supposed to dress up like a bunch of sex kittens so men will want us."

Margot wasn't entirely wrong, but she wasn't altogether right, either. I wanted to speak up, but I was the new girl so I held my tongue despite knowing there was more to Helen's message than women becoming sex kittens.

"And you know," said Leslie, "all she's going to do is turn that book of hers into a magazine."

"I've heard she's planning on firing everyone and bringing in her own people," said Penny.

"I heard that, too," said Leslie. "That's why everybody's quitting."

"C'mon now," said Bridget, "I think everyone should at least give her a chance."

"Why?" said Margot. "No self-respecting journalist wants to be any part of Helen Gurley Brown's *Cosmopolitan*. She told Liz Smith she wears falsies. What sort of person tells you something like that?"

Penny rolled her eyes and said, "I'd be surprised if *Cosmopolitan* is still being published in six months."

I learned my first day that the magazine world operated three months ahead of the calendar. So even though it was only March, the May issue had already gone to press. I was in Helen's office later that afternoon when George Walsh, the book editor, a tall lanky man with a bow tie and suspenders, delivered the page proofs. Barbra Streisand was on the cover, striking a pose with hands on hips and a foot propped up on an ottoman. Running alongside her picture were what they called "teaser blurbs": *When Dentists Are Hard to Find* and *Pants for Mermaids*.

Helen was seated at her desk, Ferragamo shoes kicked off, one bare foot tucked beneath her while she leafed through the proofs, her frown deepening when she came to each new page.

"Obviously, it's going to be a rather lean issue," said George, reaching for a chair as if preparing to settle in for a lengthy discussion. "Going forward, I'd like to see us expand the book coverage."

Just as George sat and crossed his legs, Helen flung the proof onto the floor. It landed face up, fanned open to a page with a Mutual of Omaha Insurance ad opposite an article about orthopedics.

"Very well then," George said, rising up. "We'll discuss the book section another time." He nodded, put the chair back in place and smoothed a flap of thinning Brylcreemed hair against his scalp before slipping out the door.

Helen slumped forward, planting both feet on the ground as she groaned into her hands. "Alice, do me a favor. Get David on the line."

Moments later while at my desk, trying to track down her husband, I looked up and saw someone heading down the hall that caused the secretaries to scamper to their desks in an effort to appear busy. Whoever this man was, he looked like a politician in a dark suit and tie, his graying hair combed straight back. I could smell his aftershave—Brut—and noticed the reflection of the overhead lights in the tops of his polished shoes. It wasn't until I heard one of the editors greet him by name that I realized he was Richard Berlin. The big boss. The president of Hearst. He had decided to leave his posh office in the Hearst headquarters a few blocks over and slum through the halls of *Cosmopolitan*.

"Helen . . ." he called from two yards away.

"Oh, Richard, is that you? C'mon in," she said. "Alice, dear, show Mr. Berlin in."

"You and I need to talk, Helen." He was already standing in her doorway as I rushed up behind him, a useless gesture.

"How good of you to stop by." She smiled as if hosting a country club reception. She was about to get up from her desk when he paused her with a hand command suited for a dog. Surprisingly, she obeyed and dropped down into her chair, putting him at an extreme height advantage.

"Advertising revenue is way down. We had twenty-one ad pages for May. That's it. It's got me very concerned about the June issue."

Helen pressed a demure hand to her heart. "June? Oh, never mind about June. What we need to be concerned about is this." She picked up the May proof pages like she was holding a puppy by the scruff of its neck. "We need to make some drastic changes or else the June issue won't be any better."

"And what changes do you propose?"

"First things first, we need to cut that Gore Vidal essay."

"Cut Gore Vidal?"

"It's dull, dull, dull. And while we're at it, I know you promised Rex Reed he'd be the new movie critic but his latest review is simply dreadful. I'm afraid Rex and his pippy-poo copy have to go."

"Pippy-poo?" I was surprised he'd repeated it. It had been slightly charming when Helen said it but sounded ridiculous coming from him. "So you want to cut the Vidal essay *and* fire Rex Reed?"

"For starters."

"That's nonsense. This magazine has standards we need to uphold. I'm not going to compromise the integrity and—"

Her chirpy laugh cut him off. "Oh, Richard." Flouting him, she stood up and slipped out from behind her desk. "Trust me. I have a wonderful vision for this magazine."

"That's exactly what I'm afraid of."

She smiled and tilted her head as if to say, *You silly little boy, you.* "I find it so funny that you're nervous about a woman editing a magazine *for* women." Though Berlin didn't look amused, she continued talking while managing to escort him out of her office. I admired how coolly she dismissed him while leading him toward the lobby, her voice trailing behind her. "Isn't that just too funny, Richard? Worrying about a woman editing a woman's magazine . . ."

Moments later she came back down the hall; the glib light-hearted attitude was gone, her shoulders drooped, her head hung low. She seemed to be pouting, and without a word, she went into her office and closed the door. I noticed her line lit up on my telephone extension and then blinked off. Whoever she'd tried to reach must not have been available. A moment later, I heard her sobbing.

When I got home that night, I stood in the kitchenette, leaning next to the telephone mounted on the wall. I was eating a sleeve of saltines and a tin of sardines I'd bought at the little grocer around the corner. I watched the clock above the stove, waiting for the hands to reach eight o'clock, when the long-distance rates dropped, before placing a collect call to my father.

Faye answered and I had to fight the impulse to hang up. I never knew what to say to her. Everything was always so awkward and strained. I knew she made my father happy and I didn't want him to be alone, but still. A year and a half ago, when he introduced us, Faye had been too polite and I'd been too rude, answering her overzealous questions with a string of indifferent *yes, no, I don't cares*. I was later ashamed of the way I'd acted. I was too old for that, but I couldn't help myself. In truth, Faye was perfectly lovely. Her only fault was that she wasn't my mother. And there was nothing either of us could do about that.

"Collect call from Alice," I heard the operator say. "Will you accept the charges?"

I poked a sardine with my fork, awaiting her verdict.

"Yes, Operator, I will." Faye covered the receiver, her voice garbled as she called to my father, "Herb? Herbert? Get the phone. It's Ali."

I bristled at her taking liberty with my name. I was Alice to her, not Ali. I listened while the two of them talked, mumbling back and forth. I could picture them standing in the kitchen, the phone on the counter, next to the new avocado-colored range she had to have, because my mother's blue one didn't match the other appliances.

At last my father came on the line. "Ali? Ali, honey, how are you?"

"Hi, Dad. Wanted to let you know I got a job. At a magazine. Already started." I realized I was talking in staccato sentences, as if trying to convey the most information in the most succinct manner possible. I wasn't sure if I was doing this to save on minutes—the equivalent of a telegram, where you were charged by the word—or if I simply was that stiff and awkward talking to my father these days.

"Well, good. Good for you. So this means you're planning on staying in New York then, huh?"

"Yes." *Of course I'm staying. That was the whole point of moving here.*

The line went silent. The father I knew, before Faye came along, would have had a million questions for me: Which magazine? What are they paying you? Where's your office? Do you like the people there? But then again, the daughter he knew before he'd married Faye would never have waited this long to tell him she'd landed a job.

"Dad? You still there?"

"Yeah, yeah, I'm here."

"Elaine Sloan—Mom's friend—remember her? She helped me get the job."

"Oh." He sounded surprised. "So, ah, you're in touch with her."

"She's very nice."

"Uh-huh."

I set a saltine cracker in my mouth, letting it turn soft on my tongue before I ate it. He allowed another fifty-cent-a-minute pause before he changed the subject. After clearing his throat, he mumbled under his breath, "How are your funds holding up?" I had a feeling he didn't want Faye hearing him ask me about money.

"I'm okay. I'll get paid soon." I slid my spine down the wall, grateful that the phone cord reached to the floor. The line was silent again. This time I thought it might be the connection. "Dad?"

I heard Faye talking in the background, but couldn't make out the words.

"Ah, hold on a sec, Ali. What—" He covered the phone and said something to his wife. I tapped my toes and drummed my fingertips against the hardwood floor. "Well," he said, coming back on the line, "we'll talk more on Sunday, huh? When the rates are cheaper."

After he hung up, I stayed seated on the floor, my back against the wall, the receiver still in my hand, the dial tone filling my apartment with its steady din.

CHAPTER FOUR

⎯○────────○⎯

By the end of my first week, Helen and I had begun transforming her office. She believed there was a correlation between creating the proper work environment and her productivity. The lobby, she said, we would address later, but in the meantime, she wouldn't be able to fully concentrate until she'd banished the last traces of her predecessor and made the office her own.

So out went the orange shag carpet, the heavy furniture and striped drapes, and up went the pale pink wallpaper and the floral curtains, along with plush carpeting the shade of cotton candy. Though it didn't quite go with her pink motif, she couldn't resist bringing in a few leopard print desk accessories and throw pillows for her new sofa, upholstered in the same floral pattern as the window treatments. Despite her new vanity desk, Helen would conduct the bulk of her business from a little chair that looked like it belonged in a doll's house rather than an executive's office.

When I asked about it, she said, "Oh, it's very important that I make whoever I'm meeting with feel bigger than me." I had to laugh because practically everyone was bigger than Helen. "They mustn't feel intimidated. By the time they leave my office, they need to feel like everything we agreed to was their idea in the first place," she said with a crafty smile.

After spending so much time decorating her office, I found myself falling behind on the rest of my workload. Bernard Geis Associates had begun forwarding Helen's mail to the office, thousands of letters arriving in grungy gray canvas mail bags with ropelike drawstrings and metal grommets.

As for the fan mail, Helen responded to all those herself. In addition, there were all the thank-you notes for dinner parties, luncheons, to anyone who sent her flowers, dropped off cookies and candies, which of course she wouldn't eat. But the point was that no gesture of kindness went without a thank-you note. I never knew when she found the time, but each morning a fresh stack of handwritten notes and letters on her pink stationery would be waiting for me to walk down to the mailroom, each one addressed and stamped with her *HGB* pink sealing wax.

There was other mail, too. Hate mail, which Helen asked me to handle however I saw fit. She wanted nothing to do with any "nitpicky buttinskies." Honestly, I was surprised by the volume of angry letters she received. It was hard to imagine so many people taking the time to scold her on paper, accusing her of being immoral and corrupting innocent girls. I'd just read a letter from a mother who'd found a copy of *Sex and the Single Girl* in the bottom of her daughter's drawer. *She's fifteen years old and you've got her wearing makeup and stuffing tissue paper inside her bra.*

I didn't know how to respond so I set it aside and instead started on a letter of employment for Helen's first new editorial hire. Walter Meade was coming on board as an articles editor. Walter was a former advertising man, the head of the copy department for BBDO, and like Helen, he knew nothing about magazines. But like just about every other copywriter on Madison Avenue, Meade had a novel he was writing in his desk drawer.

Through the years, he'd sold a few short stories to Bill Guy, which was what got Helen thinking about hiring him in the first place.

Walter Meade was, in a word, gorgeous. Tall, fit, dark hair, dark eyes, dimples and a smile that belonged in a toothpaste commercial. Helen took one look at my face after he walked out of her office and whispered, "Forget it, dear. He's a dandy."

I fed a piece of paper into my typewriter and cranked it in position, my fingers gliding over the keys. After finishing the Meade letter, I looked up from my desk and saw that almost everyone was gone for the day. Desk lamps were turned off, typewriters were covered, sweaters no longer hanging off the backs of chairs. It was a Friday night and everyone was eager to start their weekend. Even Helen was getting ready to leave.

"Toodle-oo," she said, closing the buckle on her yellow wicker pocketbook. "I'm off to meet David at Trader Vic's. Don't stay too late now. By the way, I meant to tell you earlier—I just love your nail polish. I've been admiring it all day."

"Thank you," I said, a bit mystified, looking down at my nails. Plain pink polish.

Helen smiled and whisked off down the hall in her orange Rudi Gernreich dress, a floral scarf tied as a headband, its ends trailing down the center of her back. When she reached the end of the hall, she turned back and called to me. "Have a wonderful weekend, pussycat."

Being new to town and not really knowing anyone, I had no plans other than a tour of the city with Trudy on Sunday, so I was content to stay late and work.

I decided to get a jump start on a memo from Helen to Ira Lansing, *Cosmopolitan*'s head of sales and advertising: *I'd like to see more feminine products advertised. Where do we stand with Maybelline, Revlon, Max Factor, Midol and Kotex?* She told him she was worried about some of the Procter & Gamble clients: *Needless to say, Ira, Crisco, Oxydol and Charmin bathroom tissue are not sexy products . . .*

As I was finishing the memo, I heard someone talking down the hall and glanced up. Erik Masterson was standing in the doorway of Bill Guy's office. I'd seen him on the floor several times that week, walking around with Dick Deems. I'd overheard some of the girls saying that Erik was the youngest executive Hearst had ever hired.

I went back to my memo, proofing it so it would be ready first thing Monday morning. Every now and again, I looked down the hall, aware that Erik was still there, hands flat against the wall outside Bill Guy's office—no wedding band. After finishing the memo, I decided to tackle Helen's mounting hate mail. I shuffled through them until I read a letter from Gretchen Hills of Indianapolis, who had followed Helen's advice, gotten her nose fixed and now couldn't breathe out of one side.

"Is she in?"

I glanced up to find Erik Masterson standing less than three feet from me. It was the first time I'd seen him up close like this, and I got why the other girls flirted shamelessly with him. Any woman would have killed for his long lashes. Plus, he had the dark eyes, the beautifully aligned white teeth, the pert straight nose and the full head of hair that made you look twice. He knew it, too. I got the sense that he liked what he saw in the mirror.

"Well?" He looked past my shoulder in the direction of Helen's office. "Is she here?"

"Oh, no, sorry. I'm afraid she's already gone. You just missed her."

He folded his arms and puckered his mouth like he was about to whistle. A cleaning woman came around the corner, pushing a large trash bin, stopping to empty ashtrays and wastebaskets. I saw that Bill Guy's office was dark now and a moment later the elevator bell dinged. That was probably him heading home. The cleaning woman had disappeared down the hall, and I realized Erik and I were the only two people left.

He turned and looked at me. There was a silence that I felt compelled to fill. "I'll let her know you stopped by."

"Actually, Alice. It is Alice, isn't it?"

I nodded, surprised that he knew my name.

He scooted some papers aside, making a place for himself on the edge of my desk. "I've been meaning to talk with you. I was looking in your file."

"Oh?"

"I saw your résumé."

"Well, that must have been a quick read."

He smiled as if he'd looked under my dress, rather than in my file. "That was some coup, landing a secretarial position here without any previous magazine experience. What's your secret?"

"I type with Olympian speed," I said, fluttering my fingers for effect. "Oh, and someone put in a good word for me."

He offered a soft laugh and consulted his wristwatch. I knew it was no Timex even before I saw the Patek Philippe on the face. "It's getting late," he said, running a hand over his jaw. "You must be starving. I know I am. What do you say we go get a bite? The Tea Room's right down the street."

I hesitated, startled by the invitation.

"Oh, c'mon, I hate to eat alone." This coming from a man who I was sure never wanted for a dinner companion. He stood up and gestured toward the lobby. "Shall we?"

A man in full Cossack regalia held the door beneath the red awning, welcoming us to the Russian Tea Room. "Very good to see you again, Mr. Masterson," he said with a tip of his papakha hat.

As soon as we stepped inside and our coats were checked, I felt underdressed. Not that the women were in ball gowns and tiaras, but they possessed a certain elegance that I'd yet to acquire. In some cases, all that separated them from me was a string of pearls, or a cocktail ring, a Hermès scarf and a sense that they belonged there, whereas I was an interloper. The men were sharp and smartly dressed, too. Handsome suits, silk ties, gemstones in their cufflinks. These chic sophisticates were standing two deep at the bar, the mix of perfume and paisley swirls of cigarette smoke gathering above their heads. The restaurant was just as packed, with more Cossack-clad waiters tending to the diners at the red booths.

I figured we'd be waiting an hour or longer for a table, but then the maître d' came up to Erik. "Mr. Masterson? If you and the young lady will follow me, sir?" And off he went, maneuvering through the crowd, graceful as a tropical fish navigating an aquarium. I, on the other hand, was more like a salmon swimming upstream, accidentally bumping into people, nearly spilling their drinks.

We were led up a flight of stairs to the second floor, where a twelve-foot glass Russian bear, looking like a giant ice sculpture, guarded the front of the room. I'd never been in such an ornate restaurant: the stained-glass ceiling, the golden tree growing out of the red carpet with colorful glass globes hanging from the branches, the decorative mirrors lining the wall of red banquettes. People mingled in the center of it all, like they were attending a cocktail party.

As the maître d' led us to our table, Erik stopped every few feet to shake hands or kiss some woman's cheek. "You're very popular," I said.

"The office is right around the corner. A lot of Hearst folks come here after work," he explained matter-of-factly as we took our seats at one of the banquettes, a gold samovar stationed next to it.

I looked across the room, watching the women in their beautiful dresses, cigarettes held gracefully in one hand, cocktails in the other, a stylish clutch tucked under an arm. I was so taken by the atmosphere, I didn't remember Erik ordering me a vodka martini. I wasn't much of a drinker but martinis were very sophisticated, very big-city-like, and a lovely glass had just appeared before me with shimmers of ice crystals floating on top along with two speared olives.

"To you," he said. "Welcome aboard."

"Anchors aweigh," I said as I clinked my glass to his a little too hard. The line and the gesture fell short, like a tossed fedora missing the hat rack. I was trying to act as if it were nothing out of the ordinary for me to be in this restaurant with a man who probably rowed crew at Harvard or Yale. No doubt he had season tickets to the Met and a family summer home in the Hamptons.

"So what do you think of the Tea Room?" he asked, setting his glass down.

"It's okay." I offered a mock blasé roll of my eyes. "But honestly, it doesn't hold a candle to the luncheonette on 74th and Third."

He laughed outright for the first time. It showed the sliver of a different, more relaxed side of him, but he quickly checked himself. "So how goes it with the new job?"

"It goes just fine," I said. "Couldn't be better."

"Really?" He tilted his head, sending a lock of hair onto his forehead. "So you *like* working for the new boss lady?"

"I haven't been there very long, but yes," I said. "She's been wonderful. And after all, I mean, look who she is."

He gave me a cryptic smile before brushing his hair back in place.

The waiter came over to take our order but Erik sent him away. I hadn't looked at the menu yet, and when I did, I was intimidated; something called lamb loin carpaccio with mâche salad, dozens of caviars, quail, wild boar.

"Do you like salmon?" Erik asked, sensing my befuddlement.

"Yes, I do."

"Very well, then." He closed his menu and gestured to the waiter. "We'll take two of the coulibiac of salmon."

Erik excused himself for a moment and I watched him work his way through the room, stopping for quick hellos with a couple of men, another kiss or two on the cheeks of a few women. I felt a twinge—not of jealousy—but more a sense of competition. And certainly not for Erik's attention. This was all about me sizing up my own worth. I knew I was an attractive woman. People told me I looked like my mother and I could see the resemblance in old photographs of her. I had her blue eyes and dark hair, the same tapered chin, the high cheekbones and good, clear skin. But even with my mother's genes, I was nowhere near as worldly and polished as the women in that room. I was questioning what I was doing there—on a Friday night, no less—with Erik Masterson.

The last man who asked me to dinner was Michael. It was my twenty-first birthday and he'd taken me to an Italian buffet. With plates in hand, we stood in line before metal bins of spaghetti and meatballs, chicken buried beneath a golden gelatinous gravy and eggplant parmesan. While the waiters were singing and I was blowing out the candle in my spumoni and making my birthday wish, little did I know that it would be the last time I'd sit across from Michael. It would take him another week to work up the nerve to tell me he didn't want to marry me.

After our food arrived, two coulibiac of salmon, which turned out to be puff pastry pies on spitting hot plates, we ate in silence.

With each bite, I could hear his front teeth scraping against the tines of his fork. The first contradiction to the pedigree I'd assigned him. It brought him a few inches closer to earth, which put me more at ease.

The salmon was delicious and I was still eating when Erik pushed his plate aside and scooted forward. Squaring his elbows on the table and lacing his perfectly manicured fingers together, he said, "Can I be brutally honest with you?"

"Sounds painful. Are you going to tell me you don't like the way I wear my hair?"

"Actually, no." He gave me a suggestive look. "I like your hair. Very much."

"Go ahead then," I said with a wry smile, "slay me with your brute honesty."

He leaned in closer still, his elbow nearly touching my arm. "Now I'm sure you've already heard all this," he began, "but once upon a time, *Cosmopolitan* was one of the most respected magazines around. It was William Randolph Hearst's favorite publication. His baby, if you will, until someone got the bright idea to turn it into a magazine for suburban housewives. That was its downfall. It's been dying ever since. And if *Cosmopolitan* has to die, shouldn't it at least be put to rest with its dignity intact?"

"What are you talking about?" I reached for my martini and took a sip. "You're giving the magazine a fresh start and a new look. That's why you hired Mrs. Brown." As I said this, I saw his eyebrow rise as if it were lifted by a pull string. "Isn't it?"

"Look, it's no secret that *Cosmopolitan*'s been struggling. Everybody knows that. Circulation's down below 800,000, and Mr. Berlin and the board of directors were prepared to close it down altogether. I probably shouldn't be telling you this, but"—he looked left then right to emphasize confidentiality—"we've intentionally put very few resources toward getting new subscriptions.

We've hardly run any advertising for the magazine. We even cut the staff. *Cosmopolitan*'s been operating on a skeleton crew."

"So you're saying you wanted the magazine to fail?"

He smiled as if pleased that I'd figured out the riddle. "That was the plan all along."

"But why?"

"A very practical business decision. The magazine's been underperforming, dragging profits down for the entire Hearst Corporation, and the board of directors wanted to see it go away—but as I said earlier"—he raised a finger—"we wanted it to go away *with dignity*."

"Then why did you bring in Mrs. Brown?"

"Let's just say her husband did a hell of a sales job on the board. He's the one who got her hired. David Brown's a big Hollywood movie producer. A real charmer. That man could sell ice to Eskimos." He took a moment, his fingers toying with his cufflink. "You're obviously a bright girl. If you play your cards right, I'm sure there's a better opportunity for you at Hearst."

With that comment, I finished my martini. This whole evening had taken a sharp turn. Despite his flirtatious glances and the clever banter, this was no dinner date. I was mildly disappointed, but in the same way a child is disappointed when his sea monkeys turn out to be reconstituted brine shrimp. My romantic expectations aside, I was curious about this *better opportunity*.

"Are you saying you want to move me to another Hearst magazine?"

He leaned in closer and lowered his voice. "I'll be brutally honest with you."

"Oy, more brute honesty? I'm not sure I'm ready for it."

"Alice," he said, ignoring my flippancy, "everyone knows that Helen—Mrs. Brown—is in over her head. The company is taking a huge gamble by bringing her in, and quite candidly, we're not convinced she's up for the challenge."

My head was swimming from vodka and confusion. "Why are you telling me this?"

"Because I need your help. I need you to be my eyes and ears."

"What does *that* mean?"

"I'd like you to keep tabs on things for me. Tell me what writers she's talking to, which photographers and illustrators she's looking at. I'd like to know who she's lunching with, who's calling for her. That sort of thing."

"You're asking me to spy on her?"

"No, no, no, nothing like that. I would *never*." He sat back and tweaked his necktie. "I just want to make sure the magazine doesn't end up looking and sounding like her book."

Now he was sounding like the girls in the office. It was obvious that Hearst wanted to rein in Helen Gurley Brown, but I wasn't going to help them. I may have had a few qualms about some of her ideas, but if I'd been rooting for her before, now I wanted to see her crush them, beat them at their own game.

"You'd be doing me and the board a big favor," he said. "And a favor like that won't go unnoticed. Or unrewarded."

"I'm sorry, but you've got the wrong girl for that job."

"Do I?" He was looking at me with those eyes, and I was sure his charisma had worked on a lot of girls, penetrating even the slightest crack in their hearts. He probably thought he could convince me that the sky was green and the grass was blue, and that it was my duty to spy on my boss. Suddenly I didn't want to be in this fancy restaurant anymore.

"If you'll excuse me," I said, reaching for my pocketbook. "It's getting late and I need to get home."

He held my gaze for a beat or two before he said, "I understand, Alice. Perhaps we'll talk about this again some other time."

"Perhaps not." I tossed my napkin onto the table. "Thank you for dinner and for putting me in an impossible position."

I got up and headed downstairs, getting as far as the coat check before realizing I'd just walked out on a Hearst executive and had probably gotten myself fired. For a moment I contemplated going back upstairs to apologize, but I couldn't do it.

I stood outside beneath the Tea Room's red awning, trying to collect my thoughts. A wind gust came out of nowhere, carrying crumpled newspapers and litter down the street. I buttoned my coat and turned up the collar. It was almost ten o'clock but I needed the walk home to clear my mind.

As I headed up 57th Street, I happened to glance at the 224 building, noticing that Helen's office light was on. She must have gone back to work after her dinner with David because there she was, her tiny frame visible through the fourth-floor window, seated at her desk, furiously typing away.

CHAPTER FIVE

———o———

That night the streetlights shone through my window as I stared at the shadows streaking across my spider-cracked ceiling. An ambulance or maybe it was a fire truck raced down Second Avenue, its siren piercing the darkness, drowning out the laughter of people—probably drunk—passing by on the sidewalk below. My eyes were burning and my body had that heavy exhausted feeling as if my bones were filled with sand, but my mind wouldn't shut off.

Each time I began to drift, anxiety yanked me awake. I rolled over and flipped my pillow to the cool side, while my thoughts alternated from worrying about my job to being furious with Erik Masterson. I flopped onto my back again, letting everything fester. By two in the morning, after another siren went by, I began crafting my telephone call to Elaine Sloan, explaining that I'd already lost the job she'd helped me get. I had visions of packing my suitcase, boarding a Greyhound and heading back home, failing to have fulfilled my mother's dream. And mine.

The last time I looked at the clock, it was half past four, and when I woke up in the morning, I was still in a foggy panic. I fixed myself a cup of instant coffee and telephoned Elaine to ask for her advice.

"I'm heading into the office in a few minutes," she said. "It's quiet on the weekends and I can actually get some work done." I heard classical music playing in the background. "Why don't you meet me down there? Just ring the buzzer on the front door and I'll come let you in."

But when I arrived at Bernard Geis Associates that Saturday morning, the front door was unlocked and all the lights were on in the lobby. People were coming and going and I heard telephone lines ringing down the hall, typewriters clacking. It seemed like business as usual.

A man in gold corduroy slacks slid down the fire pole, landing with a thud.

"Excuse me," I said. "I'm looking for Miss Sloan."

He went to get her, and moments later Elaine appeared around the corner, looking like she'd come from a horse stable, dressed in a pair of khaki slacks and riding boots. Her silver hair was loose, resting easy on her slender shoulders.

"Thank you for seeing me on such short notice, Miss Sloan."

"Please." She waved a hand through the air. "What did I tell you? Call me Elaine." She gestured for me to follow her. "So much for a quiet Saturday around here, huh?" she said, walking down the hall, nearly every office occupied. "We have a big book coming out soon, and the author has us all jumping through hoops."

She led me into her office, which impressed me every bit as much as it had that first day. Somehow I hadn't noticed the series of photographs on her credenza before, but now they caught my eye, showcasing all the celebrity authors she'd worked with. There she was, standing alongside Groucho Marx, the two of them puffing away on thick cigars. In another shot she was shaking hands with Harry Truman. And yes, there was one with Helen, their cheeks pressed together, arms clasped about one another.

As I was about to sit down, a young woman with abnormally rosy cheeks came rushing in. "Berney wants you to look at the new Jackie Susann cover right away." She held up a nine-by-twelve-inch sheet of paper with *Valley of the Dolls* in bold black type.

Elaine took the mockup and eyed it while leaning against her desk. "It's still not right." She handed the cover back to the girl. "Tell him it needs more pills."

"More?"

"Yes. More pills. More dolls."

The girl nodded and disappeared.

Elaine closed her office door and turned back to me. "So what can I do for you today?"

"I'm sorry to bother you on a Saturday."

"Don't be silly." She smiled, dismissing my concern. "I told you my door's always open. You sounded upset on the phone. Would you like some coffee?" She gestured to the chrome pot and delicate china cups resting on a tray.

I shook my head, setting my pocketbook on the corner of her desk and pressing my fingers to my throbbing temples. "I think I've made a mess of everything with my job."

"Well, in that case . . ." She reached for a crystal decanter on her credenza. "But honestly," she said, pouring a shot of brandy into two cups, "I don't think you've been there long enough yet to make a mess."

I heard someone running down the hallway outside her door. Elaine added coffee to each cup and slid one across the desk to me. With a hand gesture, she encouraged me to drink up while I explained what had happened the night before with Erik.

"Ah," she said, setting her cup down, "let the games begin."

"What do I do?"

She thought for a moment and offered a sly smile. "You do nothing. Absolutely nothing."

"You don't think I should warn Helen?" I could feel the brandy going to my head.

"Nope." She leaned forward and folded her hands. "Helen knew what she signed on for."

"But no one there seems to like her," I said, remembering my lunch with Margot and the other girls. "Not even the women."

"That's not surprising. People aren't comfortable with women being in charge. Even other women, who should be their biggest cheerleaders. I had the same problem when I was at Random House. One of the only female editors with big back-to-back books. Both of them hit the *Times* list and that ruffled a few feathers. Believe me, the reason I came to Geis wasn't because of their *fine* literary reputation." She rolled her eyes. "I just knew Berney wasn't afraid of working with strong women. He shows me respect, stays out of my way and pays me a pretty penny to boot." She took another sip of coffee. "I'm sorry this happened, but I'm not surprised. Don't worry, though. Everything's going to be fine."

"So you don't think I'm going to get fired?"

"Heavens no." She laughed. "This Erik fellow couldn't possibly get you fired. Not without giving them a reason. And his reason wouldn't sit well—even with the boys at Hearst. If anything, he should be worried that *you're* going to get *him* fired."

I hadn't thought of that but Elaine was right. That sinking feeling in my gut began to ease. I took another sip of brandied coffee.

"You have more power in this situation than he does," she said. "Unless, of course, Hearst put him up to this, which I highly doubt. Even Richard Berlin and Dick Deems wouldn't stoop that low. One word to Helen—which I wouldn't recommend—and she'd have Erik thrown out on his ear. But I have a feeling Erik will hang himself with no help needed from you. Or anyone else."

She smiled, raised her coffee cup as if toasting me. "Feel better now?"

"You have no idea." I splayed an open hand across my chest. "I didn't sleep all night. I was so worried. Thank you."

With a gentle, easy smile, Elaine took a cigarette from a gold monogrammed case and lit it with a matching lighter. After exhaling toward the ceiling, she studied me for such a long moment that I thought I had something on my face.

"What?" My fingers searched my mouth.

"Nothing. Nothing." Elaine leaned forward, elbows on her desk. "I was just thinking how much you remind me of your mother. You look just like her. But I suppose you hear that all the time." Elaine rested her cigarette in the ashtray and removed two beautiful silver rings, neither of which had been on her ring finger. "I have some old photographs of your mother somewhere. I'll have to find them and show you," she said, reaching for an elegant Le Bain hand cream dispenser on the corner of her desk.

"I'd love to see them."

She pumped a dollop of floral-scented lotion into her palm. "I meant to ask last time—how's your father doing?"

"Okay, I guess. He got remarried."

"To Faye?"

"You know Faye?" That was a big surprise.

"Well, let's just say I know *of* her."

I wondered if she'd been in touch with my father recently, but for some reason I couldn't formulate that into a question.

Elaine worked in her hand lotion, smoothing it over her long, tapered fingers, her beautifully polished nails. "Your mother would be proud of you moving here. She always wanted to raise you in the city." She replaced her rings and reached for her cigarette, rolling the ash to a fine point. "Vivian never belonged in

Ohio. But what else could she do? Your father didn't want to leave his home and she had nowhere else to go."

"What do you mean, 'she had nowhere else to go'?"

Elaine saw the puzzled look on my face and her own expression sagged. "I'm sorry." She shook her head, taking a puff off her cigarette. "I shouldn't go on like that. Forgive me."

"No, please. I don't mind." I was desperate to talk about my mother. I wanted to say *tell me everything* but I couldn't get the words past the lump in my throat.

Elaine was about to say something else when her eyes drifted beyond my shoulder and her expression brightened. "Oh, Christopher," she said. "I'm sorry we had to drag you in here on a Saturday. Come in. I want you to meet someone."

A tall man stood in her doorway. He was probably in his mid-twenties and had long dark hair that reached his collar. I noticed he had a camera hanging by its strap, bobbing at his side.

"Didn't mean to interrupt," he said.

"No, no, it's all right. This is Alice Weiss. The daughter of an old, old friend of mine. Alice, this is Christopher Mack."

We exchanged hellos and I stared at his camera, a new Nikon F model that put my mother's old Leica to shame.

"I just finished meeting with Letty," he said. "We're gonna do the new headshots and the promo shots Monday afternoon. We'll do them down at my studio."

"You're a lifesaver," Elaine said. "Jackie hated everything we did."

"You should have hired me in the first place." He cracked a smile that brought out his features: dark, intense eyes beneath a fringe of hair, nose and chin all sharp and well defined.

He finished giving her the details of his meeting, and after a few parting pleasantries between us, Elaine excused herself and walked him out to the lobby, looping her arm through his. I finished my coffee, feeling the brandy taking hold.

"I'm sorry about that," Elaine said when she came back a few minutes later, slipping into place behind her desk.

"He seems very nice," I said.

"He's extremely talented. Young, sometimes temperamental, but talented. I wish he'd cut that hair of his, though. Believe it or not, there's a very good-looking young man underneath that mop."

"Oh, I believe it." I smiled. He was attractive, more sexy than handsome. I was going to ask about his photography when I noticed Elaine had reached for a stack of papers on her desk. I sensed her getting antsy, wanting to get back to work. "More coffee? Brandy?" she asked.

"No. No, thank you. I've already taken up too much of your time. But I do feel better."

"Just remember, not a word about this to Helen. She's a big girl. She knows how to handle them over there. Make no mistake, Helen Gurley Brown might look like a feather could knock her over but she's tough as nails. An iron fist in a velvet glove."

I was reminded of how she'd broken that pencil in two.

"Helen's no stranger to adversaries. She's had her share of knocks. I remember when we were working on her book, I begged her to tone it down. And don't get me wrong—I'm all for women's lib, but Helen still thinks sex appeal is a woman's greatest asset. I used to say, 'But, Helen, what about her brains?'" Elaine shook her head and laughed.

"The thing about Helen is, she claims to be just a regular girl from the Ozarks," Elaine said, "but she's Pucci all the way and she knows it. She's as clever as they come. Every time she speaks, she has an endgame in mind. That woman is always one step ahead of everyone else. Helen has her little-girl-from-the-sticks routine down. She has a way of making you *think* she's just like you. That's part of her genius, you know. Most people don't figure out her trick until after she's pulled out the tablecloth and put it away." She laughed. "Oh, and she loves to hand out compliments."

I could vouch for that. Helen never missed an opportunity to tell me or others that she liked our shoes, our scarves, the way we'd styled our hair. She told Bridget she had good posture and asked Margot how she kept her teeth so white. She always found something to say that would stay with you throughout the day.

"And she's the first one to point out her own flaws," Elaine said. "I think it's her way of leveling the playing field. Putting her rivals at ease. You watch her, Alice—you'll see what I'm talking about. She loves to confess that she's wearing false eyelashes or a padded bra."

It was true. I'd seen Helen in action. She was calculatingly unapologetic about her enhancements. She depended on them like an artist depended on paint and brushes. They were essential in the making of her ultimate creation, which, of course, was the making of herself, Helen Gurley Brown. Millions of single girls would become her disciples, but there was only one Helen.

"Bring a scarf and gloves," Trudy said the next morning as she stood in my doorway, buttoning her coat to the top. "Sun's out but it's still chilly."

Trudy had offered to show me around the city, for which I was grateful since, really, I hadn't seen much of New York beyond Midtown and the subway that went between the 59th Street and the 77th Street stops. I grabbed my camera and a wool scarf that smelled of Shalimar, looping them both about my neck as we headed out.

Our first stop was the Lexington Candy Shop at 83rd and "Lex," as Trudy called it. Aside from the racks of penny candy, chocolate coins, candy cigarettes and ropes of licorice by the register, it was more of a diner than a candy shop, and Trudy said they had the best breakfasts on the Upper East Side.

We sat at the dingy Formica counter, scarred with knife wounds, coffee stains and scorch marks. Our red stools swiveled all the way around. We ordered two egg plates that came with hash browns, rye toast and a rasher of bacon for 35¢, along with two bottomless coffees, a nickel a cup. A powder blue radio on the back counter was playing "Do Wah Diddy Diddy" while the waitress topped off our coffees, her lips moving to the lyrics, her voice barely audible. Singing along to the radio reminded me of my mother. And of her accident.

It took the child at the counter, squealing for Milk Duds, to get me past that dark thought. The child squealed again, louder this time, until his mother gave in and plucked a box from the rack and handed it to him. *Oh, gone were the days when a box of candy could make everything all right.*

After the mother and son left, I told Trudy what had happened at dinner with Erik on Friday night and about my visit with Elaine yesterday. "You should have seen her. She knew *exactly* what I should do about the situation. I felt like the weight of the world had been lifted off my shoulders by the time I left her office." I nibbled on my toast wondering: *Did Elaine Sloan ever second-guess herself? Did Helen?* Helen was one of the most decisive people I'd ever known. She'd look at an article or a photograph and it was *yes* or *no*. Never an *I don't know*. Elaine had been the same way when she looked at that book cover. Maybe certainty came with experience, with age? "I admire Elaine. She's so confident. Wise and—"

"And did you say she's not married?" asked Trudy, missing the point I was trying to make.

"Yeah, she's not."

"Has she *ever* been married?" Trudy sounded alarmed by the prospect of that.

"I don't think so. But I'm pretty sure that's by choice. She's beautiful and successful. Elegant and smart . . ."

Trudy gave me a peculiar look and I went quiet, because it was sounding excessive, even to me. Like something bordering on hero worship or infatuation. But in truth, I was a bit in love with Elaine Sloan. And with Helen, too. And it didn't take a genius to understand why. It all came back to my mother. "I just think Elaine Sloan's a really impressive lady," I said. "I'm sure she's never had a problem getting men. She's probably not married because she doesn't need a husband."

"Doesn't *need* a husband?" Trudy slumped forward as if I'd knocked some pillar of belief out from under her. Resting her elbows on the counter, she said, "I can't imagine that. Can you?"

"The Girl from Ipanema" came on the radio.

"You *do* want to fall in love and get married," she asked, "don't you?"

"Not if I can help it."

She laughed until she realized I was serious. Or at least I'd made her believe I was.

"I've been in love," I told her, picturing Michael, his light brown hair, his boyish smile just the same as when I met him, back before his voice changed and he'd grown taller than his father. He wasn't the boy next door, but the boy across the street. I remembered when he was ten and I was eight, he thought I had cooties and ran away from me on the playground. The following year when he decided it was safe to be friends, we played games together, making a tin can telephone, stretching the string from his front yard to mine. Years later, the game was Spin the Bottle in Esther's basement. Michael was the first boy I ever kissed, and two years later when I went out with his friend, Marvin, Michael grew jealous and asked me on a date. We went together all through high school, and when he went to Ohio State, he gave me his ZBT pin first and, later, his grandmother's ring.

There were so many memories of Michael, but the one I held on to was the day he told me it was over, that guilty, sheepish look in his eyes, hands stuffed deep inside his pockets, shoulders hunched forward, the smell of bourbon on his breath. "Love is overrated," I said.

"I wouldn't know."

"Trust me, it is. You carry this other person in your heart all day long, every day, and sometimes it's wonderful and other times it's . . . it's just plain heavy. Exhausting. He has a fight with his boss or maybe his brother, but you don't know that, so you think it's something you did. That it's your fault he's gone quiet and won't talk about it. Another time he's late coming to get you—he should have picked you up an hour ago. He stopped off for a few beers and forgot to call. It's no big deal to him. But this love you carry in your heart makes you come unglued, and because your mother never came home, either, you're convinced he's been in an accident. And it's those moments—when you're worried sick over the possibility of losing him—that you realize how much you've come to depend on him. For the little things like carrying the groceries and changing the lightbulb in your closet or scratching that place between your shoulder blades that you can't reach. Just when you can't imagine your life without him, he tells you he's not ready to get married. He doesn't love you anymore. And one year later, when you think there's still a chance he'll come back to you, he gets engaged to someone else. No thank you, I don't ever want to fall in love again."

"That happened to you?" She looked at me, horrified.

I nodded, surprised that I'd just blurted that all out and afraid that if I said much more, I'd unravel. It still stung, and as much as I said I didn't want a relationship, I knew I was lying to myself. Cynical as I was, I still wanted to love and be loved. Like every other girl I knew, I wanted the fairy tale, but I also wanted a guarantee that it would be forever. I wasn't willing to risk another heartbreak. I set my napkin on my plate and pushed it away. I heard the cash register ding as the drawer sprung open. I was thinking of a way to change the subject when Trudy did it for me.

"I wonder if Elaine Sloan shops at Bergdorf's," she asked. Trudy had worked in the shoe salon there ever since she'd moved from St. Louis two years ago.

Elaine's Gucci shoes flashed through my mind. "I wouldn't be surprised if she does."

"I just had a depressing thought," she said, lifting her coffee cup. "I touch women's feet all day."

"Ah," I said, "but you're touching the richest, most pampered feet in all of Manhattan. They probably smell like French perfume."

She laughed and sipped her coffee.

After breakfast, we left the Candy Shop and took the subway to Midtown. We headed down Fifth Avenue, a roar of thunder and whoosh of air rushing up when we walked over the subway grates. We turned left onto 42nd Street, where a policeman stood in the intersection, his whistle chirping as he directed traffic.

Trudy pointed straight ahead. "There she is. Look at that."

I turned, my eyes landing on an art deco structure, regal and sparkling against the brisk blue sky.

"The Chrysler Building," she sighed with admiration. "Isn't that something?"

"It's gorgeous." My camera was already out, snapping away.

"The Empire State Building might have her by a few stories, but to me, this right here is the jewel of Manhattan."

I was still taking photographs while Trudy told me about the construction with a docent's expertise. "They built her in 1928 and she went up fast. The stainless steel came all the way from Germany. You're looking at almost 4 million bricks and 400,000 rivets."

I lowered my camera and turned to her, astonished by these facts coming from this little freckly redhead who looked like she'd be more interested in *American Bandstand* than masonry and stainless-steel cladding.

"How do you know so much about all this?" I asked, my camera paused at eye level while I studied her. Despite the cool temperature, I saw that new freckles had formed on her face in the short time we'd been out in the sun. "Seriously," I asked, taking her picture, "how do you know about all this?"

"Oh, I've always been fascinated by architecture," she said, posing while I took another photo. She was standing in front of a shoe repair shop; the neon outline of a boot on the front window framed her profile perfectly. "I mean someone made that"—she gestured to the building—"out of nothing but their imagination. They saw it in their head and now there it is. Forever. It's amazing. Have you read *The Fountainhead*?"

I shook my head.

"You should. I've read that book three times. Come"—she started off down the sidewalk—"I'll show you the Empire State Building."

We moved down Fifth Avenue between 33rd and 34th Streets. Macy's was just a short walk away. There was scaffolding up, the sounds of hammering and drilling going on behind a boarded-up storefront.

Standing in the chilly spring air, Trudy pointed straight ahead. "William Lamb was the architect who designed the Empire State Building. Guess how long it took him to design the blueprints? Two weeks. Just two weeks."

"Impressive." I raised my camera and snapped a few photographs as the smoky scent of hot dogs cooking on a nearby cart drifted our way. The vendor sat on a milk crate in a torn green overcoat, broken capillaries branching out across his nose and cheeks. He smoked a nonfilter cigarette, watching the people go by. I found that vendor more interesting than the Empire State Building. While Trudy rattled off more facts, I took a snapshot of him, hoping to capture his sad, watchful gaze. I advanced the film, adjusted the lens and took a few more of him before we left, jumped on another subway line and headed toward the Village.

I'd never been below 14th Street before. It was a different world down there, a tangle of narrow streets with no rhyme or reason as to where they stopped and started. The people were as different as the landscape. All the tailored suits and briefcases were replaced by denim jeans and guitars. There was an *anything goes* sort of energy down there. I was mesmerized by the steam rising up from the manholes, being carried away, wafting in the breeze. Garbage bags were piled up three feet high at the curb along with stacks of flattened-out boxes. I stopped and aimed my camera.

"You're taking a picture of that?" Trudy asked.

"It tells a story." I clicked the shutter. Like the hot dog vendor, my camera was drawn more and more to people and things unexpected.

"Save your film," she said, stuffing her hands inside her pockets. "We have more places to see."

The winds were picking up and the temperature was dropping; my toes were going numb. Trudy took me to a coffeehouse so we could warm up and rest our feet. Caffe Dell'Artista was old and quaint with dark-paneled walls inside. It smelled faintly of cedar and cigarettes. We ordered our coffees at the bar and went up to the second level, the stairs creaking beneath us. Upstairs a mishmash of different upholstered chairs was stationed about next to lots of little battered end tables and desks, some with antique drop handles, others with brass patina pulls. Old, yellowing maps were hanging on the walls. We took two aging leather club chairs by the window, looking down on Greenwich Avenue. French music was playing softly in the background.

Trudy took out a pack of cigarettes and offered me one. I wasn't big on smoking, but then again, I hadn't been big on drinking, either, before I moved to New York. I took one from her pack, remembering not to inhale when she gave me a light.

"I want to show you something really neat about this place. Open the drawer." She pointed to the little desk at my side.

It squeaked as I pulled it open and inside were all sorts of napkins and scraps of paper, matchbook covers and postcards, each with something scribbled down on it. She opened the drawer on another table next to her and there was more of the same.

"Everyone here writes something down and leaves it in a drawer."

"What sorts of things?"

"Whatever they want. Listen to this . . ." She read off a napkin: "'Five out of four people have problems with math.'"

"Here's one," I said, laughing, holding up a scrap of paper. "'It's not one thing after another. It's the same damn thing over and over again.'" I sorted through the drawer and plucked out another one. "This is a Winston Churchill quote: 'I may be drunk, Miss, but in the morning I will be sober and you will still be ugly.'"

Trudy burst out laughing.

"Oh, this is another good one," I said. "'Every great dream begins with a dreamer. Always remember, you have within you the strength, the patience and the passion to reach for the stars to change the world.'"

"Who said that?"

"Harriet Tubman." I looked at the handwriting, scratched out in pencil, the edges of each word smeared a bit. "What's your dream?" I asked, exhaling a plume of smoke.

"Hmmm." Trudy thought for a moment and shrugged. "I can never remember my dreams."

"No, I mean the big dreams you have when you're wide awake. Your passions and goals. Those kinds of dreams."

She looked bewildered. "I don't know. I've never really thought about it."

"Never?" I was incredulous. Practically my whole life had been given over to daydreaming. The here and now didn't satisfy me. I wanted bigger, better, more.

She exhaled and set her cigarette in the ashtray, waving the smoke away. She was blank and I could see that she'd really never contemplated that before. "Why? What's yours?"

I held up my camera. "This right here."

"A photographer?" She wasn't laughing but she wasn't buying it, either. "How are you going to do that?" Her tone said *impossible*.

"I'm not sure yet." The thing was that back home I was the only one with a camera, but New York was teeming with photographers. My competition was everywhere, their Nikons and Canons, their Kodaks knocking along at their sides while they walked the city streets. I flicked my ashes, thinking about the classes I was too intimidated to take, using the excuse that I couldn't afford them and yet I found the money for a pair of new shoes. I took a sip of coffee. "But I'll tell you something, I know what your dream is. Or at least what it should be."

Trudy looked at me, waiting and curious.

"Architecture." I raised my cup to underscore the point. "You should become an architect."

"Me?" Trudy laughed. "Girls can't be architects."

"Says who?"

"Well? I don't know of any female architects." I could tell by the way she rolled her eyes that she was already dismissing the idea.

"I'm sure they're out there. You just have to look for them. Go to the library. That's what I did. I used to sit for hours with a stack of photography books. That's how I discovered Diane Arbus, Ruth Orkin, Helen Levitt . . ." I stopped talking. I could tell Trudy wasn't listening.

She pulled out another scrap of paper. "Get a load of this," she said. "'There's light at the end of the tunnel. And it's another train coming.'"

"C'mon, Trudy, you didn't come here all the way from St. Louis to sell shoes to rich women, did you?"

"No." She started to laugh. "But I do get an employee discount."

"I'm serious. If a woman like Elaine Sloan can become a big-time book editor and Helen Gurley Brown can run a magazine, why can't you be an architect? Why can't I be a photographer?" I took my napkin and splayed it out, flat on the table. "Do you have a pen?"

"Why?" She reached into her pocketbook and handed me one. "Are you feeling inspired?"

"Yes, as a matter of fact I am. I read that you're more likely to reach your goals if you write them down, so that's what we're going to do." I uncapped her pen, and as Trudy looked over my shoulder, I wrote: *On this day, Sunday, March 28, 1965, Trudy Lewis and Alice Weiss declare that they will follow their dreams. No matter what. Miss Lewis will pursue a career as an architect and Miss Weiss will become a world-renowned photographer.*

"World-renowned, huh?" She laughed. "You're insane, you know that?"

I signed my name below it and handed Trudy back her pen. "Now's your turn."

"This is crazy," she said even as she signed it.

"I'm sure people said Elaine Sloan and Helen Gurley Brown were crazy, too."

Trudy was smiling, digging around inside her pocketbook for a stick of chewing gum. She was done discussing dreams. It was like spreading fairy dust to her, but she had no idea how serious I was. As I folded our declaration and placed it inside one of the drawers, I thought about how much I wanted to make something of myself. Maybe one day, some girl arriving in New York with a suitcase full of dreams would look to me as an example of all that she could be.

While Trudy and I finished our coffees and smoked another few cigarettes, we read through the drawers, coming across poems and love letters, random telephone numbers and silly sayings. Some of them had us laughing so hard, you would have thought we'd been drinking gin all afternoon instead of coffee.

CHAPTER SIX

B y my second week Helen and I were establishing a daily routine. It started with me bringing her coffee and sometimes a
glass of Carnation Instant Breakfast along with the morning editions of the *Daily News, The Post,* and *The New York Times.* I'd set
her newspapers down on her desk along with her coffee—usually
her second or third cup as she always seemed to beat me into the
office no matter how early I arrived.

Sometimes I'd find broken pencils on her desk, or lying on the
floor, all signs that she'd inwardly snapped without visibly losing
her temper. While she skimmed the newspapers and clipped out
articles for me to file in her ideas folder, we'd review her schedule
for the day. I'd give her a rundown of meetings, phone calls and
deadlines before we'd go through personal matters that needed
tending to, things like selecting and wrapping items from the
samples she'd received for last-minute presents or hostess gifts.
Not as easy as it seemed. Would Rona—as in Jaffe—really want
the Hermès wallet, and were the Givenchy bath oil beads too
personal for Barbara Walters? I agonized over these choices.
Something else that wasn't so simple was guarding Helen's door

and putting all calls on hold while she did her daily exercise routine: isometrics, leg lifts, sit-ups and chin lifts.

That Monday morning I followed Elaine's advice and didn't say a word to Helen about Erik asking me to spy on her. Instead, we ran through her itinerary and I gave her the advertising memo to review before delivering it to Ira Lansing.

As I left her office, I knew it was only a matter of time before I'd run into Erik and I was dreading it, wondering what kind of confrontation I'd find myself in. Turned out, I didn't have to wait long because by ten o'clock he stopped at my desk.

Leaning forward, he lowered his voice. "Listen," he said, "I thought about what happened Friday night, and well, I'm sorry. I was out of line."

"Yes, you were." I was still angry and started typing blindly, my fingers striking the keys so hard it made the coffee jump inside my cup.

He toyed with a cufflink and said, "Alice, we got off on the wrong foot. Can we start over? Pretend like it didn't happen?"

"Sure, no sweat." I ripped one page from the typewriter and cranked in another, fingers already going to town. He stood there, not saying a word, his aftershave faint but impossible to ignore. I finally looked at him. "Was there something else you needed?"

He glanced across the room and I followed his gaze. Bridget was watching us, a curious look on her face.

"Well?"

"No," he said, hands stuffed down inside his pockets. "No, I guess not."

As soon as he was out of sight and out of earshot, Bridget darted over, her pearl drop earrings swaying back and forth. "What was that about?"

"What?" I tried playing dumb and went back to typing.

"Erik Masterson. What was he talking to you about?" When I

didn't answer, she reached for my hand, making my fingers rest in place on the typewriter keys. "Are you all right?" She looked into my eyes. "Oh no. You're not all right, are you?"

I pressed my lips together hard to keep from speaking.

"What is it?"

She wasn't going to let up so I shook my head. "Not here," I said.

She waited while I got up from my desk and escorted me into the ladies' room. I leaned against the counter while she checked all the stalls. With the last door still swinging open and shut, she turned to me. "All right now, spill it."

"He's just—" I shook my head and pressed my fingers to my temples. "He rubs me the wrong way."

"Well, he can rub me any way he likes," she said, pulling a package of cigarettes from her pocket. "He's gorgeous, don't you think?"

"He might be gorgeous but he's a snake."

"What are you talking about?"

"He took me to dinner the other night."

Her eyes flashed wide behind the flame of her lighter. I detected a mixture of awe and jealousy. "And?"

I paused. I didn't want to say anything more.

"Aw, c'mon. Tell me." Oh, the look she gave me. It was like holding a candy bar out of a child's reach. "Please?"

"Okay," I said eventually. "But promise me this stays just between us."

"Of course. You can trust me. I won't say a word."

Still I hesitated. Something about people who said you could trust them usually meant you couldn't.

"Scout's honor." She crossed her heart.

She seemed almost as concerned as she was curious, and more than any of the other girls, Bridget had gone out of her way to

make me feel welcome there. "Well," I began despite my reserva-
tions, "he wants me to keep an eye on things around here for him."

"No fooling. Like what sort of stuff?"

"Anything he can take back to Hearst about changes Mrs.
Brown's making to the magazine."

"But isn't she *supposed* to be making changes?"

"That's what I thought. But he doesn't like her. I think he
wants to get her fired."

"Good God. That's terrible. I can't believe he asked you to do
that."

"Me neither. I told him to forget it. I wouldn't do that to my
boss."

She flicked her ash into the sink. It made a hiss when it hit the
drip from the faucet.

I looked at her reflection in the mirror. "You have to promise,
not a word of this to anyone. Especially not Mrs. Brown."

"Are you kidding me?" Bridget's eyes went wide. "I wouldn't
say a word." She picked a fleck of tobacco off her tongue and
studied herself in the mirror. "So what does he want from you
now?" she asked, shifting the subject back to Erik. "He certainly
was hovering around your desk this morning."

"Now he wants us to be friends. He's full of apologies." I
thought about telling her what Elaine had told me, but Bridget
changed the subject.

"So I have a little secret of my own."

"What?"

"You can't tell anyone. Promise? Especially not Margot. She's
a gossip. That girl can't keep her mouth shut."

"What is it?"

"Well"—Bridget clasped her hands—"I have an interview with
Redbook."

"What? You're leaving? Why?"

"It's just an interview but they have an opening in editorial for an assistant. And the starting salary is $80 a week."

"But you've been here for two years."

"Two years too long."

"You said you really liked Bill Guy. I thought you liked being his secretary."

"Nobody *likes* being a secretary. This is my chance to be an editorial assistant. That's a big stepping-stone and the money's good, too." She propped her cigarette in her mouth and squinted as she patted her hair in place. "Do you know what I could do with $80 a week? I'm barely able to afford anything after I pay my rent now."

I sympathized, already finding myself having to choose between a jar of Dippity-do and a roll of film or getting my pictures developed instead of going to the movies and out for a burger with Trudy.

Bridget was still going on about how she couldn't pay her last telephone bill when Margot came into the restroom.

"Well," said Bridget, dousing her hot ash under the drip of the faucet, "thanks for helping with the production schedule. I better get that report out for Mr. Guy." She winked, darted her soggy cigarette into the trash and pushed the door open with her hip.

When I got back to my desk, Ira Lansing, the head of sales and advertising, was waiting for me. He was a broad-shouldered, middle-aged man who looked like he'd played football in high school, the type that still wore his college ring, the best years behind him. He ducked his head into Helen's office, waving the memo I'd delivered to him earlier.

"Where is she? I need to speak with her right away."

"I'm sorry, but she's out of the office."

"She better not be meeting with Revlon or Max Factor."

"She'll be back in an hour," I said, trying not to show my hand. Helen wasn't in a meeting at all. At least she wasn't in a business meeting. Monday mornings she had a standing appointment with Dr. Gerson, her psychoanalyst. Not that Helen was ashamed of or secretive about this. She'd written about it in *Sex and the Single Girl*, recommending that we could all benefit from analysis. I used to think only people who'd had nervous breakdowns or were flat-out insane went to a shrink. I wondered why someone like Helen, who seemed to have everything, needed to be in analysis.

"Well," said Ira, "you tell her for me that I got this little memo of hers and I don't need her advice. I'm in charge of selling ad space here"—he poked himself in the chest—"I'm in charge of our advertisers. This doesn't concern her. She's not supposed to be involved in my business and I'd appreciate her staying out of my way and letting me do my job."

Before I could say anything, he stormed off and disappeared around the corner.

When Helen returned and I told her Ira had come by to see her, she made a *pfft* sound, discounting him. I followed her into her office and hung up her coat on the back of her door and put her pocketbook away in a drawer. Before I could even tell her that Ira was upset about her memo, she asked if he'd made a pass at me.

"No. Why?"

"Ira Lansing is a skirt chaser," she said, handing me a little baggie filled with packets of crackers she must have taken from a restaurant. "And to think they call me a hussy and tramp. And why? Because I'm a woman. I love sex. Always have. I don't think there's anything wrong with that. Sex is positively scrumptious and has zero calories. Oh, and by the way," she said, reaching for a cigarette, lighting it with her gold desk lighter, "don't believe everything you hear about me. I know people say I slept with 165 men before I married David. And that's a lie." She exhaled and smiled. "It was 166." She looked at the expression on my face. "What's the matter? Don't you approve?"

"I'm just wondering how you had time to date that many men."

"I didn't *date* all of them. I'm not talking about having relationships with all of them. Don't get me wrong, I had plenty of boyfriends and I slept with all of them, too. But the others—well, some were just men I had sex with. Sometimes they didn't even buy me dinner first or a cocktail. That was the beauty of it. No strings attached. It was just about sex and it was grand. Positively delicious." She took a puff off her cigarette and tugged on the back of her wig, as if making sure it hadn't slipped. "Men have been doing it for years. It's time women got out there and started enjoying themselves, too. I tell you, I was like a kid in a candy store. I slept with famous men, married men, rich men, poor men. Some were stunners, some"—she tossed up her hand—"not so much. Some were wonderful gentlemen, some were downright rats. I couldn't trust them as far as I could throw them. But if they were good in bed, well, then"—she laughed—"that was enough for me. Remember, great sex doesn't have to be with someone you love or even like. And don't look so shocked. You're young and single. You should be out there having fun. Your mother won't tell you this, but it's okay to be a little naughty."

The next morning on my way to the mailroom, Erik stopped me in the hallway. "What are you doing for lunch?" he asked.

"I brought my lunch."

"How about tomorrow?"

"I'm bringing my lunch tomorrow, too." I started to walk away but he grabbed my hand.

"Please?"

Margot and Leslie were coming down the hall, and both of them turned, looking back over their shoulders.

"Please?" he said again.

I sighed and shook my head.

"I'll keep asking. I'm very persistent when it comes to something I want."

Those lovely dark eyes looked at me with such anticipation and pleading, as if my response had the potential to devastate him. Or elate him. I'd never felt that powerful before where a man was concerned, but I played it cool. "And why exactly do you want to have lunch with me?"

"I told you, I feel bad about our dinner last week."

"I thought we cleared that up."

"I want to make it up to you. I want to start over. Fresh. Like it never happened."

"That's not necessary."

"Maybe not to you, but it is to me. Please?" There was that look again.

Another back and forth and I caved and ended up going to lunch with him.

In Erik's grand style he introduced me to another Manhattan hot spot, taking me to La Grenouille on East 52nd Street.

"I hope you're on an expense account," I said, after opening the menu.

"Do you make a joke out of everything?"

"Only when I'm nervous."

He looked at me, smiling and all too pleased with himself. "So I make you nervous, huh?"

"Not for the reasons you think." I gave him a stern look. I wasn't playing with him. "I'm still suspicious of your motives here."

"Alice"—his hands raised in surrender—"I come in peace. I swear." He smiled all the wider.

I broke away from his stare, glancing about the lavish room filled with flower arrangements rising out of three-foot-tall cut glass vases. Every table was full, mostly with businessmen in expensive suits, cutting deals along with their chateaubriand. There was a lot of power in that restaurant. You could feel it radiating off the tables, like heat coming off the pavement on a ninety-degree day.

The atmosphere in that room fortified my anger, adding fuel to what Elaine had said about my having the upper hand in this situation. I decided to flex my muscle and make Erik squirm. "I don't think Mr. Berlin would approve of your ethics. Do you?"

That wiped the smirk off his face. "Are you going to say anything to him?"

"I'm not sure yet," I said, though I'd already decided to follow Elaine's advice and keep my mouth shut.

He swallowed hard, and the color in his handsome face blanched out a bit.

"What exactly do you do for Hearst anyway?" I asked as I closed my menu, setting it aside.

"I ask myself that every day." He shook his head, his eyes moving side to side.

I wasn't going to let his self-deprecating response soften me. "I'm serious, what do you do?"

"If you must know, I'm pretty much a lackey and a whipping boy for Berlin, Deems and Dupuy."

"You don't say."

He looked embarrassed, even surprised, as if he hadn't meant to make such a confession.

I was trying to hold my ground, even as I felt my hard edges beginning to weaken. Administering punishment wasn't one of my strong suits. "But I heard you were the rising star of Hearst." My delivery was deadpan to show I wasn't impressed.

"Well, that's not what it feels like to me. For now it's a lot of grunt work. Every day I have to prove myself."

"Is that why you wanted me to spy on Mrs. Brown?"

He winced. "I wish you wouldn't put it that way." He pulled

out a cigarette and lit it, snapping his gold lighter shut with a solid click. "I'm not proud of what I did. I swear, I'm not a bad guy. Do you believe me?"

"Why do you care what I think about you?"

"I don't know, but I do." He shrugged, though we both knew it was because he didn't want me talking to his bosses. He gave me his best smile, like he was falling back on an old trick that had gotten him out of hot water in the past.

I wasn't moved by his ploy. We went silent for a moment.

The waiter came by and took our orders—something called Les Quenelles de Brochet au Champagne for me and Steak Tartare, Pommes Gaufrettes for Erik.

"If you want to know the truth," he began after the waiter left, "I was desperate when I asked you about Helen." He was no longer smiling and obviously felt the need to further explain himself. "Things haven't been going so hot for me lately and I can't afford to get fired. The magazine business is a small world. People talk and well . . ." He held up his hands, letting that thought float off, replaced by another. "I knew Hearst wasn't happy about the Brown hire and I was looking for a way to score some extra points. My judgment was off, and for that I am sincerely sorry."

He seemed genuine and I realized I didn't have the stomach to be cruel, even to Erik Masterson. I'd made my point, no need to belabor it.

So we made small talk instead, going on about the weather and various exhibits until our food arrived: a pile of raw filet mignon and fancy overpriced potato chips for him and fish dumplings with a creamy champagne sauce for me. It was quite good, but I noticed that Erik only poked at his meal.

"I've worked really hard to get to where I am," he said, circling back to our earlier conversation. Clearly, it was still bothering him. "It's not like anyone handed me this position on a silver platter."

"I wouldn't have thought they had." There was still a definite edge to my voice.

"Can we call a truce, Alice?" His eyes were locked on mine, and as he leaned forward, his elbow nudged his fork onto the floor. Upon retrieving it, he accidentally knocked his knife off his plate as well. For the first time, the practiced, pretentious mask slipped from his handsome face, and with a disarming shrug and his cheeks flushing pink, he said, "Wait till you see what I do to dessert." The coloring on his face only deepened. He was full-on blushing now, and suddenly the real Erik Masterson had shown up—no putting on airs, speaking French to the waiter or commenting on the latest exhibit at the Museum of Modern Art. He was being a regular guy, just being himself.

"I really am sorry about what happened," he said. "Truce?"

Despite myself, I smiled and nodded.

He took a drag off his cigarette and we let the conversation drift along with his smoke. He told me stories about Helen's predecessor, Robert Atherton, and even about Richard Berlin.

"There was the time Truman Capote threw up on Berlin's alligator shoes. Right in the Hearst lobby." He playfully slapped the table, laughing. "That was the last time he ever took Truman to lunch." He made a mime-like drinking gesture.

Erik kept talking and soon had me laughing over some of the classic typos where a recipe ran that called for *two cups penis butter* and another one for *porn and beans*. Erik's favorite, though, was the farmer who *shit a buffalo* in his field.

As my laughter subsided, he caught my eye, looking at me intently and longer than what would have been casual. I felt my heart beating just a bit faster. If he could have read my mind, he would have known just how attractive I found him. I wanted to turn away, but couldn't. It was as if he had hold of me. I didn't know what to make of this, but I got the feeling that something had just started between us. I didn't know what it was, but I knew what I didn't want it to be.

I wasn't looking for love—not with Erik Masterson. Not with anyone. Everyone I'd given my heart to—my mother, my father and Michael—had left me in one form or another. I couldn't bear another loss. Especially now that I was finally in New York and ready to put the past behind me.

But Erik was sitting across from me, smiling, sending a wave of heat rushing through me. I thought back to what Helen said the day before, about sex being just for fun. I knew I wanted to kiss Erik, to feel my body pressed to his, and wondered if I could really be *that girl*. I could tell he wanted me, too, and it had been so long since I'd felt desired. I'd only ever slept with Michael, and that was because we were engaged and I'd loved him. That made me still *a good girl*.

But Erik had me intrigued. I was drawn to him and there was definitely a flirtatious spark between us. I wanted to experience Manhattan and who better to show me a good time than Erik Masterson? Already he'd taken me to two restaurants I could have never afforded to step foot in. Besides, there certainly wasn't any danger of him looking for something serious, either. This was fun, easy, with no jagged misunderstood edges to get snagged on.

I was enjoying myself now, but I only had an hour for lunch and had to keep an eye on the clock. It was getting late, and if I walked it, I could cut up Fifth Avenue and make it back to the office in fifteen minutes.

When we rounded up to the forty-five-minute mark, I said, "I hate to do this, but I have to get back." I still didn't trust him and didn't want to tell him that Helen had called a staff meeting that day for one o'clock.

"I'll get the check."

"No, no. Stay, finish your coffee." I was already rising from my seat.

"This is twice now, Alice. You can't keep walking out on me in restaurants," he called after me.

I stopped and looked back over my shoulder, offering a coquettish shrug. "Well, maybe the third time's the charm."

B y one o'clock I was back in the office and had ushered what was left of Helen's staff into the conference room. Her only other new hire, Walter Meade, wasn't starting for another week. The editors and writers took their places at the long table, setting down their cigarettes and coffee cups, their Tabs and Diet Rite Colas. By the time the people from the art department arrived, all the seats were taken, so they perched along the window ledge like a flock of birds.

Helen lugged in a big heavy box held together with twine, while I carted in an oversize drawing pad and propped it up on the easel stand at the front of the room. Helen stood next to me in a lavender shift that exposed her delicate knees and perhaps a little more thigh than a middle-aged woman should have shown, but she pulled it off, even with the run in her stockings. She had an uncanny knack for snagging her nylons and fishnets, catching them with a fingernail or pen, or on the edge of her desk during one of her spontaneous exercise routines. She must have gone through three or four pairs a week.

She waited patiently while people settled into their seats, and with a clearing of her throat, she snuffed out their conversations. In that wispy, silky voice of hers, she thanked them all for coming as if it had been an open invitation rather than a mandatory meeting. "And now I'd like to announce that we have a new managing editor." She turned and introduced him by way of a hand gesture.

All eyes were on George Walsh. There was an audible reaction, and not necessarily a positive one, followed by some glib

congratulations. Everyone knew George had been offered the position by default. He certainly wasn't Helen's top pick. George
had been with the magazine for twenty years and was ingrained
in the old *Cosmopolitan* ways. He kept a Bible on his tidy desk,
and you just knew he thought Helen was a sinner, going straight
to hell. No one could see how this was going to work with the two
of them. She was heading into battle with Hearst, and her deputy
was a good soldier—for the enemy—who stood up and practically
saluted each time Berlin passed by.

"Now then, let's get down to business, shall we?" Helen uncapped a thick black marker, which sent a pungent smell through
the room. She faced the easel and wrote in bold letters *JULY*,
underscored with two exclamation points. She turned back
around, beaming.

"July?" George Walsh stood up, playing his new role of managing editor to the hilt. The glare from the overhead lights bounced
off the dome of his balding head. "Helen, with all due respect,"
he said with a patronizing laugh, "this meeting should be about
filling the holes in the June issue. And frankly, not everyone needs
to be here for that."

"Oh, I know, George." Helen smiled graciously, matching the
pitch of her laugh to his as she wiped his concern away with her
hand, her bracelets setting off a delicate, tinny sound. "You're
absolutely right. That's what we *should* be doing. Oh, but let's
face it, the June issue is already a lost cause. It was pretty much
set before I was even hired." Helen knew that July would be her
first chance to truly edit the magazine and introduce the country
to the new *Cosmo*. "That's why today we're going to discuss articles and concepts for the July issue."

"But we've already started the flatplan for July," said Bobbie
Ashley, her articles editor.

With a fresh spark of lightness, Helen said, "What do you say we forget about the flatplan and start with a clean slate? Anything goes. Burt, let's start with you." She clasped her hands in anticipation; her smile and expectations were earnest.

"Well," said Burt Carlson, adjusting his bow tie, which left it more crooked than before, "the home entertaining guide for executive housewives that we ran last July was well received. We could bring that back."

Everyone nodded while Helen made a face. "Oooh, so dull." She wrinkled her nose and shook her head. "Dale, what about you?"

Dale Donahue was a features writer who wore heavy tortoise-shell eyeglasses and had the ruddy complexion of a fisherman. After glancing at the backs of his hands like they were tea leaves, he said, "Lately I've been hearing a lot about fluoride, so I think something on tooth decay and—"

Helen cut him off. "Tooth decay? Hmmm, so dull, dull, dull." She smiled, casting her sights on Bobbie Ashley. "What have you got for us today, pussycat?"

Bobbie was obviously not accustomed to her boss calling her pussycat. It threw her and me both, because up until that moment, I thought that had been Helen's special pet name for me. I admit I felt slighted.

Bobbie took a moment to recover as she sorted through the scribbles on her pad of paper. Helen was still smiling, waiting. "I think it goes without saying," began Bobbie, "that women are going to want summer recipes."

"Oh really? You think so, do you?" Helen crinkled her brow. "I'm afraid my girls will find that so boring. What I'm really looking for is something fresh and unexpected. I really want something daring for my girls."

"Excuse me," said Bobbie, "I'm missing something. Who exactly are *your girls*?"

"The *girls*! My girls. Your girls. The new *Cosmo* reader is a young, vibrant, single woman. She's career minded and driven. She's sexy and fun spirited. Even a bit naughty. And I know her better than anyone because I was that girl." This was all said with dramatic hand flourishes that everyone watched, as if her fingernails were sparklers, giving off showers of glittering light on the Fourth of July.

"Bill," she said, addressing Bill Carrington Guy, her fiction editor, "what do you have lined up?"

Bill Guy was an attractive middle-aged man with a full head of light brown hair, neatly coiffed. He flipped open a folder and shuffled through some pages, and speaking like the well-mannered Southern gentleman that he was, he said, "I've got an excerpt of Michener's *The Source* and a new Ray Bradbury story."

"Are they happy?"

He squinted, as if he hadn't heard right. "I beg your pardon?"

"Are they happy stories?"

"Ah, not particularly, no."

"Oh dear, that's what I was afraid of. From now on, I want us to only publish happy, upbeat fiction."

The room filled with groans that she seemed not to hear or else chose not to acknowledge. "The whole point," Helen said, talking over the commotion, "is that *Cosmopolitan* should speak to that girl in Kansas City who's worried that her boyfriend won't marry her after she's slept with him. This magazine is for the girl in Upstate New York who's wondering if she can have sex while she's menstruating. Our reader is the girl in Phoenix who doesn't know what to do when her boss makes a pass at her. This girl doesn't care about gelatin and casseroles or gardening or fluoride. She cares about love. About getting a promotion at work. About being desirable and making the most of what she's got. She wonders why she's still getting pimples when she's twenty-one years old. She cares that her boyfriend thinks her bosom is too small.

She needs to know that masturbating is perfectly normal and that it can make her a better lover."

I heard myself gasp, but half the room did, too. Eyes were bulging, mouths were gaping. *Nice girls didn't touch themselves. Did they?*

Helen was still talking. "No one else is speaking to that girl. She's all alone out there—maybe she's right here in Manhattan. Right here in this very room."

My face grew hot as I imagined everyone staring at me, like I was *that girl*.

"Doesn't matter where she is," said Helen. "She needs us. What's she supposed to do when she finds herself attracted to a married man? Or what if she's lying awake in the middle of the night wondering why she doesn't have an orgasm every time? I'm trying to reach the girl who's worried that she's immoral because she enjoys oral sex. If we don't tell her the truth about all that, who's going to? We're here to help her, to let her know that she's completely normal and, more importantly, that she's not alone."

I took in the reactions from the room: eyes wide in disbelief, hands clasped over shocked mouths, others staring uncomfortably at their notepads, too embarrassed to look up. They thought they were listening to a mad woman, and even though I was blushing the whole time, I saw something different in Helen. I saw this tiny woman taking on all of society, starting with her staff. Starting with me. I knew Helen saw nothing wrong in sleeping with married men, but I did. And I wondered, would she have changed her tune if some young girl made a play for *her* husband? There were other things she'd preached in her book that I also felt uneasy about, like using sex to get ahead at work. But whether I agreed with her on all counts or not, I could not dispute that she'd struck a nerve. She truly cared about *her girls*. This wasn't just a job for Helen Gurley Brown; this was a calling. A personal quest. And people wondered why her book had sat at the top of the *New York Times* bestseller list for months and months. What she was saying in that conference room encapsulated all the reasons why so many young women had read and reread *Sex and the Single Girl*.

"When my girls wake up in the middle of the night with these thoughts plaguing them, I want them to reach for their issue of *Cosmo*. When our girls read *Cosmo*, I want them to feel uplifted and optimistic about their futures."

Helen snapped her fingers as if struck by a brilliant inspiration. "I want to show you all something." She reached for the box she'd brought in and untangled the twine while everyone looked on.

"When my husband and I first thought about starting a magazine, we came up with this—*Femme*." She held up what looked like a child's art project. Her homemade dummy for *Femme* was nothing more than clipped photographs and bits and pieces of headlines snipped from other publications and glued in place.

I can't say for sure if people snickered but there was eye rolling, shifting in chairs, disgusted sighs. They were missing the whole point she was trying to make and I worried that what little respect they had for her was disappearing faster than water through an open drain. She was confirming their worst fears about her and what she wanted to do with the magazine.

"Just take a look at the article ideas we came up with." She passed *Femme* around the conference room table, and I watched the expression on Liz Smith's face as her eyes landed on headlines announcing *Simple but Sexy Bedroom Tips*, *10 Ways to Guarantee a Second Date*, and *How to Have an Affair with Your Boss*. She was appalled.

Helen refused to be deterred. "From now on, every article, every movie review, book review, illustration and cartoon will appeal to our new girl readers. I'm talking about ways to make her life better. Yummier and sexier."

With that, Burt Carlson collected his things and stood up. "If you'll all excuse me."

As he left the room, I sensed others wishing they'd had the guts to do the same.

Helen didn't ease up. She carried on as if nothing had happened. "So let's see what we have."

"We've told you what we have," said Harriet La Barre, and not too kindly. "And George is right, we have holes to fill in the June issue. That should be our priority right now."

Liz agreed, so did Bobbie, and soon everyone was nodding, talking at once. I stood off to the side, watching the meeting get away from Helen like a cat escaping out the front door. There wasn't a chance for her to get it back without raising her voice, stomping her foot and breaking free of her carefully curated demure image. So she let the meeting dissolve. Some people left one at a time, others departed in clusters, and all the while Helen was the good hostess, standing near the door, thanking them for coming without ever letting the smile leave her face. If she was dying on the inside, no one knew it. Not even me.

As soon as she got back to her office, Burt Carlson was waiting for her.

"I'm not going to write about oral sex and orgasms," I heard him tell her. "I'm sorry, Helen, but I can't do it and I *won't* do it. You can have my resignation effective immediately."

Another one gone. As soon as he left her office, a teary-eyed Helen asked me to get her husband on the telephone.

CHAPTER SEVEN

○—————○

I got home that night and entered my building, eyeing its dingy cobwebs in the corners and Chinese take-out menus on the floor with footprints waffled on top. When I reached the first-floor landing, the hallway light was flickering, on the verge of burning out. As soon as I stepped inside and shut my apartment door, I felt the walls closing in on me. I went across the way and knocked on Trudy's door, but there was no answer. I was too antsy to stay in so I grabbed my camera and my coat, pulled my gloves from my pockets and headed back out.

A brisk wind gust hit me as I turned the corner and walked down Lexington. Whenever I was out with my camera, I was always acutely aware of how it made me feel. It was a prop and I, a bit of an actress: *Ali Weiss, famed photographer.* I was making a statement with that camera. Someone could look at me and assume, rightfully or not, that I was creative, artistic, talented. And I liked that. I liked being more than a secretary. The camera was my calling card, a shot of confidence. *Girl with a camera*—it said I was a someone.

As I crossed 71st Street, I saw a beautifully dressed woman

who'd buttoned her fur coat wrong so the hem didn't line up. Something about that sliver of imperfection and vulnerability made me reach for my camera as I pulled my gloves off with my teeth so I could focus in on her. I'd been struck by that same human frailty a few days before when I snapped a photograph of a man who'd lit the wrong end of his cigarette, capturing his shocked expression when he saw the filter smoking.

I'd always been observant but lately I'd begun to see the world in freeze frames, wanting to capture a single moment that told the whole story—what happened before and after the shutter clicked. Maybe I was drawn to these strangers on the streets because I, too, felt exposed and insecure in this big city. And really, it wasn't just the awkward misstepped moments that I sought to catch; it was the ordinary ones: a boy enjoying a lollipop while his dog stole a lick for himself, a woman pushing her baby stroller down the street. My eye was drawn to so much and I was running through film faster than I could buy it, certainly faster than I could afford to have it developed.

I kept walking down Lexington Avenue until I came to 63rd Street. I stopped, vaguely aware of the traffic rumbling behind me, the people rushing to and fro, a dog barking down the block. A rush of breath, white and ghostlike, hung in the air before me as I stood on the sidewalk staring at the salmon-colored brick, the arches above the windows and the green awning with gold-scripted lettering that simply said **The Barbizon**.

As I brought the camera to my eye, every thought and longing for my mother coalesced inside me. *I'm here, Mom. I made it to New York.* I had to get the picture before my vision blurred.

Just as I snapped the shutter, I heard a deep voice say, "Welcome to the Barbizon."

I pushed back my tears and looked up at the doorman as he smiled, tipped his hat and held the door for me. I wanted to toy with time, run through the doors and find my mother there. I wanted to smell her perfume when she took me in her arms and rest my chin on the ledge of her collarbone. I wanted one more look, one more chance to hear her voice.

As I crossed the threshold, all I could think was, *This was her home. This was where she lived.* My heels echoed on the marble floors as I admired the glamorous lobby with its grand staircase and the catwalk that wrapped around the perimeter of the second floor. There was a little seating area with high-back chairs, potted plants and a beautiful Oriental rug. I slipped into one of the chairs and watched the residents coming and going, trying to picture my mother and Elaine flitting through this lobby.

I wished I could have said I felt my mother's presence. Wished I could have been comforted to be there. After all, it was just like my mother had described it, down to the beautiful girls in white gloves, waiting by the front windows for their beaus to pick them up. But the ache in my heart only grew deeper. I couldn't take photos in there. I could hardly breathe.

For the second time that evening, I was on the verge of tears when a voice cut through my thoughts. "Can I help you, miss?"

I glanced up at the young woman and shook my head. "I wish you could." I got up, smoothed the front of my coat and made my way back through the lobby.

As I stepped outside, the cold air hit me full on in the face. The sidewalks were crowded and I found myself in a city surrounded by people but still I felt all alone.

I woke up the next morning to a beautiful spring day. Nothing like the night before. Now the chill that had stayed with me through the night was replaced with a mild breeze. There was hardly a cloud in sight. The darkness was gone, the loneliness tucked away, and I was back on my journey.

Even with Trudy's navigation help, I was still struggling to learn the city and wasn't all that comfortable with the subway. The graffiti, the cold stares from other passengers, the rat sightings and the frequency with which I missed my stops or boarded the wrong train made me apprehensive. I was more at ease traveling on foot, so I left early and decided to walk it.

Helen had asked me to meet her at her apartment that morning. She needed help bringing a few items into the office. I took 74th Street over and turned left on Park Avenue. Though just a few blocks from my apartment over the butcher shop, it made a world of difference. Now I understood why my mother had wanted to live here. Its glamour suited her. The avenue was wide with a manicured median in the middle filled with trees and bushes, the budding signs of crocuses and tulips already visible. Flower boxes along the window ledges were home to clusters of bright red geraniums and white hydrangeas. I made a mental note to come back with my camera and photograph the many doormen standing beneath the awnings in their crisp uniforms. I found them just as intriguing as the wealthy residents they were helping in and out of taxicabs and limousines.

Helen lived on 59th and Park, in a high-rise building adjacent to Sherry-Lehmann Wine & Spirits, where the average cost of a bottle ran higher than my weekly paycheck. She greeted me at the door in a psychedelic Pucci dress and pink shoes. Her two Siamese cats were with her. "This pretty little kitty is Samantha," she said, nuzzling one to her cheek. "And this right here"—she said, depositing Samantha and scooping up the other cat snaking about her ankles—"this handsome thing is Gregory."

From the foyer I could see a wall of tiny mirrors, hung gallery style, reflecting a spectacular view of the living room—all blues and pinks of various shades, a love seat and sofa, vases of fresh flowers, a few leopard print accents here and there.

"You have a lovely home," I said, reaching over to scratch Gregory's ear.

"Oh, I can't take credit for it. I owe it all to Michael Taylor. He cost us an arm and a leg, but as a decorator, he was worth every penny." She gently tossed Gregory to the floor, his paws landing with a soft thud on the plush carpet. There were two banker boxes resting on the floor, both packed so full that the lids wouldn't fit.

"If you take this box, I'll get the other one." She handed me a box of knickknacks, bulky but not heavy, overflowing with decoupaged boxes, needlepoint pillows and a stuffed animal shoved in head first. She hefted up the second box on her hip and paused. "Oops." She set the box back down. "I almost forgot my lunch." She darted down a hallway and returned moments later with a small brown paper bag, crinkly and limp from use. She tossed it on top of the box. "Shall we go?"

Downstairs the doorman held the gilded door for us. "Taxicab, please," I said to him, having observed that hailing cabs was their job, not mine.

"Oh, Alice, dear, no. I never take taxicabs. They're much too expensive."

I thought she was joking.

"No," she said emphatically. "I take the bus. Every day."

So with banker boxes in our arms, we walked to Lexington Avenue and waited at 59th Street for the bus. Bloomingdale's was right across the street. When the bus arrived, she pinched open her Gucci pocketbook and handed the driver two fare tokens. Helen could have afforded her own driver. It made no sense, but neither did the little brown bag lunch.

We took our seats and Helen asked how I was settling into the city and did I like where I lived. I told her I was very comfortable, staying on the Upper East Side. And yes, I had my own place.

Helen smiled approvingly. *Roommates were not sexy.* "And how is it that you know Elaine Sloan again?"

"She and my mother were good friends." I paused, flashing back to my Barbizon visit, wanting Helen to ask about my mother. I would take any opportunity to talk about her and keep her memory alive, make others see how wondrous she was.

Helen turned to me, her hand shielding the sunlight coming through the window. "Oh, before I forget, here's a word of warning about that fella you have your eye on."

"What fella?" I mumbled, knowing I'd been found out. Helen had an almost clairvoyant-like ability to read other women's minds. She knew my—and every other girl's—deepest darkest secrets.

"Oh, c'mon now, pussycat. I see the way you look at him. At that Erik Masterson. I see him hanging around your desk. Be careful, he's a Don Juan. I had a Don Juan. For nine years, I had him. Oh, that man was delicious but he treated me horribly." She winced at some particularly sour memory. "He walked all over me and broke my heart a million times because that's what Don Juans do. And remember, no matter how hard you try, a Don Juan will never marry you."

"Believe me," I said, laughing, "I have no interest in marrying Erik Masterson."

"Well, thank heavens for that. You're smarter than I was at your age."

"How do you know he's a Don Juan?"

"Oh, please," said Helen. "He has all the classic makings of a Don Juan. He's devilishly handsome and he's successful, which makes him especially lethal. He's smooth as a sheet of glass. I'll bet you he's already slept his way through half the secretarial pools in the entire Hearst Corporation."

I felt a little queasy when she said that because, since our lunch at La Grenouille, I'd caught myself fantasizing about sleeping with him. But it was all still fantasy because I kept questioning whether I could really have the kind of sex for sex's sake that Helen prescribed.

"But the thing about a Don Juan," said Helen, "is that every girl has one, so don't beat yourself up over it. Don Juans are unavoidable. No matter how smart she is, every girl has that one man that she just can't say no to even though she knows he's no good for her."

I looked out the window, studying the tree branches growing up and around the scaffolding. I observed the card tables, too, piled high with used books and incense. I knew Helen was speaking from experience. I knew she was right but I wanted to believe I was immune to my Don Juan's charms.

"Honestly," she said, "the best thing you can do is just go ahead and get it over with. Go out with him, sleep with him, get your heart smashed to bits and get back on with your life."

When we got into work that morning, Dale Donahue was waiting for Helen, his sailor-like complexion ruddier than usual. They went into her office and closed the door.

"I think he's quitting," said Bridget, setting her coffee cup down hard on my desk while she toyed with her earring. "This damn clip." She pulled the earring free and held it in her hand. The back had broken off. "Well, that's just great." She hastily unfastened the other earring and threw them both in the wastebasket.

"Easy there," I said. "They're just earrings."

"Yeah, well, they're my favorite pair and now I can't afford to replace them." She looked like she was on the verge of tears.

"Something tells me this isn't just about your earrings. What's going on?"

"Nothing. Absolutely nothing." She sighed and slapped her hands to her thighs. "I didn't get the *Redbook* job."

"I'm sorry."

"Yeah, me, too, 'cause I'm broke, and I'm sick and tired of being broke."

I was in the same boat. I had a bottle of Prell shampoo on the bathroom ledge, turned upside down to collect every last drop, and a sliver of Ivory soap that needed to last until payday.

"*What's* going on in there?" asked Margot, joining us. She leaned against my desk, sipping her coffee, leaving a half-moon of red lipstick on the rim of her cup. "I heard Dale wanted to see her. Do you think he's quitting, too?"

"I have no idea." I glanced at Helen's appointment book, thinking I might have to interrupt her meeting with Dale for a call she had coming up.

"Well," said Margot, fingering through her pixie locks, "whatever she said in that meeting yesterday really created a stir."

"People around here don't like change," said Bridget.

"That's for sure," I said, shuffling through a stack of pink message slips that had accumulated for Helen overnight.

"C'mon," said Margot, "just tell me. *What* do ya think's *really* going on in there?"

I hesitated, leery of Margot ever since Bridget told me she was a gossip. Thankfully we heard Helen and Dale talking on the other side of the door, and just as the knob began to turn, Margot and Bridget sprinted back to their desks. After Dale Donahue left, Helen handed me his letter of resignation.

"Please file this along with the other ones, will you, dear?" She had a damp tissue clutched in one hand, a fresh one in the other, which she used to dab her eyes and blow her nose. "I don't understand it. Everyone's deserting me. Tell me, am I really *that* dreadful to work for?" She smiled, casting her rod in my sea of compliments.

"Of course not." I took the bait with pleasure. "If you ask me, the people who quit weren't up for the challenge. You have a vision for this magazine, and those stuffy old men weren't right for the new *Cosmopolitan* anyway."

Her smile ripened and that did something for me, knowing I could encourage her like that. In the weeks and months ahead, we'd wind up doing this very thing, this little dance, whereby I'd confirm all that she believed or wanted to believe true about herself. Sometimes I'd respond in earnest, sometimes a little less so, stopping just short of an outright lie. She seemed to buy what I was saying either way. Bolstering Helen's ego when she was down would forevermore be part of my job description.

"Well, good riddance to him, right?" She jutted out her hip and toyed with her armful of bangles.

I reminded Helen of her upcoming call and went to get her a fresh cup of coffee. When I returned, George Walsh was in her office, along with Richard Berlin, Dick Deems and Erik Masterson. Helen was sitting in her doll's chair, looking deceptively vulnerable and fragile while Berlin and Deems sat in the two larger chairs opposite her desk. Erik and George remained standing. None of them opted for her frilly, floral sofa.

I couldn't tell if Erik was looking at me or not because I kept my eyes on the coffee cup, determined to conduct myself professionally and keep my personal life separate from whatever was going on in the workplace. And regardless of what happened outside the office, I knew I would never betray Helen's confidences and would never tell Erik a thing she wouldn't want him knowing.

As I set the coffee cup on Helen's equally tiny side table, Berlin spoke up. "George here told us about your meeting yesterday. He said you want to scrap the July flatplan and start over. He also shared the kind of articles you want in it."

I glanced at George, who brought his fist to his mouth and cleared his throat, seemingly unapologetic for tattling on Helen. I started to leave, but she motioned for me to stay and close the door. I think she wanted a witness in case blood was spilled.

"Welcome to the new *Cosmo*, fellas," she said in her silky tone, while leisurely making notations on the pad of paper in her lap.

"We've talked about this," said Deems. "We have standards here at Hearst."

"Oh, Dick," she purred, "tell me something, what was your relationship like with your mother? I only ask because you seem so abnormally uptight about women and sexuality." She looked up at him, wide-eyed and smiling. "As a matter of fact, you're all so uptight about sex. Why, you boys can't even utter the word *sex* without blushing."

Deems's face went dark, but not as dark as Berlin's. I was too shocked to check Erik's expression but I was also cheering on the inside. This was the Helen that Elaine had told me about.

"Very funny," said Deems. "I'm serious about the content of the July issue. And besides, you should be focusing on finishing up June. There are holes in that issue that need to be patched."

"Yes," said Berlin. "You need to patch those holes."

"If I hear about those damn *holes* one more time . . ." Her voice trailed off as she shook her head, exasperated. "June will be what June will be," she said a moment later, recovering with a sing-songy delivery. "But July"—she smiled slyly—"now *that* one we can do something really nifty with."

"How do you expect to execute July?" asked Erik. "You've already lost half your staff. And you went and fired Rex Reed. Who's going to write these new articles for you?"

"Hold your horses, Erik," Berlin barked. "We're not done discussing June."

Erik stuffed his hands in his pockets and took up a fascination with the floor.

I'm a lackey and a whipping boy, he'd said at lunch. I could see now that it was true.

"Helen," said Berlin, "you'll use the articles we already have in-house for June *and* for July. And that's all there is to it."

"Oh." She laughed as if the idea was absurd. "Those will never work."

"None of them?" said Deems. "C'mon now. You mean to tell me that out of all the manuscripts we have stockpiled around this place, you can't find any acceptable articles to publish?"

"That's exactly what I'm saying. Except for maybe that one piece about an estrogen pill. The rest are all just boring, dull and wrong for my girls."

"Well, I'm sorry, Helen," said Erik, trying to recover from his earlier reprimand. "But I'm afraid that's all you've got to work with."

"Oh, nonsense." Her eyes shifted to her notepad, her wrist moving back and forth as she scratched down another idea. "This city is filled with writers who would love to see their work published in *Cosmopolitan*."

"Maybe so," said Deems. "But you won't have the money to pay them."

"And why is that?" Helen looked up, drumming her pen against her notepad.

"We've made some adjustments to the budget," said Deems. "As you know, *Cosmopolitan* has been operating in the red for the past several years. Ad revenue is way down and June looks no better, according to Ira. Plus, you went ahead and hired Walter

Meade at a top salary and you certainly didn't hold back on re-decorating your office."

"That's true," Erik agreed. "You did go a little overboard in here."

"The bottom line," said Berlin, "is that the board has decided that we need to make some cuts."

"Cuts?" Her pen stopped moving, and for the first time I saw genuine concern flicker behind her big brown eyes. "You told me you haven't increased the *Cosmopolitan* budget in over twenty years. It's already impossibly tight and now you're talking about making cuts?"

"You'll have $30,000 per issue," said Berlin.

That sounded like a fortune to me and Helen must have thought it was sufficient, too. She leaned back in her tiny chair, letting her shoulders drop down into place. "Why such long faces, fellas? I'm sure $30,000 will be enough for the articles."

The men turned to Berlin.

"I don't think you understand, Helen. It's not $30,000 for the writers. It's $30,000 total. For the entire issue. That includes photography, models, retouching, illustration, editing, advertising, shipping, salaries for the staff, expenses—everything." He cracked a triumphant smile.

If Helen was thrown by this, she didn't show it. Not in the least. But George, well, he slapped his hands to his forehead and topped that off with an exasperated sigh. Helen didn't give them the satisfaction of knowing they'd gotten to her, if indeed they had.

"You forgot printing costs," she said, setting her notepad aside.

"That will be absorbed by Hearst."

"Oh, well, thank heavens for that." Sarcasm wasn't her usual style, but she was making her point as she gracefully rose from her doll's chair and smoothed down her dress. "Well, gentlemen, if it's $30,000, then it's $30,000. I can see I have my work cut out for me, so unless there's anything else, I should really get back to the July issue."

George, Berlin, Deems and Erik had barely cleared Helen's office door when I saw her break down. She went over to her sofa, curled up in the corner and wrapped her bony arms tightly around her middle as if she were about to split in two.

"Mrs. Brown?"

She sank even farther down into herself and began rocking back and forth. I noticed a fresh run had appeared in her stockings.

"Are you all right?"

She didn't respond. I went to her side and was about to ask again when she started crying. "I can't take this anymore," she said.

I'd never before met a woman who cried as often or with as much gusto as Helen Gurley Brown. Every upset and hurt, every frustration and disappointment, got washed away with her tears and an occasional eyelash or two. After a particularly hard crying jag, the kind that left her eyes puffy, she'd remove her wig and submerge her face in a bowl of ice water, holding her breath for as long as she could stand it. Afterward I'd hand her a towel and guard her door while she reapplied her makeup and reappeared, looking fresh-faced and perfectly composed.

I was shocked by her tears at first because I was just the opposite. I hadn't let myself cry since my mother died. After losing her, nothing else seemed worthy of my tears. It was as if crying over anything else diminished the depth of my grieving for her. And it wasn't that I hadn't had my share of reasons to cry. When Michael told me it was over . . . When I heard that he was getting married . . . When my father decided to remarry. Even then, I had stopped myself from crying.

Helen undid her arms and cradled her head in her hands. She was sobbing full on now, and she didn't give a goddamn that her nose and mascara were running. I reached over and plucked a tissue from a decoupaged box and handed it to her. She dabbed her eyes and blew her nose, clearing the way for the next round of tears. I handed her a second tissue, the first one balled up tight in her fist.

"How do they expect me to edit this magazine with both hands tied behind my back?" she said, choking out the words. "They're setting me up to fail." She looked up at me, her nose as red as W. C. Fields's, her painted lips quivering.

This was the one time I didn't try to convince her otherwise because we both knew it was true.

Helen was despondent and it seemed to take all her strength just to say, "Get me David."

Twenty minutes later, he appeared, a tall, older, distinguished man whom she often called lamb chop, whom she spoiled with one hand and tried to discipline with the other, weighing him every morning to determine if he could have an extra slice of toast or strip of bacon. He was certainly fit, slightly balding with a mustache and every bit as charming as she'd professed in *Sex and the Single Girl*. In the weeks and months to come, there would be many times she would have me track him down, pulling him out of meetings, making him miss luncheon appointments and flights to the West Coast. He never objected to her interruptions. He was vested in his wife. Before working in Hollywood, he himself had been an editor with *Cosmopolitan* and knew the business inside and out. She leaned on him, all 105 pounds of her, and I would come to think of him as her silent partner.

But that morning David Brown was stern with her. I heard him through the closed office door telling her to get ahold of herself. "Stop your crying, Helen. That's not going to solve anything."

Her voice was muffled and sounded nasally. I heard sobs but couldn't decipher a single word.

"No, they're not going to fire you," he said in response. "It'll cost them a fortune to buy out your contract. And even if they did, think of it this way, you'll have a nice, long paid vacation." More mutterings from her before he said, "Yes, of course I'll still write the cover blurbs for July. But first things first. You need to finalize the June issue. Then you can go to town on July. We'll come up with a plan. We'll get creative and find a way to make the budget work. We'll show them. But for now, just put June to bed."

This was followed by a long period of hushed murmurs between the two before Helen's office door opened. Despite having retouched her makeup, Helen had obviously been bawling her eyes out.

"If anyone's looking for me, I'll be back in a couple hours," she said with forced cheerfulness. "Just tell them David and I are taking a nooner."

CHAPTER EIGHT

After Helen and David left, I went down the hall to get a cup of coffee. Margot was in the kitchen along with Penny and Tony La Sala, the head art director. He had dark hair, dark eyes and a five o'clock shadow even at nine in the morning. He was stylish and wore Nehru jackets like the Beatles along with a chunky gold medallion and a healthy helping of Jovan Musk.

"Did you hear about Dale?" Penny asked, setting two saccharin tablets loose in her coffee, fizzing their way across the surface.

"We're taking bets on who's next," said Tony, reaching for a donut in a cardboard box on the counter. "I'm putting my money on Bobbie. One more *pussycat* and she's outta here."

I cracked a half smile and instantly felt guilty, like I was being disloyal to Helen. As I poured my coffee, George rushed into the kitchen, perspiration visible on his forehead.

"Has anyone seen Helen?" he asked, panting. "Alice—there you are! Where's Helen?"

"She's taking a nooner with Mr. Brown." As soon as I said it, George's cheeks turned red. Suddenly all eyes were on me and everyone was laughing. I didn't know what I'd said. Helen told me if anyone asked to say she was taking a nooner. So I did.

George scrunched up his face and hissed, "That is disgusting, young lady."

Before I could say anything, he stormed out of the kitchen, and by then the others weren't just laughing, they were howling.

"I can't believe you said that to Walsh." Tony was doubled over, clutching his sides. "That was too much."

"Did you see his face?" Margot was sopping tears from her eyes. "That was great."

Great? Too much? What did I do? What did I say?

"Of all people," said Penny, struggling to catch her breath.

I didn't know if she was referring to the fact that I'd said it to George *of all people* or that whatever it was had come out of *my* mouth *of all people*. Either way, they seemed to have developed some newfound respect for me, as if they'd underestimated my hipness. For the first time since I'd started at *Cosmopolitan*, I had their approval. They were still laughing, so I began laughing with them, hoping to solidify our bond.

Bridget walked into the kitchen, her hair swept back in a green headband that matched her top. "Is it true?" She looked at me in disbelief. "Did you really just tell George that Helen was taking a nooner?"

"Well," I said with a combination smirk and shrug, "that's what she told me."

The others were still laughing, and Bridget must have sensed the confusion lurking beneath my blithe expression.

"Alice." She pulled me aside and leaned in, whispering, "Did she really say those exact words to you?"

"Yes."

"You *do* know what a *nooner* is, don't you?"

By then, I knew enough to have been embarrassed by not

knowing. I was too proud to own up to my naiveté so instead I
gave Bridget one of those noncommittal, middle-of-the-road grins
that fools no one.

"Oh, Alice, you just told George that Helen left work to go
ball her husband."

"What?" I wasn't sure I'd heard right, but the look on her face
made my stomach drop. I felt sick inside, my cheeks and chest
growing hot. How could I have been so stupid? Innocently or not,
I had just betrayed Helen. Yes, I wanted the others to like me, but
not at Helen's expense. And what was worse, I'd lost all the
ground I'd just gained with my coworkers. I'd just confirmed that
I was nothing but a hick from Youngstown, Ohio. While everyone
else was still recovering from the hilarity, I excused myself.

When I got back to my desk, I saw that the morning mail had
arrived and I was grateful for the distraction, but the shame of
what just happened kept replaying in my head like a song you
can't get rid of.

I t was almost one o'clock when Helen returned from her nooner.
Or more correctly, from what Helen had referred to as a nooner.
I would come to learn that a nooner for Helen and David Brown
consisted of a long taxicab ride where Helen wouldn't fret about
the meter, instead taking as much time as needed for David to
calm her down and resolve whatever crisis had arisen with the
magazine. But I didn't know that yet, and neither did anyone else.

All this nooner business was still buzzing through my mind
when Helen came and stood by my desk, hand on hip and something set and unapologetic in her posture. "They want the holes
patched in the June issue—fine. I'll patch 'em up. They want me
to produce a magazine on a shoestring budget; I'll do that, too."

David was gone but Helen was back. All the way back. Whatever her husband had said, whatever he'd done to her, their nooner did the trick. She was Helen Gurley Brown again.

"Alice, come into my office. It's time to get busy." She said she was famished as she reached for her brown paper bag, removed two foiled bundles and nibbled on a carrot stick while she paced. "I want to issue a memo to the staff. We're going to tighten our belts. Effective immediately, there will be no more $8 lunches at Lutèce. They want to entertain a writer or take a client to lunch, they can go to Longchamps and be in and out of there for $2 a head. And if someone submits a bar bill from the Tea Room—or anyplace else—I expect to know who they were buying drinks for. And why." I could feel the energy stirring inside her as she reached for a celery stick and kept pacing. "There'll be no more personal long-distance telephone calls made from the office, and we're done reimbursing people for late-night taxi fares. Everyone's going to have to learn to get their work done during normal business hours or else pay their own way home." She ate another carrot stick and, in between bites, said, "From now on, everyone submits their expenses to you for approval."

I looked at the few remaining carrot sticks and the hard-boiled egg resting in a nest of tinfoil. "Would you like me to run out and bring you back a sandwich? Or maybe some soup?"

"Oh, no, no." She nibbled the last of her carrot sticks. "This is more than enough."

No wonder she was so tiny. The woman never ate. A splurge for her was an extra helping of diet gelatin.

After Helen finished dictating her memo, she reapplied her lipstick in a mirror on her desk and rattled off a number of things for me to do with an added sense of urgency.

When I left her office, I typed the memo, and while I distributed it around the office, I was collecting articles and story ideas that she hadn't seen yet.

"She's really cracking the whip, isn't she?" said Margot as she read the memo. "Next thing ya know, they'll be charging us for pencils."

Bridget came and stood behind her, reading over her shoulder. While they dissected the memo, I searched for stray manuscripts and finished delivering the bad news about expenses to the rest of the staff. By the time I'd rounded up a stack of articles and taken them into Helen's office, George was in there and he was as worked up as I'd ever seen him.

"Please," he said to her, "I beg you to use what we have in-house for July. You'll blow your entire budget trying to get someone to write your ideas. As it is, you can't even afford one or two articles from someone like Tom Wolfe or Norman Mailer, let alone a short story from Capote."

"You assume I want a Tom Wolfe or a Norman Mailer or a Truman Capote to write for me," said Helen, taking the manuscripts from me. "But I don't."

"Well, all right then, so maybe not those authors specifically. But you'd still have to pay someone to write the articles. We're just hoping you'll come to your senses and not try to publish any of those—" He pointed to the bulletin board that was wallpapered with story ideas: *Men's Naughty Bedroom Fantasies, Even You Can Wear a Miniskirt, Secrets to Snagging Your Dream Man.*

"I'm willing to look through these articles," said Helen, her palm down on the stack of manuscripts. "But I'm not going to publish just anything because it's already been paid for."

"But you have to be practical. You—"

"George." She cut him off, her voice even and measured. "Let me tell you something about being practical. It'll get you nowhere. I grew up poor as a church mouse. I wore secondhand clothes. I changed my own flat tires and my oil, too. I doctored up my broken heels with Elmer's Glue. I never left a restaurant without a doggie bag. You wouldn't believe how far I can stretch a dollar. There's not a budget I haven't been able to make work and that includes this one."

I t was getting late. The cleaning service had already come through and everyone else was gone.

"You should go home," I said to Helen, sticking my head in her office. Her desk lamp gave off a cone of golden light all around her. A pencil snapped in two was lying on her blotter. "Don't forget, you have an eight o'clock breakfast meeting tomorrow morning. Shall I telephone Mr. Brown and let him know you're on your way?" He'd called twice already, asking when she was leaving.

She shook her head and took a final puff off her cigarette, grinding it out in the marble ashtray on her desk. "I can't go home yet. I have to figure out how I'm going to put out this magazine without any money." She looked up and sighed. "I've gone through two more piles of manuscripts and there's nothing here that's even remotely publishable."

"Are you sure?"

"Here." She handed me a stack. "See for yourself."

While I began reading an article about Yosemite, Helen got up from her desk and went over to her sofa with a fresh pile of papers. "Richard and Dick want me to include a piece by Isaac Bashevis Singer in June, but that'll be the last of him. He's not right for my girls. They're also insisting I include the Rex Reed movie reviews he did before he was fired."

She cast aside the pages and stood up, her arms raised above her head, fingers laced together as she leaned to the left and then the right before bending forward, her palms flattened on the floor. She was quite flexible. Especially for a woman in her forties.

She was still lamenting the work of Singer while she kicked off her Palizzio heels and began running in place. "Any new developments with your Don Juan?"

"I'm sorry, what?" I was surprised that she'd asked.

"Well? Anything?" She was panting, running, pumping her arms.

"Not really." I was beginning to think I'd been presumptuous while at lunch with him, thinking something had begun between us. Sometimes Erik went out of his way to stop by my desk and chat; other times he breezed past me without a word, without a glance. "He runs a little hot and cold."

"That's because he's a Don Juan. You'll have to play hard to get if you want that one."

"Well, I don't exactly want him."

"Oh, c'mon now. Don't kid a kidder."

"How come you're trying to help me *get* him when you said I should steer clear of him?"

"Because, pussycat, if you're like any red-blooded female, you can't stop thinking about him, and the sooner you get him and get him out of your system, the better it'll be for me."

"Well, he seems like he could be more trouble than he's worth."

"Oh, I can guarantee you he is." Helen continued running in place, her knees reaching higher and higher.

"And I'm sure he has a million girls."

"I'm sure you're right about that, too."

"I don't think I'm his type anyway." I noticed that he always made a point of stopping by Bridget's desk. "He probably prefers blondes."

"Now that's where you're wrong. Did you not learn *anything* from my book? Type has nothing to do with it. Even a mouseburger can get any fellow she wants. At least for a little while."

Helen stopped running and was now on the floor, lying on her back, doing fluttery scissor kicks, toes pointed, graceful as a ballerina. "I landed David, didn't I? And I was the biggest mouseburger of all. I can tell you this much—no man fell in love with me at first sight. I wasn't the pretty girl with dozens of fellas lined up asking me to dance. But even back in high school, I hooked the most popular boy in my class. And you want to know how I did it? I turned on my *Plain Girl Power*. My sex appeal would sneak up on them once they got to talking with me. I could make just about any man want me."

She rolled onto her hip, lifting her top leg up and down, up and down. "The thing to remember about men is that they're a puzzle. All a girl has to do is figure them out. Find out what lights a fire under that Erik Masterson and play hard to get and he's yours." She continued with her leg lifts while she talked. "Men are really very easy to win over. I know because I got David to marry me. Oh, it took me two years and a lot of tears but he was worth it. I was living in Los Angeles when I met him. The first time I saw him was at a friend's party. I asked the hostess to introduce me and she said no."

"That wasn't very nice."

"Oh, she did me a huge favor. I'll forever be in her debt for that. You see, David had just gotten divorced and he was a big-time Hollywood producer with Twentieth Century. He was dating a lot of starlets who wanted parts in his movies. He needed some time to get all that out of his system. So I waited and waited. And then I waited some more." She finished her last set of leg lifts and returned to her position on the sofa, wrapping her arms about her knees.

"In the meantime, I was dating several men, but they were just placeholders. Then, two years later I saw David at another party. I knew he didn't want a woman who wanted him for his money or his position. I decided that I would show him right from the get-go that I was independent and self-sufficient. Which I was. I was working for an advertising agency at the time. I was one of the only women copywriters and I was good. Gosh darn good at it. I let David know that I had my own money and my own apartment. In fact, on our first date I refused to let him pick me up. I insisted on driving because I was going to have him walk me to my car after dinner and I wanted him to see that I drove a Mercedes. Believe me, that registered with him. None of his starlets could have afforded a car like that on their own. I choreographed the entire evening, and by the time he saw that car, he was hooked."

I was engrossed, and just when I thought she was going to tell me more, she reached for a manuscript, read a line or two and said, "Now see? Something like this just won't do."

I glanced at the cover page. It was an article by Tom Wolfe.

"It's wordy and complicated for the sake of being complicated," she said. "I wish these writers would quit trying so hard to sound like they're intellectuals. They're so pretentious. I want every article in this magazine to be baby simple."

She read a few more lines and set the manuscript aside. "Berlin thinks he's got me over a barrel by cutting my budget but he doesn't know who he's dealing with. If I have to, I'll write my own damn articles. And I have a camera—I'll take my own damn photographs, too." She reached for a cigarette, and while she lit it, the wheels were already turning inside my head.

CHAPTER NINE

◦────────◦

A light spring rain, more like a mist, hung in the air when I left work that night. The days were gradually growing longer—not that I would have noticed. I couldn't remember the last time I'd left work when it was still light out. My only evidence of the change of season was that it was getting warmer and I hadn't bothered to button my raincoat when I got off the subway.

I crossed 72nd Street, and as I walked up Second Avenue, my mind was racing, thinking of the best way to approach Helen about my photography. I had just gotten a new roll of film developed the day before—mostly random shots I'd taken on the subway or while I was walking about the streets, but they were the best photos I'd ever taken.

Funny how the city had changed the way I approached a photograph. I used to agonize over every shot: the angle, focus and exposure, waiting for everything to be perfect before I'd click the shutter. But New York was too fast for that. So much to see, and if you didn't catch it the instant it was happening, you'd miss it. I was becoming more and more fascinated with candid shots. To me, those captured the unexpected magic of the city, and it dawned on me that just as my mother had documented my life growing up, I was documenting New York.

When I got home, I set my pocketbook down and shrugged off my coat, slumping it over the back of the sofa. I'd been in the process of redoing my portfolio anyway, wincing when I thought about my earlier photos, embarrassed that I'd ever shown them to Elaine Sloan or anyone else. I gathered all my photographs and spread them out across the floor, eliminating dozens of them right away. I scrutinized the others and the order in which to put them. It was going on two in the morning when I mounted the last picture on the heavy black construction paper I'd splurged on a few days before.

The next morning, I brought my portfolio to work, carefully placing it in my bottom desk drawer along with my lunch and pocketbook. I had planned to show it to Helen right away, but when she arrived from her breakfast meeting and called me into her office, I grew too timid to mention it.

After I'd brought in her coffee and newspapers and we went through her schedule, there was a silence; the perfect opportunity, but I couldn't find the words to broach the subject. The day pressed on, the portfolio pulling for my attention like a child tugging on his mother's sleeve. When it was half past seven and the rest of the office had emptied out, it was just the two of us and I knew it was now or never. Holding my portfolio gingerly in my hands, I knocked on her door. "Do you have a minute?"

"Come in." She smiled, her eyes hooded. In the light of her desk lamp I could detect the dark circles lurking beneath her pancake makeup. She had her red pencil going, editing a manuscript.

I couldn't get started. I stood in front of her desk, glancing down at the case in my hands before I dared to look up.

"Oh dear." She set the pencil down, her brown eyes large with concern. "Is something wrong?"

"No, no." I offered a weak smile. "It's just that, remember

yesterday, you were talking about having to take your own photos for the magazine?"

"Oh, that." She smiled, relieved. I think she thought I was going to quit.

"Well, I wanted to let you know that I can help with that. I can take the pictures for you."

"Alice"—she cocked her head to the side—"I was kidding about taking my own photos. I just have to find a batch of writers and photographers who'll be willing to work for nothing."

"But I'm serious. I take pictures all the time. I'm good, too. And you wouldn't even have to pay me. Not a penny." I knew I was talking too fast.

"That's very sweet of you to offer." She laughed as she picked up her pencil, her eyes returning to the manuscript.

"Well, at least let me show you some of my photographs," I said, holding out my portfolio. "These are my pictures." I set my case on her desk. "I took them."

She humored me, opening the case and looking at each photograph before she closed the cover. "Oh, pussycat, I can see you're very passionate about this, but I can't have you running around taking pictures. You're much more valuable to me as my secretary." She reached for the stack of papers and went back to reading her manuscripts.

Subject closed. The possibility of shooting for *Cosmopolitan* had been extinguished as quickly as it had been sparked. I took back my portfolio, feeling foolish, my face burning. She was only being polite, going through the motions of looking at my photos. Obviously, they weren't as good as I thought. Maybe I was kidding myself, thinking I could do this at all. Maybe photography would be nothing more than a hobby for me, like it was for my mother. All I knew was that I wasn't going to humiliate myself again by showing those photos to anyone else.

Clutching the portfolio to my chest, I asked if she needed anything.

"I'm fine. I just need to read through the last of these manuscripts."

I always felt guilty leaving before Helen, even that night after she'd crushed my hopes of shooting for the magazine. I was embarrassed, though, and couldn't wait to get out of there. I said a quick good night before I grabbed my pocketbook and tossed my portfolio into the wastebasket under my desk.

As I got in the elevator that night, I knew I'd done the right thing by dumping my portfolio. But I wasn't about to give up. I just had to make my work that much better, and if ever it made sense to enroll in a photography class, it was now.

The elevator doors opened, and as I stepped into the lobby, Erik Masterson was coming through the revolving door. "Oh good, you're still here," he said. "I was just coming to get you for a drink and a bite to eat."

I was ridiculously happy to see him. After the day I'd had, dinner and drinks with Erik sounded like a welcome distraction, only I didn't like him assuming I'd be free. "Sorry," I said. "I can't tonight. I'm already running late as it is."

"For what?"

I wasn't a good liar and couldn't come up with anything on the spot, so I simply said, "I'll take a rain check."

"Oh, c'mon, break your plans." The lobby was empty at that hour and our voices echoed off the marble walls and ceiling.

"And what if I don't want to?" I smiled, remembering Helen's advice on playing hard to get.

"Alice." He put on a mock frown and brushed a strand of hair away from my cheek. "You're making this very difficult."

My face was still warm from his touch. "Maybe you shouldn't have waited till the last minute to ask me out." I raised my chin and looked him right in the eyes, and immediately knew that was a mistake because now he locked me in with his gaze. My heart sped up. I couldn't turn away.

That's when he stepped in, grabbed me by the shoulders, pulled me close and planted a long deep kiss on my mouth. His lips were soft, practiced. He knew exactly what he was doing to me, and I found myself kissing him back as he pulled me in closer still. It had been so long—I'd forgotten how fun kissing was, and here I was in the hands of a master, a true champion kisser.

"Sorry," he said, though clearly he wasn't sorry at all. "But I'm impatient and I've been wanting to do that since I first saw you." I was stunned and stumbled as he slipped his arm about my waist and coaxed me out the door.

Erik took me to a crowded restaurant a few blocks away. It didn't have the glitz or glamour of La Grenouille or the Russian Tea Room but it was very New York just the same, thick with smoke and expensive perfume.

We were halfway through our first round of drinks before a seat at the bar opened up. Erik stood next to me, keeping one eye on the room while we chatted and nibbled on shrimp cocktails and Swedish meatballs.

"You were burning the midnight oil tonight," he said. "What were you working on so late?"

"Uh-uh. I'm not falling for that."

"For what?"

"You know what. I'm not telling you what Helen's up to."

"I swear that's not what I was trying to do."

"Sure you weren't." I reached for my martini and took a sip.

"Just tell me one thing—is it true that Helen left the office yesterday for a nooner?"

"My God." I set my glass down hard, gin sloshing back and forth. "How did you find out about that? Does George Walsh go running to Hearst with every little thing? What a jerk."

"Oh, c'mon, just tell me, is it true? Did you really say that to him?"

I groaned and nodded sheepishly as he burst out laughing.

It was getting late and I'd had two martinis on a small helping of shrimp and meatballs. Erik was about to order another round.

"Not for me," I said, pushing my glass aside, looking for my jacket.

"You're not leaving yet, are you? You can't." He turned as a prism of light ricocheted off the mirror behind the bar, encircling his handsome face. His sheer beauty was unnerving and that kiss in the lobby was still stirring inside me. All I could think about was kissing him again.

"You just can't leave me for a third time," he said.

"Then maybe you should come with me."

He paid the bill and twenty minutes later had me pressed up against the doorway of the butcher shop below my apartment.

"Let me come up," he said, speaking into my lips.

I wanted to say yes but thankfully what came out was, "Not tonight."

"Why not?"

"It's a school night," I teased.

He was coming on strong, and though I wanted him, too, I was scared. What if I wasn't modern enough to sleep with a man I didn't love? And besides, I didn't want to be that easy. If I was going to give in, I was going to at least make him work for it. We kissed for another fifteen minutes. I was getting weaker, about to surrender, when he backed off and said good night.

My lips were still tingling, my body pulsing. I watched as he made his way down the sidewalk, his hand casually raised to hail a cab.

I keyed into my apartment, feeling so woozy, I ended up crawling into bed with my slip still on. As I drifted off, I thought about Erik and his kisses. All my good sense was disconnected from my brain. Maybe, just maybe, I could pull this off and sleep with him for the thrill of it. No expectations. No messy entanglements.

I was on top of the world until I thought about my photography and realized I was on the bottom looking up, with so far a climb before anyone in this town would take my work seriously.

CHAPTER TEN

———∘———∘———

made it to work the next morning by a quarter till eight. Suffering from a hangover, my head throbbed, my stomach was sour and even my bones felt parched. I dropped my pocketbook in the bottom drawer, and as I set off down the hall for coffee, I noticed Helen had already arrived. Not surprising. No matter how early I got in, Helen was always already there. That morning she wasn't in her office, but I saw the coffee cup on her desk, kissed fresh with her lipstick, and half a dozen cigarette butts crushed out in her ashtray. She was always the last to leave at night, too. She worked longer and harder than anyone I knew. I wondered when, or if, she ever slept.

After Berlin and his boys dropped the budget bomb on her a couple days before, Helen had decided she needed to find her own crop of writers and photographers. While I'd been off smooching with Erik, Helen had been devising a plan. I found a stack of newspaper and magazine clippings on my desk with a handwritten note paper-clipped to the top: *Dear A—Be a love and see if you can track down any of these writers and tell them I'd like to meet with them.*

I sorted through the clips, looking at the bylines circled in Helen's blue pencil. I didn't recognize any of the names but that was the whole point. These were unknown writers she could get on the cheap.

Later that day she produced a second pile of photographs and illustrations with a similar note attached, asking me to track those people down as well. And this time, it stung. Those calls to photographers were harder to make. It felt like they were taking something away from me, getting a chance at my once-in-a-lifetime opportunity. Each time I dialed another number, I had to remind myself it wasn't their fault. Or even Helen's. Like it or not, I wasn't a photographer. Not yet anyway. I was a secretary.

By eight o'clock the following Monday morning, the lobby was full of freelancers. They paraded in, some with newspaper and magazine clippings jutting out of manila folders, others with handsome black cases that zipped all the way around, filled with their photographs and illustrations. It made me see just how shoddy my little cardboard case had been. No wonder Helen hadn't given me a chance. A leather portfolio—that was something else I'd have to save up for.

Bridget stepped off the elevator and navigated her way through the lobby doors. "What's going on?"

"Helen's interviewing freelancers."

"I see." She surveyed the room, her neck turning like a swan's until she stopped and reached for my arm. "Who's he?"

"Who's who?" I said, my eyes scanning the list of names on my clipboard.

She nudged me and gestured with her chin toward a man I hadn't seen come in.

"I don't know who he is."

His back was turned toward me. All I could see was that he

was tall with dark tousled hair, long enough to reach the collar of his shirt—a white button-down dress shirt that he wore with a pair of denim jeans and boots instead of a suit and tie. He was standing off to the side, holding a large black portfolio, a Nikon camera slung over his shoulder, hanging by its strap.

As if sensing he was being watched, the man turned and I saw that I actually did know him. The sculpted nose and angular jaw, the dark eyes. It was Christopher Mack. His name hadn't been on my list of photographers to call. He smiled and cocked his head to the side. A subtle gesture but Bridget picked up on it.

"You *do* so know him." She shimmied off her jacket, exposing a formfitting sheath dress. "Who is he? Don't you think he looks like George?"

"George Walsh? Are you crazy?"

"No." She laughed. "George Harrison. The Beatle."

"Oh. It's the hair," I said, looking down at my clipboard.

"Well, don't just stand there. Introduce me."

So I walked Bridget over and made the introduction. "Christopher, hi. I don't know if you remember me but—"

"Alice. Sure. I was hoping I'd see you here." He shook my hand and tossed his head back to clear the hair from his eyes, though it immediately fell back into place.

Bridget cleared her throat as if I'd forgotten about her. "Oh, and this is Bridget."

She smiled, reached out her hand, shaking his and holding the grip a beat too long.

"Elaine talked to David Brown yesterday," he explained. Bridget still had hold of his hand. "He told Elaine that Helen was calling in books."

"I see you're a photographer," said Bridget, now giving a playful tug on his camera strap.

He smiled at her before turning back to me. "I hope it's okay that I just showed up here like this. Elaine thought it would be a good idea to drop off my portfolio for Helen."

"Well," I said, consulting my clipboard. "Her schedule's pretty packed but I can try and squeeze you in."

"I'll tell you what, I have to be uptown in half an hour anyway. If it's okay with you, I can just leave my case here and tell her she can look through it whenever she has a chance."

"It might be best if you—"

"Allow me." Bridget took hold of his portfolio, making a point of brushing up against him. "I'll take it, Ali." She took a few steps, stopped and looked back over her shoulder. "Nice meeting you, Christopher."

He gave her a nod as if immune to her brazen flirting. I imagined he was used to it. "In case Helen wants to contact me," he said, "my phone number's inside my book, in the back." He rapped his knuckles on my clipboard. "Good seeing you again, Alice." He turned and walked out the door as more applicants came in.

I went back to work, checking people in. My job was to confirm arrival times and take down names and telephone numbers before escorting the photographers and illustrators to the conference room, where they'd first meet with Tony La Sala. Helen had entrusted him to screen portfolios and weed out any undesirable candidates, of which there were many. Helen hadn't asked anyone to review the writers. I don't think she trusted that anyone understood what she was looking for. So far, she was ticking prospects off at breakneck speed. Writers were leaving her office as fast as I could sign them in.

Eventually I made my way over to a young freelance reporter with the *New York Post* named Nora Ephron. She had dark hair, and lots of it, so thick it looked as wide as it was high.

"Wow," she said to me, flashing a big toothy smile, "now I

know why I got a seat on the subway this morning. All of Manhattan's in here. What are you giving away?"

A petite blonde leaned in and said, "There hasn't been a cattle call like this since the Winter Garden was casting for *Funny Girl*." The tiny blonde was Judith Krantz, and she had a folder of clips from *Ladies' Home Journal* and *McCall's*.

A couple hours later, after the commotion in the lobby had settled down and the undesirable applicants had been dismissed, Helen was behind closed doors with Nora, Judith and a third writer, Lyn Tornabene.

I was back at my desk when Bridget came over, holding Christopher's portfolio in her arms. "I think he's got a girlfriend." She frowned, leaning the case against the side of my desk.

"And what makes you think that?" I asked, hefting it up, unzipping the case and laying it flat across my desk.

"There's a lot of pictures in the back—all of the same girl."

"Hmmm."

"Too bad," she said, "'cause he sure is sexy."

After Bridget returned to her desk, I looked through Christopher's portfolio. Each oversize sleeve had a clear plastic cover, protecting the photographs and catching the glare of the overhead lights. The first few pages were devoted to product shots and print ads. Mostly of high-end luxury items: a Hermès scarf, a Gucci belt, two-tone City Club shoes and a pair of Chanel sunglasses. There were some headshots of authors, too, though no one I recognized.

The photos were clean and nicely composed, but it was the photos toward the back that really showcased his talent. There was page after page of a beautiful, sultry woman, bare from the chest up, her hands strategically covering her breasts, the light shimmering off her shoulders. Christopher had devoted at least half of his portfolio to this one model.

I could see why Bridget assumed it was his girlfriend. I went back to studying his photographs, carefully turning the sleeves. All the photos were black-and-whites, stunning and artfully shot. He had captured the light in such a way that it felt as though it was moving across the model's face and shoulders. Christopher Mack's photographs had depth. They were animated. I wanted to know his secrets, his tricks. I would have given anything to take those kinds of photographs.

I was sure Helen would be as impressed as I was. Tony La Sala certainly was. She might have been, too, had she not spent the past four days in back-to-back interviews. By the time she finally got to Christopher's portfolio, she was glazed over. She closed his case and slid it across the desk to me.

"Well?" I asked as I zipped it up.

"Don't you think we're set for now?" she asked. "I sure do. But he's got something. Let's keep him on file. Just in case something comes up."

That Friday afternoon I met Christopher in the lobby when he came by to pick up his portfolio. He was wearing a pair of dark trousers and a cable-knit sweater, his hair windblown, his cheeks tinged pink from being outside.

"I'm sorry," I said, handing him his case. "If something comes up, she said she'll call you."

"That's okay. I'm booked solid for the next three weeks anyway." He smiled and I noticed that one of his eyeteeth was slightly protruding. It was the only less than perfect feature I could find on him.

"So Elaine tells me you're a photographer," he said.

"*Aspiring* photographer," I said, correcting him. I don't know why, but even though I wanted nothing more than to talk to him about photography, I felt shy discussing my own work with him.

"If you don't mind," he said, "Elaine asked me to take you under my wing, show you the ropes."

"She did?"

"How would you like to come along on one of my shoots this weekend?"

"Are you serious? Yes," I said a little too overzealously.

"It's just some headshots." I could tell he didn't want me getting too excited. "It's nothing fancy, but you're welcome to come. If you want."

"Yes," I said again, exercising a bit more control. "I would love to."

"Well, all right then." He nodded. "So, tomorrow morning. We'll start around ten o'clock. It's a location shoot. We'll be in Central Park at Bow Bridge."

Five minutes after Christopher left, Nora, Judith and Lyn arrived for an editorial meeting with some members of Helen's staff. I was asked to sit in and take notes. Despite having an empty conference room down the hall, Helen wanted to host the meeting in her office.

When they all arrived, she stood in her doorway, threw her arms open and said, "Welcome, everyone. Step into my parlor." And indeed, it felt more like a parlor than an executive's office. It seemed as though every day she was bringing in some new decorative trinket. In the month that she'd been there, Helen had the place cluttered with a menagerie of stuffed animals, scented candles and more leopard print accessories. She sat in her tiny chair, kicked off her Roger Vivier pumps with their pilgrim copper buckles and tucked her stocking feet beneath her. She was clutching an embroidered pillow that said: *I'm not arguing, I'm just explaining why I'm correct.* Bill Guy, George Walsh and her new hire, Walter Meade, were the only men in the meeting. It was Walter's first day and there wasn't a female in the room who wasn't drawn to his thick wavy dark hair, his dimples and perfect smile. All I could think was, *Oh, how disappointed they'll be when they find out he's a homosexual.* And about that, Walter wasn't shy or apologetic. He was who he was.

After Helen had introduced everyone to her new finds—Walter, Nora, Judith and Lyn—she got down to business and began throwing out story ideas at such rapid fire that even my shorthand skills were having a hard time keeping up.

"I'm thinking we need some real grabbers for the cover," she said. "Something like, *When It's Okay to Sleep with Your Friend's Ex.*"

I looked around the room, cringing. One thing about Helen— when she was on, she was spot on, and when she was off, she'd miss by a mile.

"When is sleeping with your friend's ex *ever* okay?" asked Nora.

"Oh," said Helen with a winking smile, "I'm sure we can come up with some extenuating circumstances. Or how about, *Ten Ways to Guarantee a Second Date.*" And before anyone asked her to qualify that, she said, "Or make it, *Ten Ways to Make Him Crave You.* You get the idea."

"Honestly," said George, tipping his cigarette into the ashtray, "I'm questioning why you have all these writers here. The editorial staff comes up with the article ideas and then you assign them. Not the other way around."

"But it's much more fun this way," Helen said as she sipped her coffee, dismissing him like a pestering gnat. "Now then, tell me what you're all thinking! I'm dying to hear everyone's ideas."

George glowered, his cheeks turning dark.

"I for one," said Nora, "would love to take a playful jab at the

Park Avenue set. You know, the ladies who lunch in their hundred-dollar Chanel suits. I think the rest of us *schlubs* are fascinated by them."

Oh, Helen liked that idea. "Alice, are you getting all this down?"

I assured her I was, scribbling every last detail of Nora's plan to satirize the Mrs. Vanderbilts and Mrs. Rockefellers and the rest of Manhattan royalty.

George sat off to the side, shifting in his chair, crossing and uncrossing his arms and then his legs. He smoked two cigarettes right in a row, and after Helen threw out a couple more ideas about *When You Should Fake an Orgasm* and *How to Be His Sex Kitten*, he couldn't contain himself any longer. "Might I suggest something more topical?"

"Why, George, what could possibly be more topical to my girls than learning how to make a man swoon? Don't tell me your wife wouldn't just love to cast her spell on you."

Walter Meade burst out laughing, followed by Nora, Judith and Lyn. With the addition of her new recruits, Helen finally had some people on her side and I sensed a softening of the old guard. Liz Smith and Bobbie Ashley even joined in laughing with the others.

"All right then," said George, trying to talk over them, "how about something more dignified?"

"You mean stuffy." Helen smiled, her teeth clenched, her lips barely moving. "Don't be such a drag, George."

Bill Guy, who hadn't said two words the entire meeting, finally spoke up. "I don't suppose you've given any thought to the books section yet, have you, Helen?" Now that George was the managing editor, Bill had taken over George's old role as the book editor. "I was hoping to do a feature on a new biography coming out on Prince Aly Khan."

"Ooh." Helen's eyes lit up. "Now that's nifty!"

"I like it," said Walter.

"Me, too," said Helen. "Prince Aly Khan has slept with half of Hollywood. And that was before, *during* and after his marriage to Rita Hayworth. Oh, I love it. Yes, that's perfect, Bill. Just perfect. See everyone—that's exactly what I'm talking about. We'll call it *The World's Greatest Lover.*"

"Ah, no, Helen." Bill shook his head so vehemently, his cheeks quivered. "That wasn't at all what I was suggesting."

"Oh, I know, but isn't it a real grabber? Remember, Bill, it's all in the tease."

CHAPTER ELEVEN

⊷───────⊶

Saturday morning Trudy and I went for breakfast at the Lexington Candy Shop. Lately, that had become part of our weekend routine before she went off to work at Bergdorf's and I went to the laundromat, the grocery store and ran my other errands. But that day I was heading off to a photo shoot with Christopher Mack. Over bottomless coffees and two egg plate specials, Trudy drew a map of Central Park on her napkin with arrows and directions to Bow Bridge.

After we parted ways, I followed her instructions, entering the park at 74th Street. It was sunny but windy out, the tree branches rustling, the hint of buds straining to open. I stuffed my hands in my pockets to keep warm and walked west of the Bethesda Fountain until I saw Bow Bridge coming into view. The closer I got, the more magnificent it became: an ornate design of cast iron stretching sixty feet across the lake. Already I was thinking about coming back in the summertime when all the surrounding trees and flowers were in bloom.

At the far end of the bridge, I spotted Christopher in a pair of faded jeans and a navy blue pea coat, sunglasses shading his dark eyes. He had a woman with him, carrying a paper cup of coffee. As I got closer, he saw me and waved me over. Now I could see that the woman was the same model from his portfolio.

"You made it," said Christopher. "Alice, this is Daphne."

"Hey." She smiled and waved, took a sip of coffee and handed the cup to Christopher.

They were sharing a cup of coffee. In less than thirty seconds of meeting her, even before he said, "Thanks, babe," I knew Bridget was right. Daphne was the girlfriend. They were definitely an item. And what an item they made: both of them tall, fit and sexy. Real head turners.

Naturally I found Christopher attractive, but honestly, I was relieved that he was taken. It meant I could put him in the same category as married men and homosexuals—off-limits. Otherwise, I'd never be able to concentrate and I wanted to focus my full attention on the photography and learn everything I could from him.

"I'm glad you decided to come," Christopher said as he crouched down and unlatched a suitcase packed with three different camera lenses, resting in a bed of gray foam cutouts.

"I wouldn't have missed it."

He looked up, his eyes hidden behind his sunglasses, but his lips curved upward ever so slightly. "Daphne just signed with Eileen Ford," he said as he set up the tripod and mounted his camera on top. "They need some casual outdoor shots of her."

I glanced over at Daphne, waiting on the bridge in a trench coat, collar turned up, hands stuffed in her pockets, her long brown hair blowing in the breeze. "She's very beautiful."

He smiled full on, proud, as if the compliment incorporated him, the man lucky enough to have her on his arm.

I stood off to the side while he posed Daphne, his fingertips brushing a strand of hair off her face. Such a small movement but

I felt it from six feet away. He came back over to the tripod, and after taking a reading off the light meter, he attached a long lens and began shooting with just the ambient light, calling out instructions to Daphne like, "Cheat it to the right . . . little smile, that's it . . . Look right up here . . ." He raised one hand while clicking with the other.

After a few more shots, he stopped and went back over to her, adjusting her collar, letting his fingers trail down her neck. When he'd finished shooting that roll, he pulled a reflector from the suitcase and asked for my help. "I could use an extra set of hands here, if you don't mind."

"Sure, just tell me what to do."

He handed me a reflector, saying, "I want to diffuse the light. Just hold this, like this . . ." He demonstrated, guiding my hand into position. "This'll give us softer shadows."

I held the reflector as still as I could while he snapped a dozen or so shots.

"Alice," he called to me. "Come take a look."

"Really?"

He took the reflector from me and stepped aside, leaving a space for me at the tripod. I looked through the viewfinder while he adjusted the lens. "See that?" he said. "Now keep watching and see what happens when I do this." He moved the reflector and all the shadows softened, changing the feel of the image.

"That's amazing," I said, still watching through the viewfinder.

The winds were picking up and I thought it might spoil the rest of the shoot, but Christopher loved it, wanting to capture the wildness of Daphne's hair streaking across her face even as it pulled threads of lipstick against her pale skin. He took the camera off the tripod and leaned against the railing while he snapped a series of shots. A gust of wind carried a bite with it, and I buttoned my coat and stomped my feet to keep warm. Daphne must have been freezing standing on the bridge, but she kept turning this way and that, tilting her head and pouting her full lips while Christopher worked the camera.

At one point he twisted out of his pea coat. "Hold this for me, will you?" He was in a T-shirt, and as he hoisted himself up on the bridge, the bottom of his shirt hiked up, exposing a band of pale skin just under his navel. He was performing quite a balancing act to get the angle he wanted. One slip and he'd fall, but that didn't seem to faze him. He was determined to get the shot. He finished off that roll of film, hopped down, and we were done.

Daphne came over and looped her arms around his waist, leaned in and kissed him on the lips. "Thanks, babe."

I wondered how long they'd been together and if she still felt a flutter when he touched her, or was it all too familiar by now. I could remember that initial spark radiating through me the first time Michael let his fingers brush against mine and when, at last, he kissed me—*really kissed me*. It was all so new and exciting, but over time the spark faded, replaced by something richer and deeper. Or so I thought. I didn't need the spark to feel in love, but Michael did. Among other things, I had made the mistake of becoming too familiar.

Daphne and I made small talk while Christopher packed up his gear, collapsing down the reflector and tucking it back inside the case along with the lenses. He hoisted up the suitcase, slipped the tripod under his arm and still managed to reach over and hold Daphne's hand. As we were leaving the park, they invited me to join them for coffee. I started to beg off, already feeling like a third wheel, but Christopher insisted.

We went to a quaint place on West 72nd and Central Park West that felt like we'd stepped into a European café with French windows along the front and a glass case of pastries, cannoli, rugalach and other baked goods. It was warm and cozy inside; the scents of fresh coffee brewing and homemade bread mingled in the air. Classical music played softly in the background.

We took a corner table, the two of them sitting on one side, me on the other. He put his arm around her, rubbing her shoulder to warm her up. She was digging around in her handbag for something.

"Order me an espresso, will you?" she said, getting up, a dime in her hand. "I have to make a quick phone call."

We ordered our coffees and talked about the mechanics of the day's shoot. His arm was still resting on the back of her chair, still feeling for her like an amputee longing for their lost limb.

"What got you interested in photography?" he asked.

"My mother. She wasn't a professional or anything, but she loved taking pictures. Or really it was more like she loved having pictures. Loved having her memories frozen in time."

"I can't remember the last time I took any personal pictures. Just for myself," he said, smiling before his eyes shifted toward the back of the café, where Daphne was leaning against the wall, receiver to her ear, nodding while resting her fingers in the holes on the dial wheel.

"How about you?" I asked. "How'd you get started in photography?"

"I don't really think it was any one person or any one thing. It was probably out of boredom and loneliness more than anything," he said. "I wasn't very sociable as a kid. Pretty awkward so I kept to myself a lot. Never really felt comfortable around other people. I liked watching them more than dealing with them." He laughed. "I remember my dad had this camera. Just an old Yashica. I found it in the back of a closet one day. I taught myself how to use it, and once I got the hang of it, you'd think I'd found my new best friend. Seemed like it filled up all the emptiness. I didn't feel so alone anymore. That probably sounds weird, doesn't it?"

"No. Actually, not at all."

"Really?" He gazed over at me with a curious expression.

I was reluctant to talk about my mother's death directly, so instead, I circled around it. "When I was growing up, something happened that made me aware of how temporary and fleeting everything is. It was my mother's camera and taking pictures that gave me a way to capture moments. To preserve people and things so they wouldn't slip away and be forgotten." I was going to say more but Daphne came back.

"I hate to do this," she said. "Gary wants me to come look at a script. I have to go see him now." She turned to me. "Nice meeting you."

"I'll see you at home then?" he said.

At home. They lived together.

"Daphne wants to be an actress," he explained after she'd left.

"Oh really."

"Gary's her agent. Not a great one. He's young, just starting out, but he's trying to get her some auditions." He nodded and reached for a cigarette. "I think she's gonna get a lot of work from the Ford Agency. She's got a good look, you know? Fresh. Different." He lit his cigarette and set it in the ashtray, a ribbon of smoke rippling between us. "Daphne's just so"—he raised his hand, as if grasping for the right word—"so natural in front of the camera."

"How long have you two been together?"

"Two years. Off and on, three. But, no, really two years now. We met right after she came to town. From Montreal. I'm a sucker for a girl who speaks French." He smiled and there wasn't a doubt in my mind that he was a man in love. It was in the way he spoke about her, the way he'd been looking at her while she was on the phone. He'd never hurt her, never leave her. He was devoted. And I was fascinated. There was something about them. Like they were the perfect couple. It renewed my faith that relationships like theirs really did exist.

Christopher and I got back to talking about photography and I told him how inspiring it was being in New York. "I hardly know what to photograph first."

"That's the thing," he said, "there's almost too much here. It's all fodder. What's great is, the two of us could be looking at the same thing and we'd end up taking two completely different photographs because your eye would go to one thing, and mine would go to something else. As photographers, we're not creating something out of thin air like a writer or a musician or a painter. Our art is derived from what already exists. We're actually *stealing* from what's already there and turning it into our own expression. So really, all you have to do is figure out what you want to say and zero in on it. Frame it and crop it with the lens . . ."

We talked for another half hour or so about things like composition and negative space and ways to manipulate the image. I'd never had this kind of conversation with anyone before. It was the language of photography and I couldn't get enough.

"What would you say your style is?" he asked.

"Me? Mine?" It was the first time anyone had ever asked that. The first time I'd ever been regarded as a photographer. It felt validating and strange. "Oh, I don't know. Lately, I guess I've been shooting quirky things like street vendors and strangers on the subway. Piles of garbage."

"Sounds like you're starting to develop your eye. You'll have to let me see your work sometime."

I shook my head. "It's not good enough to show anyone."

"You have to get over that. You know, criticism can be a good thing."

"I'm just not quite ready for that yet."

"Okay, all right. I'll let you off the hook. For now."

We talked awhile longer, and after we'd finished our coffees and left the café, I thanked Christopher for letting me tag along.

"Bring your camera next time," he said.

"Next time?"

"Yeah, it'll be fun. Give me a call. We'll just knock around, take some pictures. I can show you a few things."

We said good-bye, and after he'd disappeared around the corner, I was dancing on a cloud. In Christopher Mack, I'd found a mentor. I wanted to run home, grab my camera and go out shooting, but I was out of film and broke until payday.

So there I was, standing all alone on the sidewalk, all this energy with no place to go. I had no idea what I was going to do with the rest of the day. It was only then that I thought about Erik. I'd hardly seen my Don Juan that week and he hadn't called. I didn't know if he'd ask me out again, but after spending the day with this perfect couple, my mind was flooded, remembering the intensity of Erik's kisses.

CHAPTER TWELVE

○———○

Helen had just come back from a breakfast meeting and asked me to join her at the wall. The wall was where the flatplan resided, tacked up in the back of the art department. And by now, we both knew exactly what the flatplan was: the editorial lineup, driven by the advertising, so we could see what was already in place. There it was, a page-by-page, spread-by-spread layout of the July issue with notations for *F.O.B.*, or Front of Book, and *B.O.B.*, or Back of Book. In between there was a series of pages, some left blank, others already set for *a Pyrex Ad, a Mr. Clean Ad, a Gerber Coupon Ad*, two pages for *Book Reviews*, a page and a half for *Movie Reviews*.

The flatplan changed by the day. Helen would reserve three pages for a feature on *How to Make Your Bedroom Sexier* and someone from Hearst would come by and strike it out. That morning I noticed some new articles had been added. Three pages were set aside for *You Too Can Be a Witch*, one page for *Lipstick Telling Tales* and four double spreads devoted to *Aly Khan, The World's Greatest Lover*.

I walked with Helen as she reviewed each page. She crossed

out the question mark that someone had put next to the Aly Khan headline. The cover was blank with a big *TK—To Come—* scribbled in. Inside front cover: *Bell System Ad. Full Page.*

Helen leaned forward to pencil in an upcoming article she'd pulled in as a favor from her friend Doris Lilly: *How to Marry a Millionaire.* She had also asked another friend to write a piece about Picasso's lover and had begged Jacqueline Susann to contribute something.

"I can't imagine Jackie won't come through for me," said Helen. They were both Bernard Geis authors, and Susann's book, which Elaine Sloan was working on, about starlets hooked on amphetamines and barbiturates hadn't come out yet. "It would be wonderful advance publicity for her."

Helen made a few more notations about articles and columns she wanted included. We stood back looking at it all. Page by page, July was beginning to fill in like a pruned houseplant.

We had just returned from the art department when Ira Lansing came racing down the hall and tore into Helen's office before I could announce him. I was on his heels apologizing to Helen.

"We have a serious problem, Helen."

"Please," she said, looking up from her perch on the sofa, "come in, Ira. You, too, Alice. Come in and close the door. No need to disturb everyone else out there."

I did as she said, leaning against the closed door while Ira started in on his tirade. "I hope you're proud of yourself. You've just put the entire magazine in jeopardy."

Helen had a manuscript in her lap, her pen in position to make an edit. "Now take a deep breath, Ira, and tell me what seems to be the problem." She sounded like she was speaking to a child with a skinned knee.

"I'll tell you what the problem is. Pampers and Mr. Clean are

pulling their ads from the July issue. Procter & Gamble got wind
of the article lineup for July and they're out."

A stunned look washed over her as she set aside whatever she
was editing. "How on earth did they hear about the lineup?"

I was asking myself the same thing.

"Someone out there"—he pointed toward her door—"is talking. I just got off the phone with P&G and they're not happy.
Neither am I."

"Who would do a thing like that?" she asked, sitting up straight
now, tugging her bracelets free from her cuff.

"How the hell should I know, but I'll tell you one thing, you
better learn how to control your staff. Stop them from flapping
their gums. P&G is a wholesome company. They don't want all
this sex and gossip mixed up with their products. You just better
hope no one out there's talking to Swanson's. They're scheduled
for a full-page ad."

"Oh, Ira, relax." She was on her feet now, padding across the
room for her cigarettes. "Those aren't the only advertisers on the
planet."

"In case you didn't know," he said, "it's advertising that keeps
a magazine afloat. You're losing money for this publication before
you've even put out a single issue."

"Those advertisers were all wrong for the new *Cosmo* anyway,"
she said clicking her table lighter and blowing a plume of smoke
toward the windows. "We need to be as particular about our advertisers as we are about our articles. My girls don't care about
diapers and mopping the kitchen floor. And they aren't going to
plop down on the sofa and eat a frozen TV dinner." She took
another puff. "Really, Ira . . ." She shook her head. "Pampers?
Mr. Clean? Swanson's? Not sexy."

"I don't give a damn about sexy. This magazine needs advertisers and we were light to begin with. Thanks to your brilliant ideas, you've just lost about a third of that revenue."

"We'll get it back."

"And how do you suppose we do that?" You could see the panic in his eyes. "I had relationships with those people. They're very disappointed. I don't think there's any way to make them change their minds."

"Oh, Ira, let them go. It's all right. There's far bigger and better advertisers to be had."

"I see. Just like that, huh?" He huffed, hands on his hips. "It took me years to build up the confidence of those advertisers. There's a reason why editors don't get involved in any of this. The clock is ticking and this magazine can't afford to have another advertiser pull out for July."

Helen waltzed over and picked an imaginary piece of lint off his lapel. "If you can't find the right advertisers for this magazine, then I will."

"You're so sure of yourself, aren't you?"

"Actually, no, I'm not." She smiled brightly as if she hadn't a care in the world. "I'm not at all. And you and your colleagues remind me every day that I've never done this before. But I'm not going to just roll over and give up. If you can't bring in some new advertisers, then I'll do it myself."

"Lots of luck, Helen. It's not so easy. Now if you'll excuse me, I'm gonna call American Home Products and make sure they're not pulling the Preparation H ad."

"Hemorrhoids?" Helen shook her head. "I have no interest in advertising hemorrhoid cream in *Cosmo*. The only thing Preparation H is good for is reducing bags under the eyes."

I was still standing in front of the door when Ira headed toward me. I stepped aside just as he tugged the door open and marched out of Helen's office.

I had fully expected Helen to dissolve into a puddle of tears, but instead, she puffed on her cigarette, the wheels turning inside her head as she said, "Get Walter Meade. And my Rolodex. Oh, and do me a favor, make a reservation for a private dining room this Thursday. Twelve noon at Jack and Charlie's 21."

Despite her moratorium on expensive lunches, Helen hosted an elaborate spread for some of Madison Avenue's finest at the famed 21 Club. Helen and Walter had gone back through their advertising contacts and invited the decision makers from Max Factor, Palmolive, Chanel, Maybelline, Clairol as well as the key advertising executives from agencies like BBDO, DDB, McCann-Erickson, along with David Ogilvy from Ogilvy & Mather. This was the first of what would become Helen's legendary weekly advertising luncheons at 21.

I accompanied her that day as I did to most meetings, always on hand to take notes, offer support, do whatever she needed. Helen and I were greeted by the lawn jockeys looking on from their rod-iron gate as we entered the restaurant. I saw that David Brown was already in position, deliberately dining that day in the bar room. He was with another gentleman, the two of them at a corner table with a red and white checked tablecloth, a menagerie of toys suspended overhead, dangling from the ceiling: model airplanes, soccer balls, football helmets, tennis rackets, trains and dolls. If anything went sideways, I was to get David so he could come in and save Helen's meeting.

The maître d' led us downstairs, beyond a concrete facade door, where the secret wine cellar, from its speakeasy days, was located. It was a handsome room lined with wooden wine racks along the walls and a long lacquered table sporting a golden 21 emblem inlay in the center. The table was set for twenty with an array of silverware along with red and white wineglasses and crystal water glasses, too. I reached into my tote bag and placed a notepad and pen before each plate. Four tuxedoed waiters stood at the corners ready to take cocktail orders and tend to Helen's every need.

As the guests began filtering in, Helen stood in the doorway in a cream-colored Norman Norell dress with a matching sweater draped delicately over her shoulders. As if by magic, her sweater stayed in place whether she was shaking hands with this one, hugging that one, or offering her cheek. She knew all the men and had worked with most of them in her former life as a copywriter, creating their advertising campaigns.

I had studied all the attendees' bios prior to the luncheon and the one guest who intrigued me most was the only woman on the list: Mary Wells. An attractive blonde, she was smartly dressed in a pale pink suit, probably a Chanel. She was an award-winning copywriter from Jack Tinker and Partners who had grown up in Youngstown, Ohio. I'd read that she had started her career writing copy for McKelvey's Department Store, the very store my mother used to take me to. Never satisfied with the quality of the merchandise, though, my mother always prefaced each trip with, "When we move to New York, I'll take you to Saks and Bloomingdale's." But those memories aside, I was inspired that someone who had started out in Youngstown had gone as far as Mary Wells. It gave the budding photographer in me hope.

Once everyone had their cocktails, Helen stood at the head of the table with a glass of champagne, which I knew she wouldn't drink for fear of going over her daily 1,200-calorie allotment. But the drink in hand did add a nice, celebratory touch. As she welcomed everyone, the waiters brought out sterling silver buckets piled high with steamers.

"As you know," said Helen in her whispery voice, "I've entered into a new venture as the editor in chief of *Cosmopolitan* magazine. This marks a wonderful new beginning for the magazine and an exciting new opportunity for you.

"I know you've heard rumors about what the new *Cosmo* is going to be, so let me set the record straight. Shall we start with the facts? What if I told you that this magazine can put your products in front of 27 million women. That's the number of readers this magazine is going to reach. Almost half of them are single and the rest are either divorcées or widows. Together it gives us a grand total of 27 million women. That's a lot of potential consumers for you, and I'm here to tell you that the new *Cosmopolitan* can put your goods and services in the hands of each and every one of them."

That was my cue to pass out the special dummy comp of the July issue that we had prepared despite resistance from Ira Lansing and some of the Hearst men.

"This is a huge mistake," Berlin had said when he found out about the luncheon. "Don't show your hand. It's simply not the way we do things."

But Helen had gone ahead and done it anyway. She'd compiled twenty samplers of the July issue: a sneak peek of headlines, introductory copy lines and some photos. It was just meant to give them a taste of the new *Cosmo* format. After I'd distributed the dummies, I went back to being inconspicuous and took my place by the door.

"Now, you might ask, who are these 27 million women? Who is the woman we're trying to reach?" Helen smiled, her eyes twinkling. "Allow me to introduce you to the *Cosmo* Girl." She paused for a moment and that's when I realized she was gesturing toward me. "Alice?"

When she called my name, I panicked, thinking I'd forgotten to do something.

"Come here, dear." She summoned me to her side with her fingertips.

I quickly realized that, like the untouched glass of champagne in her hand, I was about to become a prop for her presentation. Knowing Helen, the idea had just come to her.

"Alice here is my secretary, but she's also a *Cosmo* Girl. Why, just look at her."

All eyes were upon me and I felt I owed them something in return—a little soft shoe or a magic act. Maybe I was expected to light up like a Christmas tree. I didn't know. All I could do was smile.

"She's smart, independent, always striving for more," said Helen. "She's bold and daring. She loves men and she *loves* sex."

I could feel my cheeks going red, the blush crawling up my neck.

Helen continued. "Like Alice, the average *Cosmo* Girl is any-where from eighteen to thirty-four and she's hungry for your products. She has a job and her own money, and she's looking to make her life bigger and better. Here's a girl eager to buy the lat-est shade of lipstick and nail polish. She cares about the brand of shampoo she uses. She's not waiting for a man to take her on that trip to Hawaii, and she doesn't need him to test-drive that new car, either. Yes, she wants to travel, drive a nice car and do it all in a stylish pair of shoes."

Thankfully she dismissed me after that and I scurried back to the door, next to the waiters who stood at attention, hands clasped behind their backs.

Helen continued to paint the portrait of the *Cosmo* Girl while her guests dined on onion soup gratiné, the Gruyère cheese bub-bling and oozing over the sides of the crocks. She didn't have any soup but she did occasionally pluck a lettuce leaf from her salad bowl. And with her fingertips poised and pointed like she was having tea, she'd tear off the tiniest shred and make a seductive yet dainty show of placing it in her mouth. She could make a single lettuce leaf last three minutes, sometimes longer. Only Helen Gurley Brown could get away with eating with her hands. And in a restaurant like 21.

By the time the sirloin steaks had been polished off and the brandy was poured and cigars ignited, Helen had everyone excited about the new magazine. And she had a lunch bill for $278.

When we returned to the office, Ira Lansing was waiting for Helen like a puma stalking its prey, waiting to pounce.

"How dare you!" he said, practically spitting with rage. "How could you have held a lunch like that and not include me?"

Helen was unflappable. With a tilt of her head, she calmly said, "What would you have done there?"

I had to agree. Even if Ira had been invited, I wasn't sure what he could have contributed. Though I wasn't thrilled about being part of her act, I had to say, Helen was at her best that day. It was her show. She was the star and her performance was brilliant.

"That's not the point," Ira said. "How do you think it looks? I'm the head of sales and advertising."

"And you told me you were losing accounts. I simply wanted to do what I could to bring some new advertisers on board."

"But that's not the way it's done, Helen."

"Oh, I know, but we did just pick up Philip Morris, Helena Rubinstein, Kimberly-Clark's Kotex brand and Cover Girl." Helen smiled and sashayed her way into her office, leaving Ira standing in the hallway, speechless.

CHAPTER THIRTEEN

⊶——⊷

"Oh, pussycat? Where are you?"

It was the following Monday morning and Helen had just returned from her analysis appointment. Something in her voice, always velvety smooth, sounded a bit off.

"Is everything okay?" I asked, standing in the doorway, leaning against the jamb.

Helen was sitting in her favorite spot on the sofa, her wig tilted a little off center. She reached for a cigarette and tapped the end on the coffee table before she placed it in her holder and lit it. "Come in and close the door, would you please?"

"Did I do something wrong?" I asked, taking a few tentative steps closer.

"Not at all." She smiled. "I have a special assignment for you."

"Oh?" *A special assignment?* I perked up. She'd changed her mind. She was going to give me a photography assignment. I waited patiently while she puffed on her cigarette and shot a stream of smoke toward the overhead light.

"I need you to go out and get me a copy of *Playboy* magazine."

"What?" It was like someone had just knocked a stack of books off a high ledge. All excitement tumbled and collapsed inside me. The disappointment must have shown on my face.

"Uh-oh. What's the problem?" Helen asked, flicking her cigarette ash.

"No problem."

I went back to my desk feeling a bit put out. Of all the things Helen had asked me to do, including buying socks for her husband, picking up her wigs from the beauty parlor, doing her grocery shopping and scooping her cats' litter boxes, this request to buy a copy of *Playboy* seemed like the most unnerving. *What kind of nice girl looks at* Playboy, *let alone goes out and buys one?*

I took a dollar bill from the petty cash drawer and went to a newsstand on the corner. It was a mild, sunny morning. Dozens of newspapers in dozens of languages were hanging off a display tree to the side, their pages rustling in the breeze. A middle-aged man with a turban on his head stood inside the stand behind a sliding glass window peppered with fingerprints. Cigarettes, candy bars and chewing gum were piled high on either side of him. With just a glance, I saw the current issues of *Esquire*, *National Geographic*, *Mad*, *Highlights* and the *Saturday Evening Post*. He had to have *Playboys*, too, but apparently, they were behind the counter, kept out of the hands and eyes of curious adolescent boys. It was obvious that I was going to have to ask for it.

"*Playboy*, please," I said, slipping a dollar in the little metal gully beneath his window. "And would you put it in a bag?"

"No bag." He dropped a quarter in the change bin.

After he handed me the magazine with a barebacked woman on the cover, draped in a sheer bed sheet, I rolled it into a tight cylinder so no one could see.

I slipped into Helen's office, handed the magazine to her and was almost out the door when I heard, "Oh, and Alice?"

"Yes?" I said, walking backward toward her.

"One more incy-wincy favor?" She was already leafing through the pages. "Could you be a little lamb and round up as many back issues as you can find?"

"Back issues of *that*?"

"Mm-hmm." She reached in her top drawer for a pair of scissors and began clipping out pictures of half-naked women. "And I'll need them right away. Tomorrow at the very latest. David doesn't keep any old magazines lying around. Says it's too much clutter."

"Well, I suppose I can check the library and see if—"

"The library?" She cracked a smile and held up her scissors. "Pussycat, I'm not planning on returning the issues."

"Oh. I see."

I left her office and went back to my desk, feeling like I was being tested. I thought about the various things I did for Helen on any given day. I took good care of her—and she knew it, too, often telling me that I was spoiling her. And I was. Picking up her dry cleaning without her having to ask, running home to pay her housekeeper because she'd forgotten to. I ran out and got her lunches that she never ate. And sometimes dinners, too. I brought her endless cups of coffee and had ducked out in the pouring rain to buy her cigarettes. Noticing she'd run her stockings again, I'd dash over to Bergdorf's for a new pair. I made sure her newspapers were on her desk every morning. I set out extra pencils for her to snap whenever she was about to lose her cool and picked them up afterward so she wouldn't trip over the carnage. I shielded her from phone calls and visitors she didn't want to deal with. I kept people out of her office and kept her on schedule, minute by minute. I made it so she didn't have to think about a thing other than running that magazine.

But those *Playboys*—I feared this would be the one request I couldn't accommodate. I hated the thought of letting her down, but I didn't have any idea where I was going to find back issues of *Playboy*. She said she needed them right away and there wasn't time to order them from the headquarters in Chicago. Dentists' and doctors' offices were graveyards for old magazines but not magazines like that. After more contemplation, I realized there was only one place I could possibly get them.

"Do you read *Playboy*?" I asked even before our drinks arrived. Erik and I were seated side by side at the bar of the Russian Tea Room.

"I've been known to. Yes." He gave me a quizzical look. "Why are you asking?"

"I need your back issues."

"Oh, you do now, do you?" He began laughing.

It was the first time I'd been alone with him since the night he'd kissed me, and that was more than two weeks ago. I had wanted to hold out and make him come to me, but I needed those magazines, and in truth, I was grateful for the excuse. My eyes kept wandering to his mouth, remembering the feel of his kisses, the way his lips brushed mine, the sweet taste of his tongue and the way he'd worked me into a frenzy.

The bartender set our drinks down and Erik plucked his olive clean from the glass. "And why is it that you need my back issues of *Playboy*?"

"It's for research."

"I'll bet. What kind of research?"

I didn't say and took a sip of my martini, letting the icy gin race down my throat while I thought of a suitable explanation.

"Well," he said, "if it's research you need, I'd be happy to give you a hand with it."

"Very funny. So can I have your back issues?"

"What'll you give me for them?" He arched a suggestive eyebrow and I fell right into it.

"Just wait and see."

"Oh, really?" He laughed. "Tell me the truth. Is this just some cheap ploy to get invited up to my apartment?"

I smiled. The innuendos were going back and forth. We were facing each other now, his leg was pressed against my thigh, and the heat coming off that touch point could have boiled water.

With our drinks still half-full, he peeled off a couple bills and left them on the bar. I slid beside him in the back of a taxicab, which dropped us off at a doorman building on Park Avenue.

"Good evening, Mr. Masterson." His doorman nodded as we passed through the marble lobby.

Erik's apartment was on the nineteenth floor; the type of place I'd fantasized about living in. It was the complete opposite of my efficiency. If I had to guess, I'd say he was paying at least $350 a month for rent. Everything in his apartment was sleek and modern with black-and-white Orla Kiely walls and thick shag carpeting. A straight-back sofa with Barcelona chairs completed the look. He had brass candlesticks, cigarette holders and table lighters. Every ashtray was clean, not a stray newspaper lying about or a glass left behind on his kitchen counter. I wondered if he had a housekeeper who came in every morning, picked up his socks and shoes off the floor, did his dishes and laundry and put the place back together.

He slipped into his kitchen and reappeared with a silver shaker. "Martini?" he asked, sorting through the array of bottles along his well-stocked bar.

"Why not?" I sat on one of the black swivel chairs and rested my elbows on the bar.

It took us one martini apiece before he mentioned the *Playboys*.

"They're back there, in the bedroom." He gestured with his head and I followed half a foot behind him.

Given the rest of his apartment, I wouldn't have been surprised if he'd had a circular bed with satin sheets and a mirrored ceiling. But his bedroom was perfectly normal, even understated compared to the rest of his bachelor pad. A Magnavox TV stood in the corner, rabbit ears stretched in a wide V. I took the only seat available, on his bed, my hands resting on the pale blue chenille spread. The room smelled faintly of talcum powder.

He went into his closet and came back with a stack of magazines. I could tell they'd been read more than once, the pages curled and dog-eared. Miss January had the ripple of a glass ring on her bare thigh.

"You ever seen one of these before?" he asked, setting the stack aside, picking up the top one.

Miss March was a pouty blonde in a sheer negligee with a plunging neckline, her breasts heaving forward. He opened the magazine, letting the centerfold tumble down with all of Miss March hanging out. I looked at her body, the curve of her waist, the fullness of her breasts, the dark triangle between her legs. I glanced at Erik and noticed a vein in his neck throbbing. I hadn't counted on him being nervous though I wasn't surprised that I was. Neither of us said a word. The moment hung there, seeming to last forever.

"I should really be going," I said, not wanting to leave but unwilling to make the first move.

He nodded and cracked a slight smile as if to say he understood. For a practiced Casanova, I was taken aback that he'd let the opportunity to bed me get away so easily. He closed up the centerfold and put the magazine back on the stack with the others and carried them out to the living room.

"So," he said, hanging on to the word like a lifeline. I was already reaching for my pocketbook when he said, "How about a nightcap before you go?"

Moments later we were side by side on his couch, gimlets in hand, enjoying the view of the city with all those high-rise buildings and their windows, little panels of light twinkling like stars. It was surreal to think that here I was, on Park Avenue, in this glamorous apartment, in the center of all this. He opened a box on the coffee table, offered me a cigarette and took one for himself, serving up a blue-white flame from a lighter shaped like a speedboat.

"Where did you grow up?" I asked as I exhaled, picturing him as a young boy waterskiing off the back of a Charger, chopping its way across the Atlantic.

"Here and there," he said.

"Well, that's informative."

"Mostly here," he said. "I'm sorry. I guess I don't like talking about myself."

"Makes it hard to get to know someone that way," I said. "What about your family? Siblings?" With just my father left, I was always interested in other people's families. I noticed he didn't have any photographs, no portraits on the wall or end tables.

"I have some half brothers, a couple half sisters."

"Oh, I see." It was clear that he didn't want to talk about it, so I let it go. It was becoming obvious that nothing was going to happen between us, and this confused me. Admittedly I was disappointed and slightly embarrassed. It was hard to believe that I'd misread the signals this whole time. One more puff off my cigarette before I ground it out and took the last sip of my gimlet. "Well, I should really be going."

He nodded, and just as I was about to get up, he made his move, reaching over, grazing my cheek with the back of his hand. I leaned into his touch like a kitten being stroked. My heart began beating faster when he stood up, pulled me to my feet and kissed me. Wrapping his arms about my waist as he walked me back into his bedroom.

As he started to undress me, unhooking my bra with a quick pinch and slipping the straps down off my shoulders, I covered my breasts with my hands.

"Don't be shy," he said. "You're beautiful." He reached for my hands, bringing them to my sides, leaving me exposed. "Let me look at you."

As his eyes traveled across my skin, taking in the fullness of my breasts, the curve of my waist, I felt that I was something to be admired. I glanced down at my body, trying to see what he was seeing. The lamp threw a golden glow around me. I reached for the zipper on my skirt and slid it down over my hips. Now I wanted to show him all of me. He came and kneeled before me, his lips pressed to my flesh as I ran my fingers through his hair. Everything coming alive inside me.

Afterward I lay in his bed, replaying it all in my mind. I'd never experienced anything like that before. Michael and I had been each other's firsts. Everything was tender but tentative. Sweet and sincere. The best part for me was just being close to him. That was all I wanted. That had been enough. But not anymore. I'd just been with a man who knew his way around a woman's body. Unlike Michael, Erik was skillful, almost artful in his caresses, his kisses. He'd brought me to near delirium before I shattered in his arms. Now I got it—I was let in on the big secret. At last I understood why sex was such a big deal and why it drove people to extremes.

I wanted Erik again but it was getting late. I glanced at the alarm clock on his nightstand. It was almost two in the morning. I began to ease out from beneath the covers when he reached for me and pulled me close. The second time was even better than the first, making it even harder to leave his bed.

An hour later he watched me get dressed, his hair crumpled, the dark shadow of whiskers coming up on his face. "You sure you don't want to stay?"

Oh, I wanted to but I couldn't. "I have to be in the office early."

"Wait—I'll get dressed, get you a taxicab."

"It's okay. I can do it."

"Well, at least let me pay for it."

That I accepted, because otherwise I would have had to walk. As I put on my shoes, he said, "Don't forget your *Playboys*."

"I won't."

"Are you going to tell her who you got them from?"

"Tell who?"

"Oh, c'mon now, Alice. I know the *Playboys* are for Helen."

Now I understood what the *Playboys* were for. Two days later, per Helen's instructions, I was waiting for Mr. Hugh Hefner when he stepped off the elevator.

Helen knew that *Playboy* stood for everything Hearst detested. Their greatest fear was that she would turn *Cosmopolitan* into a *Playboy* knockoff for women. When she'd first asked me to schedule the meeting with Mr. Hefner, I had looked up from my steno pad and said, "Are you sure you don't want me to make a lunch reservation somewhere instead?"

"Oh, please." She'd fired up a cigarette and laughed. "Berlin and his minions will find out I'm meeting with Hugh anyway. I might as well do it here in my office and save the company the expense of taking him to lunch. Especially after that bill we got for 21. Sheesh. Besides," she'd said with a mischievous grin, "I like making Hearst nervous. Throws them off balance and gives me the upper hand."

Hugh Hefner was a good-looking man with a square jaw, a prominent nose and a full head of dark hair that spilled onto his high forehead. He was suave and charming, a dashing figure in a tailored suit and tie. The pipe parked in the corner of his mouth gave off bursts of aromatic smoke.

"I'll take you back to Mrs. Brown's office," I said. "If you'll follow me—right this way."

A lot of famous people had walked the halls of *Cosmopolitan*, especially since Helen Gurley Brown took over. Lauren "Betty" Bacall stopped by once just to say hello. Same was true for Henry Fonda and Tony Curtis and some of the other stars who had appeared in the movie version of *Sex and the Single Girl*. But Mr. Hefner's visit stirred the most commotion. Everyone in the office knew who he was, and even the most conservative of the lot paused to watch him pass by; the question marks were practically visible to me, hovering above their heads.

When I led him into Helen's office, she sprang up from her sofa and hugged him as if they were old friends, and perhaps they were.

"Oh, Hugh," she purred. "It's so good to see you."

I brought them both coffees and left, closing her door behind me. They were sequestered for several hours and the whispering around the halls was growing louder.

Margot stopped me just outside the ladies' room. "What's he doing here?" she asked.

"I don't know. She just told me to schedule the meeting." I started to walk away but Margot grabbed my arm and pulled me aside.

"No, wait. Is it true?"

"Is *what* true?"

"Is she gonna turn *Cosmopolitan* into *Playboy* for women?"

"If you're asking if she intends to fill the pages with photos of half-naked men with their rumps in the air, I doubt it."

"I'm serious." She was wringing her hands, her anxiety palpable.

"Why are you so worried about all this?"

"It's just that . . ." Margot paused and looked around before she said, "I just don't want to see you lose your job. And you know if she tries to copy *Playboy*, Hearst'll fire her and you'll be out the door with her."

I would have been touched had her concern been sincere. But I didn't trust Margot and I wouldn't dare tell her that Helen would never get fired because it would cost Hearst a fortune to buy out her contract.

"You worry too much," I said. "It'll all be fine. Helen knows what she's doing."

I walked away thinking about how Helen enjoyed making Hearst nervous, and I was satisfied that at that very moment, someone, most likely George, was already on his phone, reporting the Hugh Hefner sighting to Deems.

CHAPTER FOURTEEN

———o———o———

One Saturday morning, after breakfast with Trudy, I entered my apartment building, stopping before the wall of mailboxes just inside the doorway. I was surprised to find something other than bills waiting for me.

I recognized the handwriting immediately and opened the envelope while climbing the stairs. A crisp $20 bill fell out, landing on the floor at my feet. The note inside, scribbled on a single sheet of paper, simply said, *I think you dropped this*. He didn't sign it. He didn't have to. This was something private, just between my father and me. I picked up the bill, a smile on my face as the memories came racing back.

From the time I was a little girl, for no apparent reason, he would hold up a quarter or a fifty-cent piece, sometimes a silver dollar, and as he'd press it into my palm, he'd say, "I think you dropped this." It was our little secret or so I thought. My mother may or may not have known he did this. Sometimes the coins went into my piggy bank, sometimes straight into my pocket to be spent right away on chocolates and ice cream sodas.

I went into my apartment and reached for the telephone to

thank him. "You didn't have to do that, Dad," I said, still holding his note.

"But you dropped it." He laughed over the murmur of the TV or maybe it was the radio in the background. Sounded like the Cleveland Indians game, and I pictured him in his chair that reclined back, his slippers dangling off his feet. How many times did I sit on his lap and, in later years, lie on the area rug beside him, propped up on my elbows, watching the game, happy as could be, even though I hated baseball. That was the kind of contentment that could only be appreciated in retrospect.

"I figured you could use a little help," he said. "And I knew you wouldn't ask for it."

"I'm okay, Dad, really I am. But I can't lie, the extra $20 will come in handy."

"Good. Just don't waste it on taxicabs and all those fancy restaurants."

"I won't. I promise." I smiled, choked up, as I opened a cupboard, a tin of saltines and a jar of peanut butter on the shelf. The refrigerator wasn't any better stocked.

"How's Faye?" I asked, just to keep him on the line.

"Just getting over a cold," he said. "It's this *mshuge* weather we're having. Hot one day, snowing the next. And you know spring colds are the worst . . ."

We talked a few minutes longer and I managed to keep my father on the phone for a full five minutes before we said good-bye.

When I hung up, I took my $20 to the drugstore around the corner and bought eight rolls of Kodak Tri-X film, thirty-six exposures each, for $10. After I got back to my apartment, I put the change in the jar where I stashed my grocery money, pulled out my address book and dialed Christopher's number. I had to do it now before I chickened out.

"Oh, Ali. This is a surprise. Good to hear from you," he said.

"I remember we talked about getting together, you know, to do some shooting." I squeezed the receiver, feeling nervous about taking him up on his offer. I was worried he'd said it just to be nice. Or maybe he forgot he'd said anything in the first place.

"Sure. You free today?"

Today! I glanced at my reflection in the tea kettle on the stove. "Today?"

"Yeah, it's perfect. Weather's great. Why don't you meet me down in the Village?"

I hung up the phone, amazed at how easy that was.

Twenty minutes later I hopped on the subway, and when I passed through the giant arch in Washington Square Park, Christopher was waiting for me, standing next to a lamppost. His hair was windblown and he wore a black T-shirt and jeans, his Nikon hanging at his side. He rolled a copy of the *Village Voice* in his hand, holding it like a baton.

"You ready for your photography lesson?"

"I am." I smiled, holding up my mother's camera.

We walked through a cluster of pigeons and sat on a bench looking out onto the fountain shooting a geyser into the air while droplets skipped and danced on the water's surface. It was a beautiful day, the temperatures in the high sixties. Flowers were coming up; buds were opening on the shrubs and bushes. Spring green leaves appeared faint, almost like shadows on the trees in the distance. People were riding bicycles; others were stretched out on the grass, heads resting on their bunched-up sweaters and jackets, listening to a cluster of street musicians playing folk songs.

"Let's see what you got here. May I?" He reached for the strap, sliding the camera off my shoulder. "Wow," he said, unsnapping the case. "A Leica IIIc MOOLY. What year? '46? '47?"

"1945. It belonged to my mother."

"Wow," he said again, looking through the viewfinder, aiming at me.

I laughed and raised my hand, blocking his shot.

"Ah, c'mon," he said, teasingly reaching for my hand, pulling it away.

"I'd rather be behind the camera than in front of it."

"Then let's do it," he said, pushing up off the bench.

We wandered about taking pictures of elderly men playing chess, of a vendor roasting nuts, a ghost of smoke blowing before his weathered face.

"Do you ever feel a little weird, like you're spying on people?" I asked as I focused my lens on a banjo player, bent over his case, counting up his tips. "You know, like you're intruding on their privacy?"

"Some of the most memorable photos of all time would fall into that category. Remember that great shot of the sailor kissing the nurse in Times Square after the war?"

Funny he would mention that photograph. "That one always reminds me of my parents. My dad was a sailor back from the war when he met my mom."

"See? Or what about the photo of the U.S. troops raising the flag at Iwo Jima? Or the Hindenburg? Those are moments that would have been lost forever if someone like us hadn't been there with a camera."

"Excellent point." I smiled, thinking only a photographer would see the world that way.

We left Washington Square Park and headed down Waverly Place, taking pictures of anything and anyone that caught our eye: a group of boys on roller skates, a cat perched in a doorway. At one point, we traded cameras and he let me use his Nikon.

"Hey, look here," he said, stopping on the sidewalk, aiming my mother's camera at me.

I turned around, thumbs in my ears, fingers wiggling at him while I stuck out my tongue.

"Beautiful. Got it."

"Good thing it's on my camera. I can destroy the negative," I teased.

"Damn. There goes my blackmail plan."

The afternoon flew by and we lost track of time, shooting until we ran out of film. I was sure Christopher had no idea what that day meant to me but he had helped me over a mental hurdle. As we stood near the subway, talking while people rushed up and down the stairs, he told me I had a good eye and he pointed out things I should work on. But more than all that, he took me seriously. For the first time since I'd arrived in the city, becoming a photographer didn't seem so far-fetched.

CHAPTER FIFTEEN

A week later Trudy knocked on my door, asking to borrow some nail polish remover. As soon as she stepped inside, I saw her face and hoped my expression didn't look as alarmed as I sounded.

"What happened?" I pinched my bathrobe closed, eyeing the bright red splotches and open sores along her cheeks and chin.

"Oh, that." She brought her hands to her face as if she'd forgotten about it until I brought it up. "I gave myself a facial."

"Using what? Sandpaper?"

"Very funny. No, it was a mask. Just buttermilk, honey and lemon juice. It was supposed to remove my freckles but I left it on too long."

"Why would you want to get rid of your freckles?" I asked, heading to the bathroom for the polish remover.

"Because I hate them."

"But they're so cute."

"Yeah, that's the problem. I'm sick and tired of being *cute*. I've heard that my entire life and I'm sick of it."

"Being cute isn't necessarily a bad thing," I called to her as I sorted through the bottles of Anacin, Vick's cough syrup and milk of magnesia in the medicine cabinet. "I'm sure there's lots of women who would love to be cute."

I brought the bottle to her and she dropped down on the side of the bed. "I just want to look sexy and sophisticated for once. But that's impossible when you're covered in freckles."

"But you're adorable," I said, realizing that was the last thing she wanted to hear. But it was true, and the more upset she got about being adorable, the more adorable she became.

I stepped into the closet and shimmied off my bathrobe before slipping into my dress with the blue princess panel in the front and the gusseted sleeves.

"Wow, look at you," said Trudy. "Is that new?"

"I treated myself. Found it on the sales rack at Alexander's." I did a quarter turn, inspecting myself in the mirror on the back of the closet door.

"You should have come to Bergdorf's. They give us sales girls a discount, you know. I could have bought it for you and have you pay me back."

"Even with your discount, I couldn't afford anything at Bergdorf's. I shouldn't have even bought this," I said, thinking how I'd used what was left of the $20 my father sent me to buy it. "It set me back almost $9."

"Well, you sure look swell. I didn't know you had a date tonight. Is it with Erik?"

"Oh, no. No, I don't have a date." Not that I hadn't tried for one.

The night before, Erik had sat on the edge of his bathtub while fragrant soap bubbles grew up out of the hot water, surrounding me. When the tub was full, he'd stood up, removed his towel and said, "Scoot over."

The water had sloshed around us, some of it splattering onto the tiled floor as we kissed and he'd brought my legs around his hips, rocking me back and forth. *Sex in a bathtub*. Something else I'd never imagined I'd do. But Erik was full of surprises and un-expected ways to please me.

I had wanted to please him, too, and later, as he dried me off in his monogrammed thick pile towel and wrapped his arms around me, I said, "Why don't you come over for dinner tomorrow night? I'll cook for you."

"Really? You cook?"

"No, not really." I'd shrugged. "But I can."

He'd laughed, like it was charming. "That's sweet, but why don't I take you out instead."

"You're going to spoil me," I said.

"That's okay, isn't it? I bet you'd love Tavern on the Green."

"Wow." My mother had told me about that restaurant and I'd always wanted to go there. I'd been so pleased when he'd suggested it.

"Only I can't make it tomorrow night."

"Oh." I hadn't known what else to say. I busied myself with the towel, wrapping it tighter around me, grateful then that Bridget had invited me to a party that Saturday night.

"Another time, though," he said. "I promise." He had kissed my neck and tickled me until he had me laughing in spite of myself, squirming out of his arms and out of my towel, letting it drop to the damp floor. We had sex again and I had stayed the night, waking Saturday morning to sunny-side-up eggs in bed.

"No date, huh?" Trudy said. "Well, you sure look real smart."

"Thanks." I tilted my head while I clipped on my earrings. "I'm going to a party."

"Oh."

I glanced at Trudy through the mirror. She looked a little wounded and I couldn't say I blamed her. We had an understanding that unless we had a date or some other obligation, Saturday night was girls' night. The two of us would go to the movies or a play or sometimes splurge for a dinner out. Trudy had always included me in her plans, and I would have been lost my first few weeks in New York without her.

"Why don't you come with me?" I said.

"Looking like this?" She pointed to her face. "No, but thanks. I'm going to go hide out in a dark movie theater. The new Frankie Avalon and Annette Funicello picture just opened." She looked in the mirror and turned away. "Need help getting to your party?" she asked, knowing I was still leery of the subway, especially at night and when it involved transferring trains.

"Bridget's meeting me at the 77th Street station."

Before I left that night, I looked at Trudy and said, "And about your freckles, don't get rid of them. They're part of what makes you *you*. And someday some man is going to fall in love with those freckles. Mark my words."

The party was at Katie Murphy's, a secretary at *Town and Country*, who lived at 33rd and Madison. Bridget and I met Margot, Leslie and Penny at the Herald Square subway stop, and together we all walked the few blocks to the party. It was a cool spring night. The weather called for rain but so far it had been holding off. None of us wanted to carry umbrellas so we were taking our chances.

As we were climbing the stairs, I heard music blaring: Herman's Hermits, "I'm into Something Good." When we reached the third-floor landing, we saw people dancing in the open doorway and spilling out into the hallway. Peering into the apartment, I felt as if I'd just stepped into one of Holly Golightly's parties. Cigarette smoke hung in the air like fog rolling in off the Hudson. Everyone had a glass of something: wine, whiskey, gin or beer. The

men were handsome, the women stylish. A redhead in a psychedelic pantsuit was dancing by herself with an inch of unbroken
cigarette ash waiting to fall with each gyration.

Bridget leaned in with an elbow nudge and said, "Let's mingle.
There's a guy over there who does the hiring at Doubleday."

We dumped our jackets on a chair serving as a coat rack and
off we went, dresses swishing as we maneuvered through the
crowded apartment. I recognized a few people from the office.
Liz Smith, in a mod high-button dress, was talking with Lyn
Tornabene, who was perched on the arm of the crowded sofa. She
was wearing a pair of floral culottes with a matching scarf. Rex
Reed was with them. He was dark and handsome, but not in the
classic sense. It took a moment for his looks to register, and when
they did, they stuck. I remembered seeing him the day Helen
fired him. Apparently, he still wasn't over it.

"And what do you think she tells me?" Reed said, standing on
an ottoman like an orator, arms dramatically flung to his sides.
"She tells me I write 'pippy-poo' copy."

"What the hell is that supposed to mean?" asked Lyn, laughing.

"I have no idea. But then get this. She has the nerve to say
they're still running my last reviews because she *has to* and then—
then she turns around and asks me for one last favor before she
cans me. She wanted me to fly to Los Angeles and interview some
hypnotist to the stars."

"Oh no." Liz Smith laughed into her hands. "Helen's been trying to push that *Hip Hypnotist* story off on everybody."

"Well, I told her I was taking my pippy-poo copy elsewhere,
thank you very much."

They were laughing and I didn't want to embarrass Rex Reed
or myself. After all, Helen's secretary didn't need to be seen
standing there, overhearing it all, so I drifted away.

Since the hostess worked for a Hearst publication, most of her guests were in the magazine business, but I also met book editors and advertising executives, stockbrokers and a few lawyers. One of the ad guys was performing card tricks, pulling a jack of hearts from behind a girl's ear.

I ran into Bridget, who had struck out with the Doubleday man. She handed me a glass of something green with crème de menthe. "No job," she said, clinking her glass to mine, "but I did get a date out of it, so I guess it wasn't a total loss. I sure hope he takes me for a steak. God knows he can afford it."

The party carried on, the hour grew later, records were changed, bottles were drained and ashtrays overflowed. People continued to come and go. One of the stockbrokers, Ray something or other, was trying to get my telephone number. He was wearing an argyle vest and moved stiffly like a man accustomed to three-piece suits. "Or," he said, handing me his business card, "you can call me."

I happened to look over and spotted a couple in the adjacent room. Ray was still talking while all the air caught inside my chest. I saw the back of the man's head and something inside me just knew. A beat later, as if he sensed he was being watched, he slowly turned around. It was Erik. With another woman. A blonde. Exactly the sort of beauty I would have expected for him.

The stockbroker was still coming on strong, telling me about his Fifth Avenue apartment overlooking the park, but his voice was muffled in my ears, drowned out by the sound of my heart pounding. I was crushed and humiliated, with no one to blame but myself. What did I expect? He was a Don Juan. Of course he was seeing other women. All along I told myself Erik was just for fun, but the body doesn't lie. I felt sick to my stomach and that's how you know you care.

I couldn't take my eyes off Erik and his date, not knowing if I wanted him to see me or not. The blonde wore an expensive gold watch with diamonds along the band. I knew it was a ridiculous assumption, an illogical leap, but I wondered if he'd given it to her. Maybe a birthday present or possibly an anniversary gift. They looked familiar and natural with one another, like they had been together forever.

My face was burning hot and I excused myself from the stockbroker. I was leaning against a bookshelf, the empty glass in my hand feeling suddenly very heavy, when Bridget came up to me.

"Is something wrong?" she asked, resting her hand on my shoulder.

I didn't say anything as I watched her gaze reach across the room in Erik's direction.

"Ali, are you okay?"

I nodded. She didn't know about Erik and me. None of the other girls did. The only person I'd told was Trudy. "I think I just had too much to drink."

"Do you need to get some air?"

I nodded again and closed my eyes. I couldn't torture myself by watching them anymore.

"Do you want me to come with you?"

"No. No thanks. I'll be fine."

I sorted through the pile of coats until I found my jacket and left the party. Down on the sidewalk, I tried to get my bearings and remember which direction to head for the subway. It was drizzling lightly and I could still hear the music from the party, the Four Tops singing "Baby I Need Your Loving." A couple strolled by with their fingers laced together. The lump was rising in my throat but I swallowed it down. No way would I shed a single tear over Erik Masterson.

The front door opened, and when I looked up, I saw Bridget standing beneath the streetlamp, raindrops visible in the light.

"I'm worried about you," she said. "Tell me what's wrong. What happened up there?"

I'd had just enough to drink to get me talking. Even though I felt foolish telling her about Erik, I couldn't stop myself. Every last detail came tumbling out.

"Men are rats," she said as we stood beneath the awning, shielding ourselves from the drizzle. "Just tell me one thing—is he as good in bed as everyone says?"

I closed my eyes and winced, listening to the sounds of cars going by, their tires rolling over the wet pavement.

"Well? Is he?"

I refused to answer. I didn't want to think about his other conquests. "I feel like such a fool. I had his number from the start. I shouldn't be surprised. I just don't understand why I'm so upset."

"Because you slept with him and that changes everything. And it's not your fault. It's physiological," she said, speaking with an air of great authority. "I read somewhere that when you have an orgasm, your body releases this hormone that attaches you to the man who gave you the orgasm."

I hoped that was true. I thought I was in control of this situation but all these feelings had snuck up on me.

"And the part that really stinks," said Bridget, "is that it's not the same for men. They don't have the same hormone so they can just sleep around and walk away. But not us girls. Think about it. How many women do you know who meet someone and all you hear is how *he's too old, too short, too poor, too this, too that*. But then"—Bridget raised her finger—"she sleeps with him and suddenly he's a god."

"Well, make no mistake, Erik Masterson is no god. He was just someone to have a little fun with. He was handsome and—"

"And he takes you to expensive places."

I cringed. "That sounds terrible."

"Let's face it, they use us and we use them."

I half nodded and half shrugged, remembering what Helen had told me about her 166 lovers. It was okay for her, but could it be okay for me? I wasn't using Erik, was I? I shuddered thinking of how I'd offered to make him dinner when he knew he had a date with that blonde. I looked at the clock on the bank sign across the way. It was after midnight.

"Listen," I said, "it's getting late. I'm going to head home. Why don't you go back upstairs?"

"You sure you're all right?"

"I'm sure."

She stepped to the edge of the awning and held her hand out, checking for raindrops. "Looks like it's easing up. If you're going to make a run for it, do it now."

I rode the subway and, for once, didn't care if I missed my transfer or if the car was filled with muggers. I leaned my head against the window and watched the graffitied tiled stations flash by like movie frames.

It was raining full on when I got to my stop, and by the time I made it back home, I was drenched. I slipped the key into the lock, raindrops dripping off the tips of my hair, puddles forming at my feet. As soon as I got inside, I hung my soggy jacket on the coat tree in the corner and slipped out of my shoes, soaked through so that my damp feet left a trail of footprints on the hardwood floor.

I took a couple more steps and thought I heard someone out in the hallway. Trudy, maybe? I turned toward the door, but it was just a creak, the building settling. I stood there, staring at my jacket, its collar hanging by the hook on the coat tree, shoulders and sleeves drooping, raindrops still puddling on the floor next to my wet shoes. That image said it all, summing up exactly how I felt.

I reached for my camera, and as I focused the lens, I knew I was onto something, something I hadn't been able to capture before. For the first time, a title for a photograph came to me: *After the Party.*

CHAPTER SIXTEEN

◦――――◦

Monday morning while at my desk, sorting through Helen's fan mail and separating out any critical letters, I caught myself thinking about Erik and about the photos I'd taken when I got home from the party—nearly an entire roll devoted to my soggy shoes and jacket hanging off the coat tree. I couldn't wait to get the film developed and see if those shots were as good as I thought.

"Alice?" Helen called to me from her office. "Be a lamb, would you, and go get Bobbie, Walter and George. Ask them to come down here. I have an article idea I want to discuss with them."

"Right away."

I went down the hall to Bobbie Ashley's office first. I found her hunched over a manuscript, its pages scattered across her desk. Bobbie was stylish, one of those women, like Elaine Sloan, who knew how to add a scarf or a cuff bracelet to chic up an outfit. Her office smelled of Chanel No. 5. I'd always had a keen sense of smell and knew my fragrances after weeks of spritzing myself at the Bloomingdale's counter. I realized I was beginning to associate fragrances with my coworkers. Helen was L'Air du Temps, Bridget was Shalimar, Margot, Rive Gauche, and Penny, Coty.

Bobbie was deep in concentration and didn't notice me standing in her doorway. I eventually cleared my throat to get her attention.

"Yes?"

She was still scrutinizing the manuscript before her, scratching out a line or two with a red pencil, while I explained that Mrs. Brown needed to see her.

"Mmm-hmm." She still hadn't bothered to look at me. "Tell her I'll stop by this afternoon."

"Actually, she'd like to see you now."

Her eyebrows rose slightly. "Did she say what it's about?"

"She has an article idea she'd like to discuss with you and Mr. Meade and Mr. Walsh."

Bobbie set her pencil down with considerable force. "Someone needs to tell her there's no money for any more articles. There's no money for anything." She got up from her desk and brushed past me.

I stopped by and got Walter and George, following them down to Helen's office. As I was about to close the door, she called me back in. "Come have a seat, dear. I'd like you to take notes for us."

Helen was in her doll's chair, shoes kicked off, feet tucked beneath her. Bobbie and Walter sat on the sofa while George took one of the side chairs, knees pressed together, cigarettes in one hand, coffee cup in the other. I was next to him, pen and steno pad ready for dictation.

"I have a marvelous story idea for July," said Helen.

"There's no money to assign any more writers."

"George, it would be so lovely if, just once, you stopped worrying about the money."

"Well, someone has to. Do you realize what you've already spent on those writers for this issue? That is, if you can call them writers. You offered one freelancer $500 for a piece on a career girl who goes to a psychiatrist."

"I'm very aware of what I'm paying her, George. Now, let me tell you all about this new story idea. It's a real grabber."

"I'm all ears," said George, taking a sip of coffee.

"I want us to do an article about how to properly handle a bosom."

I nearly dropped my pencil, and George almost spit out his coffee.

"Oh, my goodness," said Walter, already blushing.

"You're not serious, are you?" asked Bobbie. "Who would you even get to write a piece like that?"

"It's exactly the sort of article we need," said Helen. "A woman's bosom isn't just a couple of melons. They need attention and especially during lovemaking."

I could see how uncomfortable this discussion was making everyone. Everyone but Helen. She talked about sex the way other people talked about the weather.

"Men need an education on how to caress the bosom, and what's pleasurable to the nipple and what isn't. I have a feeling there's a lot of biters out there. And, after all, who better to teach them the right way to handle the bosom than women?"

"You don't have a dime to spend on a story like this," said George.

"Then I'll write it myself."

"You won't have time to do that," said Bobbie.

"Wanna bet?"

"I don't know a thing about bosom fondling," admitted Walter, "but you know I'll help you write it."

"This is ridiculous," said George. "You can't just pull a story like this out of thin air."

"I have an office full of women," said Helen with a laugh. "Women who I'm sure enjoy having their bosom fondled by someone who knows how. I've got a test kitchen right outside my door and I'm going to use it."

Bobbie and George, and even Walter to an extent, were bewildered when they left Helen's office, but she was inspired.

"Alice, let's issue a memo. Just for the female staff members.
Mark it confidential."

Helen was talking fast, like she did when she got excited about
something, and I was capturing it all in shorthand. I went back to
my desk and began typing it up, thinking, *I came to New York to
become a photographer and I'm typing up boob memos.*

TO: My Girl Staffers
FROM: HGB
SUBJECT: Highly Confidential!!!

We need your help for an upcoming piece about bosoms
and foreplay. Please tell me how you would like men to
handle your bosom during lovemaking. I want to know
what arouses your desire as much as what you don't like. I
see this as a crucial guide for men and an opportunity for
us to educate them on what will make our bosoms happy.
You will be doing women everywhere a great service by
participating in this. Please submit your replies to Alice no
later than 5 p.m. on Friday. If you prefer, you may respond
anonymously.

had just finished distributing Helen's bosom memo when Bridget
invited me to join her and some of the other girls to attend a
lecture up at Barnard College. "Betty Friedan's speaking there
tonight," she said, gazing into her compact mirror, applying a
fresh coat of cherry red lipstick.

Helen had left the office early that day so I accepted the invite.

On our way to the lecture, Helen's memo was all the girls wanted to talk about.

"I thought it was a joke at first," said Margot. "She's our boss. How can she expect us to tell her about our sex lives?"

"And what about how she makes it seem like it's our duty to respond to her memo? Like it's our responsibility to educate the men for all of womankind," said Leslie.

"I think it's funny," said Bridget. "I mean, c'mon, she's talking about publishing an article about boobs. *Boobs!* No woman's magazine has ever done that before."

"I'll respond to the memo," said Penny. "But I'm not signing my name."

I kept my mouth shut and took in the landscape. I'd never ventured that far on the Upper West Side. The Barnard campus was within spitting distance of Columbia University. It was lovely, with red brick and limestone buildings, meticulously manicured walkways and regal proud pillars.

The speech was in the Julius S. Held Lecture Hall on the third floor, a spacious room of wooden floors, freshly polished and still smelling of beeswax. There were rows of squeaky wooden fold-down chairs and a blackboard that stretched the width of the room. The lecture hall was packed and we had arrived just in time to get six seats together, toward the back.

When Betty Friedan was introduced, the audience, mostly young women, stood up, cheering and clapping. She moved to the podium, her hands to her sides, modestly trying to silence everyone, motioning them back down in their seats. I hadn't read *The Feminine Mystique*. All I knew about Betty Friedan was what I'd read in newspapers and heard in passing comments by other women.

In person, she was not what I'd been expecting. On sight alone, she was rather bland, even a bit homely, with a hooked nose and close-set, owl-like eyes. She was dressed smartly, though, in a simple A-line skirt and a beige sweater set. Her hair was short, her jewelry basic, and other than some lipstick, she wore little or possibly no makeup. In other words, she was the complete opposite of Helen Gurley Brown.

Betty Friedan spoke for close to an hour. The women inched forward in their chairs while she talked about both single and married women, putting themselves second and third behind boyfriends, husbands and children. "We all know women who dropped out of college the moment they got married. They're in the same boat as the housewife in the suburbs who worked to put her husband through college and quit as soon as he landed a job."

She spoke with great passion about young women with a world of choices before them who go through the motions of their days, feeling restless, bored and unfulfilled. "These bright, educated, capable women have been reduced to shells of their ideal selves. Society has told them that nothing will make them happier than having a clean house and a hot meal on the table."

And according to Mrs. Friedan, the solution was not to be found in sexual fulfillment, either. "Many of the women I surveyed reported having satisfying sexual relationships with their husbands. And yet"—she paused to punctuate the point—"that did nothing to ease the overwhelming doom of their day-to-day existence."

In the end, her talk was thought provoking and disturbing, as I was certain that we all saw bits and pieces of ourselves in the women she described.

As we were leaving the lecture hall, inching our way toward the exit, someone called my name. I turned around and there was Elaine Sloan.

"I thought that was you, Alice," she said, pulling me in for an embrace. She was wearing a low-cut black linen dress, her silver hair beautifully pulled back off her face, makeup flawless. She was so slender I could see the outline of her sternum through her suntanned skin. I wondered if she'd recently come back from vacation. She looked like she'd stepped out of a magazine, an advertisement for the Breakers in Palm Beach.

After I made a quick round of introductions, I saw the way Bridget and the others eyed Elaine's Louis Vuitton pocketbook tucked beneath her arm, her silver bracelets and diamond earrings. Everything about Elaine Sloan said style, success and money.

"I heard you went on a couple photo shoots with Christopher," she said.

I felt Bridget's eyes on me. "He's been helping me, giving me some pointers."

"You didn't say anything about going on any photo shoots with him," said Bridget, as if I'd been keeping a secret from her.

"Elaine put him up to it," I said for Bridget's benefit. "She knows I'm interested in photography."

"Speaking of which," said Elaine, "I finally found those photos of your mother that I've been wanting to show you. Come have dinner with me tomorrow night."

"I'd love to."

"Wonderful. Cocktails around six, dinner say seven-ish. I'm at the Dakota. Just give the doorman my name."

As I thanked her for the invitation, she embraced me again, kissed my cheek and made her exit as the others watched her disappear into the crowd.

"Who is she?" Margot asked with a bit of wonderment, as if she'd never imagined that a small-town girl like me might know such a woman.

"She's an editor at Bernard Geis. She was a friend of my mother's." I waited, hoping they'd ask me to elaborate, but all I got was Bridget pulling me aside to ask if Elaine could get her a job in publishing.

It was still early and a beautiful evening so the five of us sat outdoors at a coffee shop on 96th and Amsterdam near the subway stop. Crowded around a rickety table, with our hands clasped about our coffee mugs, we took turns dissecting Betty Friedan's lecture.

"Do you ever feel like we're part of the problem?" asked Margot.

"How are *we* part of the problem?" Penny looked perplexed, a deep line etched between her eyebrows.

"Well, think about it. We work for a magazine that's been spoon-feeding all this idealism to women. Every month they open their magazines and see the life they should aspire to and what they should be happy with."

"Ah," I said, "but that's exactly what's so exciting about the direction Mrs. Brown wants to take *Cosmo* in."

"Oh, you can't be serious." Margot was incredulous, the mild breeze stirring the tips of her pixie. "She's only perpetuating the problem."

"Exactly," said Leslie. "Forget about that ridiculous bosom memo, don't you see the difference between what she preached in *Sex and the Single Girl* and what Betty Friedan was talking about tonight?"

"Of course they're saying different things," I said. "But the overall message is the same. Helen Gurley Brown is all for a woman having a career."

"Yes, so she'll be more interesting to men," said Leslie.

"And she believes that a woman should be independent," I countered. "She believes a woman should live on her own, have her own apartment."

"Yeah, so she'll have a place to entertain men," said Margot. "Don't you see? Helen Gurley Brown is still telling us that we need a man to be fulfilled. Betty Friedan is telling us that we already have everything we need within ourselves."

I understood what Margot was saying, and while I didn't agree with everything Helen said, she was my boss and the underdog and I had a soft spot for anyone trying to beat the odds. When people attacked what she stood for, my knee-jerk reaction was to defend her.

Margot interrupted my thoughts. "Take that woman—your mother's friend—you can't tell me that she's sitting around waiting for her husband to make her happy."

"She's not married," I said.

"She's not?" Bridget looked shocked.

"That just proves my point," said Margot.

"But," I said, "I think that Helen Gurley Brown and Betty Friedan are both urging us to have full, happy, exciting lives with or without men. They just have different methods of getting there."

"I'm not sure what we're all arguing about," said Carole, a new secretary in the circulation department who had started a week after I did. "Can any of you honestly say that you don't want to get married and have a family?"

At first no one said anything. I stared at the traffic inching along Amsterdam as I shifted in my chair, thinking about Michael, the only man I ever thought I'd marry, the man I thought would be the father of my children.

"Sure, I want a husband and a family," said Penny eventually. "But not yet. Not now."

"Me neither," said Margot.

Leslie nodded. "I'm with them. There's things I want to do first."

"Like what?" asked Carole.

"I want to be a writer," said Penny.

"An editor," said Bridget.

"I want to be a photographer," I said.

"I'm going to be a fashion designer," said Margot.

We were all looking at Carole, her hands wrapped tightly around her coffee mug. "I'm sorry," she said sheepishly, "but I'm not like the rest of you. I don't have these big, glamorous goals. Sure, there's things I'd like to do—I'd like to travel and maybe take a painting or sculpture class. I don't want to just sit home and bake cookies. But at the end of the day, I'd be happy just to meet a nice man, get married and raise a family."

I expected the others to jump on her, but to my surprise, no one said a word. We grew quiet, the sounds of the city—the horns, people shouting, dogs barking—suddenly filtering in, but still our silence was impossible to ignore. It was as if Carole had just spoken some shameful truth that we were all harboring. Even me.

The Dakota was an impressive address to call home. Between the sweeping courtyard, its gables and dormers, the ornate spandrel archways, it looked like a Gothic castle to me. When I approached the main entrance, I was greeted by the uniformed doorman, who telephoned Elaine, announced my arrival and showed me to the elevator, where another uniformed man delivered me to the fifth floor.

Elaine answered the door before I rang the bell. Her silver hair was loose upon her shoulders and she was dressed in a flowing cream-colored tunic with black piping along the sleeves and collar. There was soft music playing on her hi-fi system, some sort of jazz.

"You have a gorgeous home," I said, stepping into a room enveloped by emerald green drapes, an elegant sofa and matching overstuffed chairs. The crystal chandelier, suspended in the foyer, shimmered down on the rich mahogany floor. I wasn't a good judge of spatial calculations but I would have guessed her ceilings were twelve feet high.

"I'm glad you like it. What can I get you to drink? A martini?" She walked over to a glass cart sporting brown and blue bottles of gin, bourbon, vodka and wine along with a sterling silver ice bucket just beginning to bead up with condensation, as if freshly filled.

"A martini would be great."

Noting that I was careful to sidestep around the zebra skin area rug sprawled out on the living room floor, she laughed and said, "It's okay. He won't bite. You can walk on him." She poured some gin and vermouth in a silver shaker. "I'm almost done decorating. At least for now. I suppose I'll get bored again soon enough and redo it all."

"You did this? Yourself? Without a decorator?"

She smiled as if it was no big deal and poured two martinis, leaving the perfect amount of room at the top for an olive. "It's a hobby." She handed me my drink and gave my glass a delicate clink with hers. "Now tell me," she said, "how are things going at work?"

"Much better, thanks to you."

"I hope that young man—what was his name again?"

"Erik."

"Erik, right. I hope he's been behaving himself."

"He won't be bothering me again." I took another sip of my martini. I hadn't seen Erik since the party and that was fine by me. I was sad that it was over, but I was done with him and grateful that I hadn't gotten myself in any deeper. I was safe now. My heart had moved, far outside his reach.

We took our drinks into the living room, the two of us sitting on her overstuffed chairs. I was hoping she'd bring out the photos of my mother soon, but Elaine seemed in no hurry to get to those.

"What did you think of the lecture last night?" she asked.

"It was a lot to take in. Makes you think. We were talking afterward about how Betty Friedan says one thing and Helen Gurley Brown says another."

"They're as different as night and day. Or so they'd like to think. Betty loathes Helen. She says Helen's obscene and disgusting. Personally, I lean more toward Betty's way of thinking, but Helen's not all wrong. Oh, but enough of that," said Elaine, shaking her head. "It was good to see you last night. Looks like you're meeting people and making friends."

"Everyone at work's been so nice and welcoming," I said. "And again, I can't thank you enough for helping me get the job and for asking Christopher to help me with my photography."

"No need to thank me. Christopher's happy to help you out. Besides"—she paused and lit a cigarette—"he owes me a few favors."

I looked at her, my eyebrows rising, asking her to elaborate.

"I've known Christopher since he was a little boy," she explained. "His parents divorced when he was a baby, and I met his father, William, shortly after that. I was mad for William." She smiled as if picturing him in her mind's eye while she flicked her ashes. "I almost married that man."

"What happened?"

She cocked her head toward the ceiling, as if the answer were waiting for her up there. "I guess, in the end, I didn't love him enough. He expected me to give up my career and raise his son, which I practically ended up doing anyway. I was also mad for Christopher. I don't talk to William anymore," she said, a certain sadness passing over her face. "But Christopher will always be in my life. He's like a son to me."

"What happened to Christopher's mother?" I couldn't resist asking. Now that I didn't have my mother, I was either fascinated by or resentful and envious of other people's relationships with theirs.

"His mother . . ." Elaine's voice trailed off for a moment, as if she was deciding how best to answer. "Christopher hasn't seen her since he was a baby. You see, his mother didn't just leave his father, she left him, too. After the divorce, she remarried. She and her husband have two children now. They live right here in the city, and she's never once reached out to Christopher. Not even a phone call. A letter. Nothing."

I felt some vague kinship to him, only his mother had left him on purpose. Mine was taken away from me.

"How she did that to him, I will never understand. Anyway"—Elaine wiped the thought away with her hand—"Christopher always wanted to be a photographer but his father didn't approve. William's a stockbroker and he wanted his son to follow in his footsteps, or at least work in finance. They had some terrible arguments over it. I was always playing referee. William thought Christopher would starve trying to make a living as a photographer. And believe me, Christopher's done very well for himself. And he's still so young. As you can see, I'm proud of him." She smiled, satisfied, as she leaned back and rubbed the nape of her neck. "And I can always say I gave him his first photography job. That was when I was at Random House. I had a young author who needed a headshot."

I was still trying to picture Christopher as a young boy, remembering the conversation we'd had that day in the coffee shop where he'd talked about being awkward around people, keeping to himself.

"He's a good kid," Elaine was saying now. "And talented. Not to mention handsome. Underneath all that hair. And let me tell you, those good looks run in the family. You should have seen his father when he was younger."

I smiled and said, "Christopher's girlfriend's awfully pretty, too."

"Oh, Daphne." She made a mocking pout. "That's gone on

longer than it should have. And you can't tell me his mother leaving doesn't have something to do with that."

"Don't you like Daphne?" I was surprised.

"No, she's fine. Perfectly fine. I just don't like her for Christopher." She stubbed out her cigarette. "Not that he'd ever listen to me when it comes to Daphne. I hope you're hungry," she said, changing the subject, getting up and motioning for me to follow her into the kitchen, which was larger than my entire apartment.

"Smells delicious," I said, taking in the scent of garlic filling the air. Three copper pots were simmering on the stove, the gas flame lapping up the sides of them. More pots, of varying sizes, were hanging from a cast iron rack above a butcher block island. Fresh basil, oregano and bay leaves sat on the counter, waiting to be added to the sauce.

"I can't believe you know how to cook, too. Is there anything you can't do?"

"You're very good for my ego." She laughed and flung a strand of spaghetti at the wall. I remembered my mother used to do the same thing. I felt a pang, staring at the noodle clinging to the tile.

"Done," Elaine said triumphantly and proceeded to drain and toss the noodles into a savory sauce of olive oil and white wine, garlic, herbs and shrimp.

We sat beneath another crystal chandelier at a dining room table that could have comfortably sat twelve. Elaine poured two glasses of chilled Chablis and raised her glass. "Cheers."

The meal was delicious, and afterward Elaine said, "Why don't we take our coffee into the living room and I'll show you the photos I found of your mother."

At last we were getting to it. I had studied all the photographs I had of my mother, memorizing each smile, every glance and hand gesture. I had pieced together my own version of her life, my own story. But I knew my story was incomplete. Other than my father, who wasn't big on talking about my mother, Elaine was the one person who could fill in the blanks.

She went to another room and came back a few minutes later with a flat lacquered box. "Now I know I have some others. Somewhere." She raised her hands as if saying *somewhere* could have been anywhere. "Come." She patted the seat cushion next to her. "Take a look . . ."

I sat down and she handed me a photo, the corner creased and bent.

"I think that was shortly after we met."

I looked at the black-and-white snapshot, the two of them standing in the doorway of the Plaza Hotel. It gave me goose bumps when I held it.

"See how much you look like her?"

I swallowed hard. Of course I saw the resemblance. But to me, my mother was always much more beautiful. There was something about her, an enchanting quality that people were drawn to. Especially men. Women—at least the women back in Youngstown— were leery of her and probably jealous. They regarded my mother as the big-city girl who thought she was better than them, and in truth, my mother did think that about herself. There wasn't one thing back home that she didn't compare to New York: The restaurants weren't as good, the bagels weren't real bagels, the selection of cheese was nonexistent, the clothes were a season behind.

"You know, there weren't a lot of us Jewish girls at the Barbizon," Elaine was saying, "so your mother and I stuck together. I remember on Yom Kippur the other girls wanted to fast with us so they could lose weight." She picked up another photo. "Oh, would you look at this? This must have been taken in one of our rooms."

Elaine handed me the photo of my mother lying at the foot of a bed, propped up on her elbow, smiling into the camera. Whoever took the photograph had perfectly captured that rascally look in my mother's eyes. It was a look I had cemented in my mind, the look she got right before she'd burst out laughing.

"Oh, how the camera loved your mother. She couldn't take a bad picture if she tried. Even Harry Conover used to say that."

"Who's Harry Conover?"

"You've never heard of Harry Conover?" she asked, surprised. "Before there was an Eileen Ford or John Casablancas, there was Harry Conover. He owned the biggest modeling agency in New York. I got my first job through him. For Pond's Face Cream— that might have been when we took this one." Elaine laughed, handing me the next photo. It was the two of them with cold cream on their faces, a playful look in their eyes, mouths forming exaggerated O's. "You know your mother could have done very well as a model if her father hadn't put the kibosh on that."

"Why? He didn't want her to model?"

"Oh, heavens no. Her father, the judge," she said with finger quotes, "was very strict. Always worried about what other people would think. He didn't like the idea of his daughter posing for money. In his mind, she might as well have been a pin-up girl."

Elaine was so casual, so matter-of-fact, but I was hanging on her every word. Other than him being a judge, I knew next to nothing about my mother's father.

"No one ever talked about my mother's side of the family," I said. My mother's parents had both died right before I was born. "What is it about my family and car accidents?" I said.

"What do you mean?"

"Well, first my mom's parents die in a car crash and then she does, too. It's like car accidents are hereditary in my family."

Elaine gave me a cryptic look as she poured a dollop of cream in her coffee and gave it a long, leisurely stir.

"My dad's parents are gone, too," I said. "So I've never had any grandparents."

"Well, all I know is that your mother's father completely over-reacted when she met your father. You would have thought she'd committed a crime."

"He didn't like my dad?" I pictured my father, kindhearted and soft-spoken, the most nonconfrontational person I'd ever met. "I thought everyone loved him."

"Oh, honey, it was the circumstances more than anything. I don't know how her mother felt about everything, but I can tell you her father was a real shit. Sorry," she said, reading my pained expression. "But it's true. He just about broke your mother's heart. Trust me, your parents did the right thing."

"About what?" I had no idea what she was talking about. It was like we were having two separate conversations.

"Like I said, her father was a real shit. And her mother should have stepped in but she didn't." Elaine looked as if she was about to say something else but had lost her train of thought. After a moment, she raised her cup. "More coffee?"

I tried to find out more about this awful thing my mother's father had done, but Elaine kept dodging it, and by the end of the evening, I left with more questions than answers.

I supposed I could have asked my father about it, but I was never able to keep him on a long-distance call long enough for a serious conversation. And he wasn't big on letters, either, so there was no point in writing to him about it. I would have to wait until I saw him next, whenever that would be.

CHAPTER SEVENTEEN

○———○

Responses to Helen's bosom memo were trickling in all week long. I'd leave my desk to get a cup of coffee or go to the ladies' room, and by the time I came back, more would appear, folded in half, sealed with a piece of tape. Others were stapled shut or else in envelopes. Most were typed so no one would recognize the handwriting.

My telephone line buzzed and I was summoned to the mailroom to retrieve a package for Helen. When I returned, two more anonymous bosom confessionals were on my desk.

I was slicing the first one open when Mr. Berlin came charging down the hall. "Helen! Helen, this time you've gone too far." He was waving a copy of *Women's Wear Daily* in his hand, his face blood red, his heavy jowls quivering. "You're making us the laughingstock of the entire magazine industry."

Before I could intervene, Helen was standing in her doorway, her Pucci ruffles all aflutter, her voice still silky smooth. "Richard, what on earth is the problem this time?"

"How in the hell did a memo of yours end up in *Women's Wear Daily*?"

"What memo? What are you talking about?" Though she tried keeping her voice calm, I could tell she was alarmed.

"It's right here. In their gossip column." He opened the magazine and began to read aloud, not caring who heard: "'We need your help for an upcoming piece about bosoms and foreplay. Please tell me how you would like men to handle your bosom during lovemaking.'"

I watched the color drain from Helen's face as he recited her memo verbatim along with the editorial heckling that accompanied it. By now, everyone had stopped what they were doing and had gathered around, speechless, while Richard Berlin continued to ream her out.

"I hope you're proud of yourself, Helen. You've got everyone laughing at us. At you. What the hell were you thinking? You know perfectly well that I never would have let you run an article like that in the first place."

And that's when Helen exploded. "That memo was confidential," she screeched, her delicate voice unable to muster any real power. "They had no right to share that with anyone outside this office." Her eyes were turning glassy even before she ran into her office and slammed the door.

"What the hell are you all staring at?" Berlin barked at the onlookers. "Everybody back to work." They scattered like billiard balls after a clean break.

Once Berlin stalked off, I went to Helen's door and knocked tentatively. "Mrs. Brown? Mrs. Brown, may I come in?" There was no answer so I slowly turned the knob and opened the door. She was curled up in the fetal position on her sofa, sobbing into clenched fists. "I'm so sorry that happened. Is there anything I can do?" I asked, inching closer, holding out a handkerchief for her. "Would you like a glass of water? A cigarette? Anything?"

"How did this happen?" she mumbled, taking the handkerchief. "Why would someone do such a thing?"

"I don't know," I said, sitting beside her. She seemed so fragile, like a little bird. "I only gave that memo to the girls here in the office."

"And one of those girls gave it to *Women's Wear Daily.*" She started rocking back and forth. "This is a nightmare. Do you know how many people read *Women's Wear Daily*? And the timing." She sat still, letting the repercussions sink in. "My God, I'm trying to save this magazine. I have to bring on writers and photographers. I have to convince advertisers to spend money with us, and now no one is going to take me seriously." Her lashes had come unhinged, hanging cockeyed like broken window blinds. She reached up and gently peeled them away, setting them on the coffee table—two curved caterpillars.

As she blew her nose and dried her eyes, I sat there, witnessing a shift in her. I'd never seen her that angry before.

"I don't care who it is," she said, her voice turning hard and brittle, finding the strength that had eluded her moments before in front of Berlin. "I'm going to find the little bitch who leaked that memo. I'm going to find her and fire her on the spot."

First thing the next morning, while a group of us were getting our coffees, Helen marched into the kitchen holding a piece of paper. It was like the parting of the sea the way everyone moved to let her through. Without saying a word, Helen went over to the bulletin board and stabbed a thumbtack through a note: *There's a viper in our nest!!!!!*

She turned and left without making eye contact with anyone, not even me. Everyone crowded in closer to the bulletin board as if there were something more there to see. I leaned against the counter, my coffee turning cold while I watched the girls, my colleagues and friends, wondering which one of them could have done such a thing. I knew a lot of them had issues with Helen, but I couldn't imagine someone would have disliked her enough to blatantly sabotage her editorship like this, not to mention the entire magazine.

When I came back to my desk, Erik was walking about the floor. I was certain he was loving the whole *Women's Wear Daily* debacle. I'd been doing my best to avoid him ever since the party and, given the bosom memo, that felt like a lifetime ago. I watched Erik from the corner of my eye. He stopped to chat with Bill Guy and with Bridget and some of the other secretaries. When he started making his way toward me, a rush of heat flushed through my body. I thought I'd made peace with all this, but I was fuming.

"There she is," he said, acting all chipper, as if nothing were wrong. His glib tone only infuriated me more. "Haven't seen you around lately."

"Yeah, well, I sure have seen you."

He furrowed his brow. "What's *that* supposed to mean?"

"I was at Katie Murphy's party last weekend."

"You were? I didn't even see you."

"I know you didn't."

"Well, why didn't you come over and say something?"

"Because you were busy. I didn't want to interrupt you while you were on a date."

He twisted up his handsome face. "What? Who? You mean Sharon?" He laughed. "I wasn't on a date. Sharon's an old friend. I ran into her at the party. That's all."

I picked up my pen and jotted down some random nonsense on a notepad just for the sake of having something to do.

"C'mon, Ali, it's no big deal."

I gave him a harsh stare and then wanted to rewind the last few minutes and start over so I could come across indifferent and unfazed.

"You believe me about Sharon, don't you?"

I stopped writing and set the pen down. "Do I look stupid to you?" So much for defusing the situation. Now I was only making it worse.

"Ali, c'mon now, why are you getting so worked up over this?"

I sighed, planting my elbows on my desk, resting my head in my hands. I was bewildered. "Maybe I don't know how to have a casual fling. Maybe I—"

"Ali—"

I held up my hand. "Let me finish." I looked into his eyes, lovely as they were, and said, "I'm not looking to fall in love with you. I'm not interested in some deep, complicated relationship." I could tell by the way his mouth hung open that he wasn't expecting me to say that. Or else he didn't believe me. "I mean it," I said. "I'm not looking for a relationship. I'm all for something fun and easy—no strings attached. But"—I lowered my voice to a whisper—"we're sleeping together and I'm sorry, but I can't do that if you're having sex with other women. It makes me feel dirty. Like I'm using someone else's toothbrush."

He laughed and rubbed his chin. I had no idea what was going through his mind.

"If you want to sleep with other women, that's fine," I said. "We don't have to see each other. No hard feelings."

He laughed again. "I don't want to sleep with other women."

I kept talking, like I hadn't heard him. "I'm just not interested in sharing you when it comes to that department."

"I don't want to sleep with other women," he repeated as he looked at me and smiled. It was his bedroom smile, the smile he gave me when he knew he was thrilling every inch of me. I hated myself in that moment, but heaven help me, I wanted the thrill again.

Later that night I ended up at Tavern on the Green with Erik because he'd promised he'd take me there, and plus, according to him, "You can't really call yourself a New Yorker until you've dined there."

The decor played off its Central Park locale with pinks the shade of blooming flowers and greens that matched the grass outside. It was like sitting in the middle of a garden. Just as my mother had described it. She'd told me that a lot of celebrities ate there and I was pretty sure that was Ava Gardner across the way, dining with a young actor-like type.

It was all so over the top, so absurd. So very Erik. None of it was real but that was fine by me. It fit the fairy-tale New York I'd always imagined—me in a glamorous restaurant with a handsome man. This was exactly what I'd wanted from him and I was sure Helen would have approved. My mother would have, too. It was pure single girl fun.

After he'd ordered two champagne cocktails at 95¢ apiece, I said, "You certainly do live well, Mr. Masterson."

"I work hard, might as well enjoy the fruits of my labor, right?"

"I don't suppose you ever get a craving for peanut butter and jelly, huh?"

He smiled. "Not lately, no." He raised his champagne glass to mine and said, "To one of the most challenging women I've ever met."

I brought the glass to my mouth and paused. "Is that a compliment or a complaint?"

"For now it's a compliment. Ten years from now, it might be a complaint."

"Ten years? Don't you think you're getting a little ahead of yourself? I doubt we'll even remember each other's names in ten years."

"See? That's what I'm talking about. Nothing gets past you. You don't suffer fools gladly. I'm not used to that but I'm beginning to think I like it. You definitely keep me on my toes."

We both sipped on that sentiment, and in between the cherrystone clam cocktail and the frog legs sautéed in butter, we danced to the Milton Saunders Orchestra. I glanced down at our feet, the tips of his shoes unapologetically bumping into my new baby dolls.

"I should have warned you," he said, "I have two left feet."

It was true. He was a terrible dancer, and I teased him mercilessly about it through one more song before returning to our table in time for the pineapple cheese pie and an ice cream roll with Nesselrode sauce. The bill came, but Erik called the waiter back over and ordered two brandies.

His apartment was a short taxicab ride from the restaurant and we kissed and groped the whole way. Once upstairs, we wasted no time. We undid each other's buttons and zippers, eagerly as children opening Christmas presents. I was on his bed, half out of my dress and nearly out of my mind. He was leaning over me, the tips of his hair brushing against my cheek, when the telephone rang.

He groaned.

"Do you need to get that?"

We both looked at the phone on his nightstand, ringing.

"Nah, it's probably work." The phone rang another half-dozen times before the caller gave up.

We were back at it and five minutes later the phone rang again. He paused for a moment, propped himself up on his elbows, eyeing the receiver.

"It's okay," I said, scooting out from under him. The shrill ringing filled the apartment with a sense of urgency. "You should
answer it. It might be important."

When the phone rang for a third time, he picked up. I heard a
man's voice on the other end and felt a rush of relief. "Yeah," Erik
said, running his fingertips over my shoulder and down my arm.
"I know you've been calling, but I can't talk now. Why?" He
peeled back the sheet and eyed my body, shaking his head in a *my
oh my* kind of way. "Because I'm busy." He hung up the phone,
deliberately leaving the receiver off the hook.

"Not important, I gather?"

"This right here"—he leaned in and kissed me—"this is what's
important."

Afterward we lay in his fine bed making shadow puppets on
the wall.

"That's not a dog," I said, teasing him. "It's supposed to be a
wolf."

"Now this is a wolf," he said, demonstrating.

"Not fair." I laughed, pulling his hand down. "You have longer
fingers than me."

We kissed some more after that and he held me and it felt like
heaven. He had a way of making me believe I belonged there in
his Park Avenue bed.

CHAPTER EIGHTEEN

○━━━━━━○

Once again Helen broke her own expense account rule. She had me set up a luncheon meeting at Patsy's on West 56th with Jack and Sally Hanson, the husband and wife team who'd founded the Jax clothing line. Everyone from Ann Margret to Gina Lollobrigida wore their sexy, curve-hugging slacks, and Helen wanted to feature the couple and their clothes in the July issue.

With Helen out for lunch, I had decided to slip out for a bite myself. I was touching up my lipstick at my desk when Bridget came up from behind, appearing in my compact mirror.

"Who are you getting all dolled up for? Special lunch plans?"

Actually, I was meeting Trudy, but before I could explain, my phone rang.

"Saved by the bell," said Bridget with a laugh.

"Mrs. Brown's office." I closed my compact and tucked it back inside my pocketbook.

"I hope it's okay to call you while you're at work."

"Who is this?"

"How quickly we forget. It's Christopher. Christopher Mack."

"Oh." There was no hiding the surprise in my voice. I looked at Bridget and made a yapping gesture with my hand. She got the message and went back to her desk.

"So there's a gallery opening down in the Village on Friday night," he said. "I thought you might like to go. It's no big deal. Some of my photography's gonna be on exhibit there so I'm inviting people I know. You can bring anyone you like. I think Elaine's going to be there."

I immediately thought of bringing Trudy and not Erik. I didn't want to introduce Erik to Elaine, and until that moment I hadn't realized how sheepish I felt about seeing him. That notion traveled to my gut and settled there, something hard to digest.

Christopher gave me the address, and as soon as I hung up with him, Helen called. She was on a pay phone inside the restaurant. I could hear dishes clanking in the background, bits and pieces of conversation. She had forgotten her Jax folder on her desk and would I be a little lamb and bring it over?

After canceling plans with Trudy, I gathered Helen's folder, stuffed thick with notes, tear sheets and the same dummy she'd shown at the 21 Club luncheon. When I arrived at the restaurant, the maître d' led me to her table. Along the way, I noticed David Brown dining there with another man, and that was no accident. I'd never made a luncheon reservation anywhere for her without first making sure David was dining there, too. Same time, same place. Always on call to bail her out if needed.

But things appeared to be going smoothly as I approached Helen's table. She was smiling, laughing, an untouched martini she'd never drink and a salad she'd maybe pick at, waiting patiently for her. Jack and Sally Hanson, with their California tans, were eating their entrées while Helen did the talking, stopping only when she saw me with the maître d'.

"Oh good, you're here."

I smiled at the Hansons as I handed Helen her folder and quietly began backing away.

"Oh, wait a minute, dear. Have a seat." She gestured to the empty chair beside her and, after consulting the file, proceeded as if I wasn't there.

"Basically," she said, "we want to reinforce the Jax brand as the leading line of sexy clothing for career-minded girls." She paused and picked a lettuce leaf from her salad bowl, her fingers delicately raised while she shredded that leaf into itty-bitty bites, which she daintily nibbled. Her fork and knife were at her place setting, untouched. "How do you like that?" she asked, selecting another lettuce leaf.

"I like it very much," said Jack, dabbing his napkin to his mouth.

"Why do I feel like there's a catch here?" asked Sally.

"There's no catch." Helen smiled and shredded another lettuce leaf. "I'm talking about a beautiful fashion spread—eight full pages—including a magazine article. We'll do a full profile on the two of you—Hollywood's most exciting couple—the jet set, only we'll call you the 'Jax Set.'"

"The Jax Set." Jack smiled. "Now I know why you were such a brilliant copywriter. I think it's very clever, Helen, but eight pages? Why are you willing to give us so much precious real estate?"

"Because look at what you've done." She went for another lettuce leaf. "The two of you have completely changed the way women dress. What a stroke of genius to take that side zipper and move it to the back of the slacks. Now that really shows off a woman's figure. With this campaign, every one of my girls will be running out to buy Jax slacks."

"You said campaign," Sally noted, sipping her martini. "So is this an advertisement we're talking about?"

"Ah," said Helen, "that's the brilliant part. It won't look like one. It's an advertisement disguised as a fashion feature. And the best part is, it'll cost you a fraction of the price of running even one full-page ad. All I'm asking is for you to cover the photography. Of course, you'll provide the clothes, but I'll handle all the rest."

I sat back, watching the Hansons. She had them. Helen finished eating her salad with her fingers and walked away from that meeting with Jack and Sally Hanson agreeing to foot the bill for her first fashion spread.

"So this is an art gallery opening," said Trudy.

"Not quite what I was expecting, either," I said as we stepped inside.

It was a raw space that looked like it had been all but abandoned before this pack of artists descended upon it. Small and cramped, it smelled of cigarettes, incense and stale beer. People stood in clusters, smoking, drinking from paper cups. I'd never seen so many goatees before, and compared to the beatniks with their sunglasses, striped T-shirts and berets, Trudy and I looked out of place, which tickled me. I couldn't help but smile, recalling how I had telegraphed *Ohio* when I first moved to New York and now, here in the Village, in my new blue shift and Rhonda's slingback shoes, I looked pure Uptown.

I scanned the crowd but didn't see Elaine Sloan. She would have stood out in this room, too. The same was true for Daphne, whom I hadn't seen, either. But I did spot Christopher—or at least a glimpse of him. He stood off to the side, looking very mod, like he belonged in London with his black sports jacket, straight-legged black trousers, handsome leather boots and thick brown hair perfectly tousled. He was shaking hands with one of the beatniks while two women looked on, probably hoping to catch his eye.

"That's him." I gestured with my chin. "That's Christopher."

"Wow," said Trudy. "You didn't tell me he was so—"

"He has a girlfriend."

She gave me a downturned smile. "Drats. Why are the good ones always taken?"

"That's just the way it goes," I said.

Trudy and I were drifting about, observing the hodgepodge of paintings, sculptures and photography. I didn't care much for any of the artwork; some of the canvases had pieces of broken chairs or light fixtures sticking out of them. Others looked like they weren't finished, or had been a mistake. We were both laughing at one piece when Christopher came up to us.

"You're here." He took a step toward me, arms open. "I'm glad you made it," he said, hugging me.

I introduced him to Trudy, and after they'd said hello, I turned back and looked at one of the paintings. It had something shiny protruding from the canvas. "What's that supposed to be?" I asked.

"I think it's a hubcap," said Christopher with some authority.

"Oh, so it is." I turned back to face the painting. "But why a hubcap? What's it supposed to mean?"

"I haven't the foggiest idea," admitted Christopher. "I suppose we'd have to ask the artist."

"I'd like to ask *somebody* where the ladies' room is," said Trudy.

Christopher gestured toward the rear of the gallery. "All the way to the back and down the stairs."

After Trudy left, he pulled a pack of Lucky Strikes from his pocket, offering me one. While he lit my cigarette, I pointed to a sculpture: a bunch of pieces of rusted-out scrap metal soldered together. "And what about that?" I asked. "What's *that* supposed to be?"

Christopher followed my gaze and made a face. "Oh, please. Sculpture is something you bump into when you're backing up to look at a painting."

I laughed. "That's very clever."

"I can't take credit for it." He smiled. "It's not my line. I stole it from Ad Reinhardt."

"Well, at least you're an honest thief."

We moved on. He followed close behind me as we came to the next painting: a bunch of stripes in varying shades of green.

"I'm sorry but I don't get contemporary art. Or pop art. Or whatever you call it."

"You might want to keep that to yourself in this crowd," he said with a slight grin.

We paused to look at another painting, white with flecks of wood sticking out of the canvas.

"So?" he asked. "What do you think of this one?"

"Not much." I laughed. "I could do that. How is this even considered art?"

"Ouch. Now that one hurt." He pointed to the signature.

I looked down. *Christopher Mack.* "You did this? It's yours?"

"Guilty."

"Oops. Sorry." I was embarrassed and laughed, because what else could I do? Fortunately, he was laughing, too. "I don't really know anything about art," I said.

"Well, that's obvious." He was still laughing.

"I didn't know you were a painter."

"According to your standards, I'm not. Honestly," he said, "I just fool around with it. The gallery threw me a bone, said I could show a piece if I let them exhibit my photography."

"Speaking of which, where are your photos?" I stepped away, hoping to put some distance between me and my faux pas.

He walked me over to another section of the gallery. "Let's see if I can redeem myself." He held out his hand, displaying a series of black-and-whites.

I looked at them, astonished, my mouth gaping open.

"What can I say? You inspired me." He smiled, offering a modest shrug.

They were the photos we'd taken that day in the Village: a woman whose dog was tugging on his leash, a group of boys roller skating down Waverly Place. Two old men sitting on a park bench, playing chess. There were some others, too, some I hadn't seen before. I was surprised though that Daphne wasn't in any of them.

"Where's your girlfriend?" I asked, meaning both *Why isn't she in your photos?* and *Why isn't she here tonight, for your opening?*

"Something came up," he said, like it was no big deal. "Oh, and Elaine sends her regards. She had another Jackie Susann crisis at work."

"I feel like I'm hogging the guest of honor," I said, turning to another photograph. "Don't you have people you need to mingle with?"

"I suppose. It doesn't really matter, though—mostly they're just all into being part of the scene down here."

"It's very different from uptown."

"Just wait till the poetry starts," said Christopher. "You ain't seen nothing yet."

I smiled. "Seriously, I should really let you get back to your guests."

He nodded. "Tell your friend it was nice meeting her. Oh, and let me know when you want to go shooting again."

We said our good-byes without making definite plans. Trudy reappeared moments later, just as the lights grew dim and more people crowded in toward the center of the room. The place was packed, people standing shoulder to shoulder. Some sat on crates and others on the ground, arms circled about their knees, leaning back against the brick walls. A young man stood on a makeshift bandstand. He had shaggy light brown hair and an equally shaggy beard. He smoked his cigarette down to his knuckles while reciting a poem about the soullessness of modern life, the fleeting nature of our existence and its impermanence. He snapped his fingers between each stanza, as if advancing the poem.

When he'd finished, I was entranced. There was a pulse in the air, a different kind of energy. I liked it and suddenly regretted having worn my new dress and Rhonda's fancy shoes. I would have liked to have stayed for more poetry, but it was getting late and Trudy was antsy, looking at her watch and smoking back-to-back cigarettes.

We left the gallery and made our way toward the subway. It was a beautiful clear night, just enough of a breeze to stir the mild spring air. Cars lined the streets, bumper to bumper, and Villagers filled the sidewalks, jackets flapping open, the smell of marijuana trailing behind them.

"I think he likes you," said Trudy while we were waiting on the platform for the subway.

"No. Who? Christopher? No." I shook my head. "We're just friends. I told you, he's got a girlfriend."

"A girlfriend who wasn't there tonight."

"It's not like that. He loves Daphne. You should see them together. He's crazy about her."

Our train pulled up and we got on board, took our seats. I was still thinking about the poetry.

"Okay, fine," said Trudy. "I won't say another word about Christopher Mack. But I think you're kidding yourself."

"Enough, Trudy. Christopher's helping me with my photography—that's it. That's all I want it to be."

"Wow." She looked at me, mystified, her eyes big and round. "You really don't want to fall in love, do you?"

"Like I told you before, not if I can I help it."

CHAPTER NINETEEN

———◦————◦———

The Jax photo shoot was set and Helen had asked me to join her along with Harriet, Tony and George. We were shooting at J. Frederick Smith's studio on West 87th Street. It was an enormous white room with the morning light streaming through the windows, streaking across the wooden floor. Smith's illustrations and photographs lined the walls as you walked in. His work possessed an overtly sexy pin-up style that reminded me of the images I'd seen in those *Playboy*s. Several pieces of Smith's work had wound up on the covers of *Esquire*. His wasn't the sort of photography you'd ever see in a *McCall's* or *Ladies' Home Journal*. Not even in *Mademoiselle*.

Hearst would not have approved of Helen's choice of photographers if they knew, and I made sure I'd kept that information away from Erik. Though he'd been impressed that Helen had managed to get the Hansons to pick up the tab for the shoot. How he knew that, I wasn't sure, because I didn't tell him. Each time he asked who was shooting the Jax spread, I outright lied and said I didn't know.

It seemed as though there were hours of preparation before a single shot was taken. Sitting off to the side, behind Helen and the Hansons, I was fascinated by the process.

There were racks of clothes next to steamers on long poles, puffing away. Stylists were on hand to make quick alterations, stitch up hemlines, let out darts and clip back excess fabric with clothespins. A hair stylist had set up a table in the corner, full of rollers, brushes, combs, wigs on Styrofoam heads and gadgets for curling, straightening and smoothing. The makeup artist was next to her with cases of rouge, lipsticks, eye shadows, false lashes and pancake foundation.

Smith had his own entourage of assistants to load cameras, set lights and tripods, move sweeps and props about. They'd take a Polaroid or two and make adjustments before checking the light meter again. They'd repeat that same process until they got it perfect.

Then there were the models, stunning even with their hair in rollers the size of soup cans and no makeup yet on their flawless features. I watched those beautiful creatures, thinking of my mother and what Elaine had said about her father cutting her career short. I was still thinking about that when, much to everyone's surprise, Erik showed up along with Dick Deems and Frank Dupuy.

"What are they doing here?" Helen whispered to me, her lips barely moving.

"I have no idea." I didn't even realize they knew the shoot was that day.

Helen breezed past me with a forced smile. "Dick, Frank, Erik—welcome. Have you met Jack and Sally Hanson?" Helen put on a perfect performance as if she'd intended to have them there all along.

Erik and I said hello but that was it. I wondered if Helen knew I was sleeping with him. She had to have known. She had a sixth sense when it came to those things.

I was standing next to her when she instructed Harriet and Tony on how to handle the Hearst executives. "Just reassure them that everything's going fine," she said. "And whatever you do, don't let them wander about. I don't want them trying to direct this shoot."

As soon as Harriet and Tony went to talk to the men, Helen called Smith over. He had two different cameras hanging about his neck, beads of sweat visible on his forehead.

"Will you be a dear and do me a special favor?" I heard Helen say to him. "Just take some nice clean shots of one of the girls— just to satisfy Deems and his lemmings. I don't even care if you have film in the camera. I'll make them—poof—go away as soon as I can and then we can get back to work."

"Got it." He nodded and called out, hands cupped about his mouth, "Where's Renata? Somebody get Renata."

Renata was a tall blond German beauty whose last name I couldn't pronounce. She came out from behind the changing curtain in a pair of hip-hugging white Jax slacks and a red and white gingham top with a high collar that reached all the way to her chin.

Smith posed her against a white sweep, having her sit on a stool, hands in her lap, her long blond hair pulled back in a sleek ponytail, the expression on her face wholesome and innocent. I had to hand it to Helen—she knew what she was doing. After twenty minutes or so, the Hearst men stopped asking questions and stood back watching, the tension on their faces fading.

While Smith pretended to photograph Renata, I looked over and noticed Erik had cozied up to one of the models, standing a good two inches taller than him in her high heels. Innocent flirting or was he going to get her phone number?

I waited ten seconds, which was about all I could take, and walked over. "Hey, how's it going?"

He got the message, stuffed his hands in his pockets. "We were just talking," he said when the model was out of earshot.

"So," I said, softening my tone, "I was thinking we could go hear some poetry tonight."

"Poetry?"

"Yeah, there's this great club down in the Village and we—"

"The Village? Poetry?" He made a face. "I gotta work late tonight."

I don't know why this bothered me. I knew he didn't like the Village and he probably liked poetry even less. I turned away, desperate to change the subject. "Looks like they're setting up lunch," I said.

They had a lavish buffet of sandwiches and salads, fruits and slabs of hand-carved roast beef. I fixed Helen a plate though I knew she wouldn't touch it, just as she hadn't eaten anything from the breakfast spread, either.

After the Hearst folks had finished lunch and left the studio, Helen excused herself from the Hansons and walked over to the set. George marched up behind her, but she ignored him. Thanks to her advertising days, it was clear that she was in her element. With one arm wrapped about her waist, her opposite hand propped up beneath her chin, she stood there, studying Renata.

After a moment she turned to Smith. "What can we do to make this juicier? More like one of your *Esquire* photos?"

"Now Helen . . ." George was shaking his head. "You know we can't do—"

"Oh, don't worry." Helen gave him a patronizing, dismissive smile. "I'm just having a little fun is all. You should try it sometime."

George walked away, shaking his head even more emphatically.

Smith stood back, thinking. "Renata, honey, stand up, will you please?"

When she did, Helen pulled the stool out of the way and walked around the glorious creature, eyes sweeping the length of her body as indiscreetly as a leering man on a construction site. She turned Renata around; her gingham top was cut low in the back exposing her shoulder blades and the subtle nodes of her vertebrae.

"Too bad we can't shoot her from behind," said Smith. "The back of that top's sexier than the front."

Helen looked at Smith, her eyes twinkling. "Renata"—she held out her hand—"come with me, dear."

Helen went behind the changing curtain with Renata and a few minutes later reappeared with Renata's blond hair tousled and wild and her gingham top now on backward so that it was plunging in the front, showing off her heaving cleavage and the round slopes of her breasts.

George's eyes about popped out of his head.

"How's that for juicy," said Helen.

The Jax photo shoot was still going on when Helen sent me back to the office to tend to other matters: letters and thank-you notes to be sent out, meetings to be scheduled, that sort of thing. I was inspired by what I'd seen at Smith's studio, and after weeks of procrastinating, I was ready to enroll in a photography class. I'd been carrying the application around in my pocketbook and was about to fill it out when Bridget rushed over, asking about the shoot.

"It was fascinating," I said, tucking the form in my drawer, where I'd conveniently forget about it for several weeks. "Although

the guys from Hearst showed up out of nowhere and almost ruined the whole thing."

"Did Erik go over there with them?" asked Margot, stopping
by my desk, a stack of folders in her arms.

"Oh, I'm sure he was there," said Bridget. "Erik Masterson
would never pass up an opportunity to be around a bunch of
fashion models."

That stung. They continued talking while I shuffled through
the mail for fear they'd see the hurt in my eyes. After Bridget and
Margot had gone back to their desks, I focused on Helen's mail
and ended up reading a letter I shouldn't have opened.

Dear Helen,

*I hope this finds you well. I can't remember the last time I
spoke with you or received one of your letters. You used to
write all the time but lately it seems like I have more
contact with David than I have with you. I saw your
picture in one of the magazines, either* Time *or* Newsweek.
*I was at the doctor's office with Mary. She had an
appointment that day. The doctor wants to send I wished
they'd used a better photograph. You look so tired and
haggard. David tells me you're always working. Even on
the weekends. Be careful there. Don't forget to tend to your
marriage and your husband. You'll wear yourself out
working all the time and you don't want to end up losing
David over this job of yours. If you drive him away, don't
think it will be easy for you to find another man. Need I
remind you that you're no Grace Kelly or Jayne
Mansfield. You've got your smarts but that will only carry
you so far. And, my goodness, the things you said in that
article. Helen, must everything that comes out of your*

mouth be so vulgar? I'm worried that you're making a spectacle of yourself. In the future, I urge you to think before you speak or you're likely to find yourself out of a job, out of a marriage and up to your eyeballs in debt. Speaking of which, I mentioned that I took Mary to the doctor's recently. He wants to send her to Warm Springs but of course that costs money and I'll never be able to afford it. Just wanted to let you know. Here's some clovers from her yard. We need all the good luck we can get. Pray for your sister, will you please?

Love,
Mother

By the time I reached the end, a dozen or so clovers had fallen out of the letter and landed on my desk, wilted and shriveled from their travels. A trace of green petal blood appeared where some of the leaves had been crushed. I picked up one, holding its limp stem between my fingers, and realized it was a four-leaf clover. I glanced at another clover. It also had four leaves. All of them did. I'd never seen a four-leaf clover before, let alone a whole collection of them.

I folded the letter, tucked the clovers inside and stuffed it back in the envelope, wondering how it had gotten mixed in with Helen's fan mail. It was an innocent mistake and I was sure she would understand, but still I shouldn't have read the whole thing. I should have stopped as soon as I realized it was a personal letter, but I couldn't help myself.

When Helen returned from the photo shoot around six o'clock that evening, she wasn't upset about my accidentally opening it.

"Hmmm." She looked at her mother's handwriting on the envelope. "I wonder how much money she's asking for this time," she said, taking a seat behind her desk while reaching for a cigarette. "That's the only reason she ever writes—to ask for money or to tell me what I'm doing wrong."

Helen was prescient; her mother had ticked off both boxes with a few swipes of her pen.

"Oh, mothers," she said, skimming the letter while holding up a clover. "Would you like one? They're from my sister's place. Mary's backyard is covered with four-leaf clovers. Can you imagine?" She smiled at the wonder of it. "Every now and then I have my mother clip a bunch to send to me. I like to press them and give them to people who could use a little good luck. Although"— she frowned—"they never did poor Mary any good. Did I tell you she has polio?"

"No. I'm so sorry to hear that."

"It's a shame. She's a dear, dear girl and really quite pretty. Much prettier than me—just ask my mother, she'll tell you." Helen pursed her lips and leaned back. "Poor Mary's in a wheelchair. I guess it's no surprise that I should feel guilty for being the healthy one. I'm always sending her and my mother money but that doesn't alleviate my guilt. My psychoanalyst says it's my cross to bear. And you know my mother—not Mary—but my mother was the reason I went into analysis in the first place. I love her, I do, but I tell you, there's not one session—not a single one— where I don't end up talking about her." Helen went into a luxurious yawn, stretching her arms overhead. "Are you close with your mother, Alice?"

Her question was jarring. "Ah—ah, no. Not anymore. She died." Even after all these years, I dreaded uttering those words.

"Oh, pussycat. I'm sorry. That's terrible." She set the clover aside and gestured to the chair opposite her desk. "When did she die? How old were you?"

"It happened a while ago," I said, sitting down and pushing back on the lump in my throat. "I was thirteen."

Helen's shoulders sank. "You poor thing. It's dreadful to lose a parent and at such a young age. I know." She smiled sweetly. "I was ten when my father died." Her eyes instantly began misting over. "He was killed in an elevator accident." She shook her head at the freak nature of it.

"Oh no." My hand went to my chest. "How tragic."

"Oh, it was awful. Such a shock. We were caught so off guard. It's the sort of thing you just never expect to happen."

"That's how it was for us, too," I said with some awe. I never would have guessed that Helen Gurley Brown and I would have had anything in common, and here we had both experienced the same kind of sudden loss. "My mother died in a car accident. She was just going to the store. She said she'd be right back but she—"

"I was terrified of elevators," said Helen. "For years I took the stairs, no matter how many flights up." She shook her head again.

"I know what you mean," I said, trying again to make her see this connection we shared. "I always avoided the intersection where she was hit. The other driver ran a red light. He walked away without a scratch. They said my mother was killed instantly."

"I used to have nightmares that I was in an elevator and falling story by story. I'd wake up just before it crashed."

I realized I'd mistaken Helen sharing her father's accident for being empathetic about my loss, but the truth was, she wasn't listening to me. And perhaps that was a good thing because I'd already said more than I had in years about my mother's death. Still, I wanted Helen to *hear* me, and for once, I wanted to feel like I was more to her than just her secretary.

"My father's accident made front page news in our hometown

papers," she continued on. "Everyone came to pay their respects and I kept expecting him to come through the front door, thinking he'd be so pleased that everyone was there just for him. I was so young. I didn't realize I would never see him again." She plucked a tissue off her desk to catch the tears.

"I'm sorry," she said as she dabbed her eyes. "It still chokes me up, even after all this time. But I'm sure you understand," she sniffled. "Such a terrible thing to lose a parent. The pain never really goes away, does it?" She looked at me and I couldn't tell if she wanted me to respond.

I was about to say something when she shifted her focus and picked up her red pencil, glancing at a manuscript on her desk.

Session over. Just as well. One more minute and I might have cried.

"Well," I said, getting up from my chair. "I'll let you get back to work."

"Oh, and don't forget to take your clover," she said, returning to her bright, cheerful self. "They never helped Mary but I still believe in them. Besides, you'll need all the luck you can get with that Don Juan of yours." She gave me a knowing look, and I couldn't tell if she was pleased that I'd followed her advice or if she thought I was just another foolish girl with a hard lesson to learn.

CHAPTER TWENTY

○───○

The next morning I was at my desk by half past seven. Helen was already in her office, and after I brought her a cup of coffee and a glass of Carnation Instant Breakfast, we went to the wall. No one else from the art department was in yet. I turned on the harsh overhead fluorescent lights, gleaming down on the floor. Instead of desks, people back there worked at slanted drafting tables with high-back swivel chairs. There were T-squares and rulers mounted all over the walls, a lightboard in the corner and a Xerox photocopier machine.

As soon as we approached the wall, Helen saw that a cover had been added to the July flatplan. Tony must have pinned it up the night before. She stood back, eyeing the pretty brunette, smiling and holding a beach ball.

Helen picked up a red marker and drew a big X over the model. "When Tony gets in, let him know we're redoing the cover."

With her red marker in hand, she went page by page, X-ing out an article on *Simple Summer Picnics* and another one about *How to Treat a Sunburn*. I noticed a couple other new articles had appeared overnight, too, which all passed Helen's inspection: *How to Break into Advertising, The Non-Disastrous Affair, Judy Collins: Folksinger Profile.*

We were finishing up when Tony La Sala walked in, jacket slung over his shoulder, cigarette in his mouth and briefcase in hand. He smiled, about to say good morning when he looked at the wall and saw the red X over the cover.

"What's going on?" He dropped his briefcase with a heavy thud. "Helen, what are you doing? That cover has been planned for months."

"Oh, I know." She frowned as if she shared his disappointment. "But we just can't use that for the cover. I'm sorry, Tony, but it's back to the drawing board."

He tossed his jacket onto his chair with too much force and it slid off the other side and onto the floor. He left it there and parked his hands on his hips. "Back to the drawing board with what? At least give me some direction. What's not working for you? Is it the background color? The typeface? The drop shadows? The image? I have other shots of her. We could—"

"It's the girl, Tony. It's the girl." She went to his side and placed her hand gently on his arm. "We need to start from scratch. Think sexy, Tony. Sexy."

She turned and walked out, leaving Tony and me staring at his cover. "Hearst is not going to be happy about this," he said, whistling through his teeth. "I hope she's planning on telling Berlin she's changing the cover because I'm sure as hell not going to."

Later that week I was asked to join Helen once again in the art department. We were standing at the wall, looking at some new ad pages, illustrations and *TK*s added to July as well as preliminary ideas for the August flatplan.

I was taking notes while Helen reviewed three new options for the July cover that Tony had mocked up. Each one was beautifully mounted on easel backs and he had added in place-holder type for the copy lines. George and Harriet stood next to me, watching for Helen's reaction while Tony made his presentation.

"I think this one right here is terrific," said George, pointing to the cover with a pretty brunette, sitting in a white wicker pea-cock chair, a bouquet of daffodils in her hands.

"She might be a little too sweet," said Harriet. "Even for me."

"Thank you," Helen agreed as she paused before setting the comped-up cover facedown. She looked closely at the other two. "Nope. Uh-uh. Oh, darn, I'm afraid not."

"What are you talking about? That's a beautiful chick," said Tony, indicating the last one she'd rejected.

"Beautiful isn't the same as sexy," said Helen. "Pretty isn't the same as sexy. I want steamy. Sultry. Sexy. What happened to all the photography from the Jax shoot?"

"Those aren't cover shots," said George.

"Besides," said Harriet, "Tony and I already looked through them. Trust me. There's nothing that'll work for the cover."

Helen turned out her bottom lip. "Oh, but are you absolutely sure, kittens?"

"Positive," said Tony.

"Well, let me have a quick look. Just for fun. Just to satisfy my curiosity."

"Fine. Suit yourself." Tony gave her a stack of contact sheets with twenty-five photos per page, each one no bigger than a post-age stamp.

"Here"—Harriet handed her a loupe—"use this."

Helen, in a bold pink Mary Quant shift and yellow shoes, leaned over the lightboard, loupe pressed to her eye, meticulously studying each image. No one said a word but I noted the looks the others exchanged behind Helen's back.

It was on the third contact page that she said, "Ah-ha! There she is! This is perfect!"

I looked at the picture she was pointing to. It was a shot of Renata with her red and white gingham top on backward.

Harriet looked over her shoulder. "Are you out of your mind?" She laughed, thinking Helen was pulling her leg.

"This is exactly what we need for the July cover."

"You can't use that," said George.

"Why not?"

"Because," said Tony, as if it were obvious.

"Your eye goes right to her breasts," said Harriet. "That's the only thing people are going to look at."

"Exactly," said Helen, smiling. "She has a marvelous bosom. I don't go for those flat-chested models. She looks like a woman. Of course, we still had to stuff her top with half a box of Kleenex, but just look at the results. She's sexy and spirited. Now that's a cover shot!"

"Need I remind you," said George, "we're not selling this cover to men."

"You're absolutely right. We're selling it to women. Women who *want* men. And men want a sexy girl like Renata. And, George, all those women want to learn how to be sexy like her."

George waved her argument away. "Hearst will never go for it."

"They will if it's served up to them in the right way," said Helen.

"There is no *right way* to serve up a platter of boobs to Berlin and Deems," said Tony.

"Have ye little faith?" Helen grinned, courting the challenge. "Do you know how many breakthrough advertising campaigns I sold to clients? Clients who were just as stubborn and conservative as Richard Berlin and Dick Deems. I can sell this cover. Trust me. Just don't let anyone at Hearst see this until I have a chance to present it to them. Understood?"

In the days following, while Tony worked on the new cover, I was trying to justify why I still hadn't enrolled in that photography class, telling myself that I was learning more from Christopher, which in part was true. We'd gone out shooting a couple more times, and thanks to him, my work was improving, but deep down, I was afraid of getting into a class and seeing just how far behind I was.

Besides, I told myself that Helen needed my full attention now. She was finalizing the July issue, starting on August and the preliminary flatplan for September. She was also juggling close to thirty articles in various stages of production. All week I'd watched writers and editors come and go from her office. Liz Smith had seemed perfectly content when she'd walked in, but thirty minutes later she left, her shoulders broken down, her manuscript covered in Helen's red pencil. Even Walter Meade's articles got delicately ripped to shreds.

I was in Helen's office, bringing her a fresh cup of coffee, when Bobbie Ashley and George Walsh handed her an article about ten doctors' favorite crash diets.

"Well, you get what you pay for," said George, an obvious jab about hiring inexperienced and inexpensive freelance writers.

"I'm afraid he's right," said Bobbie, plopping down in a chair. "This article is—well, it's just not publishable."

"Let me have a look." Helen was curled up in the corner of her sofa as she started to read.

George folded his arms across his chest and shifted his weight from one leg to the other. "Obviously the first paragraph is—"

"Shssh." Helen held up her hand and continued reading, her lips curving into a measured smile. When she finished, she looked up. "Well, it just needs a little love is all. We'll just punch it up a bit and use it for August."

"What?" Bobbie's mouth gaped open.

Helen picked up her pencil and made a notation in the margin. "Oh, it's a fine little piece."

George slapped his forehead. "It's not fine."

"It reads like a child wrote it," said Bobbie.

"Why?" countered Helen. "Because it's not gushing with a lot of big highfalutin words? That doesn't make for good writing. My girls don't want to have to run to a dictionary just to get through an article."

"But we have to maintain some standards," said George. "This is *Cosmopolitan*."

"I'm sorry," Helen purred. "But the piece stays in. I'm slating it for August."

Later that same morning, she came out of her office and walked up to my desk. "Will you be a little lamb and type this up?"

Helen handed me eight pages of handwritten notes paper-clipped to a manuscript that had been discarded for a past issue. I saw that Lin Root had written the original article about a gynecologist in New York City touting an estrogen pill called Premarin. He claimed that it saved women from the discomforts of menopause and was the way to stay youthful and womanly forever.

Helen kept the original facts, but had rewritten the rest of it in her usual style, using as few monosyllabic words as possible along with lots of italics, ellipses and exclamation points. She referred to Premarin as a "honey of a hormone."

As I began typing, Bridget came up to me. "How about lunch today?" She was wearing a blue miniskirt that I'd never seen before. For someone who said she never had any money, she'd been buying a lot of new clothes lately. She extended her leg, toes pointed as she pulled up her tights, inch by inch.

"I can't. Sorry."

"What are you working on?" Before I could stop her, she had picked up Helen's notes and began leafing through the pages. "*Oh, What a Lovely Pill!*—what's that about?"

"A new contraceptive pill."

"Interesting. It's about time. Do you know that I've been to four different doctors and not one of them will prescribe any form of birth control for me? One doctor told me it was immoral for an unmarried woman to be engaging in sexual activity. He said he wouldn't give me a license to ruin myself. Those were his exact words. *Ruin myself.* Can you imagine?"

"Thank God for rubbers, huh?" I said as my fingers clacked away.

"And what about those poor women in Connecticut? Even the married ones. It's *illegal* for them to use *any* contraception. That *includes* rubbers. And it's not like they're living in some Podunk town. My God, they're within spitting distance of Manhattan. Wake up, people. It's 1965."

"Well," I said, feeding a clean sheet of paper into the typewriter, "if this pill does even half of what they claim, I want it."

"What all does it do?" she said, clearing a corner of my desk and settling in to read.

"Things like stopping menstrual cramps and bloating."

"I'm all for that." She turned the page and kept reading.

"Helen says it's the fountain of youth for older women. It's supposed to keep your hair shiny and thick. And keeps your eyebrows and your lips full, too."

"My lips? What do you mean? Are they supposed to get thinner?"

"Apparently so." I paused with my fingers on the keys. "I'm getting the impression that everything that's nice and thick when you're young gets thin, and everything that's nice and thin gets thick."

Bridget grimaced. "Great. So that's what we have to look forward to?"

My phone rang. It was Erik, also asking me to lunch, which had to be code for sneaking over to his place for a quickie. The last time he'd taken me to lunch for lunch's sake was that day at La Grenouille. Bridget was still perched on the edge of my desk, reading through the article.

"Sorry but I can't today," I said, the receiver cradled between my ear and shoulder. He persisted and got a little snippy when I said no a second time. It was okay for him to decline a poetry reading but not okay for me to work through lunch. "I'm swamped. Maybe later in the week."

When I hung up, Bridget pointed to the manuscript and laughed. "Would you listen to this—'Keeps a girl's libido in tip-top shape and makes her private parts extra juicy.'"

"Please tell me I don't have to type that."

CHAPTER TWENTY-ONE

○——————○

Helen had left early to attend a dinner with the head of Revlon, in hopes of getting him to advertise in *Cosmo*. I had finished up for the day, and since Helen was gone, I decided to leave early. At least early by Helen's standards. It was close to six o'clock and Erik was meeting me at Keens Steakhouse on Herald Square in half an hour.

I was already down in the lobby when I remembered I'd left my keys on my desk and called for another elevator. The cleaning service was making their rounds and there were only a handful of people still working when I went back up to the office. Whoever was left was on deadline, reworking their pieces so Helen could edit them and possibly rip them to shreds.

As I turned the corner, I was surprised to see Margot still there. The hairs stood up on the back of my neck. She rarely stayed a minute past five, and she was standing at my desk, going through my top drawer. When she saw me, she jumped, a hand splayed across her chest.

"Oh *Gawd*, you scared me half to death."

"What are you doing?" My tone was harsher than I'd expected.

"I just got my monthlies," she said, shaking her head. "I thought you might have a napkin."

"Other side, bottom drawer." My voice still had an edge I couldn't shake. I didn't like the idea of her rummaging through my things.

"You're a lifesaver." Retrieving a Kotex, she said, "At least I know I'm not pregnant." She laughed, trying to lighten things up.

"Anything else I can help you with?" I consulted my watch to keep from looking her in the eye.

"Thanks again. You really are a lifesaver."

"Well, it's a good thing I came back when I did."

"You can say that again."

She'd missed my sarcasm, or maybe ignored it on purpose.

I grabbed my keys, looking around my desk to make sure she hadn't helped herself to anything else before I left to meet Erik.

'd never been to Keens before, another one of Erik's top restaurant picks. He said they were known for their mutton chops and an impressive collection of churchwardens. I had no idea what churchwardens were until I arrived and saw all the white, long-stemmed clay pipes mounted on the ceiling. Some of the stems were more than a foot long.

There was no sign of Erik, so I sat at the bar and waited for him there. It was a masculine place with dark paneling and, of course, those racks of pipes. The bartender was a kindly-looking man with large, round eyes, and I noticed he blinked rapidly while he explained that Keens had once been the meeting place for a pipe club.

"Keens's Pipe Club had over 90,000 members in its heyday," he said, rinsing some glasses in a bin behind the bar. "Some of those pipes date back to the 1800s. And anyone who was anyone belonged to Keens's. We've got Teddy Roosevelt's pipe up there. And Albert Einstein's, J. P. Morgan's, even Babe Ruth's."

He continued to chat with me, something I noticed a lot of bartenders did whenever a young woman was by herself. It seemed to keep other men from bothering the fair maidens. While he was chatting and making a martini for me, my eye kept going to a portrait on the wall behind him. It was a woman, nude, lounging suggestively on a chaise, keeping watch on the activities at the bar.

"I bet she's seen a thing or two through the years," I said, gesturing with my glass.

"Ah, that's Miss Keens." The bartender smiled and blinked, pointing over his shoulder with his thumb.

"Who's the artist?"

"One of the great mysteries. No one knows who painted her. Some say the artist tried to copy a Goya nude. Ain't she a beaut?"

He continued talking about the nude and the pipes while I finished my martini. Still no sign of Erik. My friend, the bartender, produced a second drink for me. "You'd be wise to eat a little something," he said, handing me a menu. The only thing I could afford was the Miss Keens steak burger for $1.75.

"Comes without a bun." He winked. "Get it? She's served naked."

"And I suppose you could order a tomato slice or lettuce leaf with it if you like lingerie."

He laughed.

My Miss Keens burger was delicious but did little to offset the gin. I kept my eye on the door while I ate, even glanced about the restaurant thinking I might have missed Erik when he came in, but there was no sign of him. By the time I'd finished my burger, it was a quarter till eight, and I was done waiting. I paid my bill, grateful that the bartender hadn't charged me for that second martini, and made my way to the Herald Square subway station.

I sat on the train, my head leaning against the cool glass on the window. I was furious with Erik—*he'd* been pushing to see *me*. Was this some game he was playing? Was he punishing me because I hadn't been available for lunch? I wondered how everything got so complicated? What happened to us just having fun? Now I was annoyed with myself and questioning how far was I willing to go for great sex.

The walk from the subway to my apartment took some of the edge off my anger but didn't really sober me up. Now I just wanted an aspirin and sleep. It was stuffy inside my place, but before I could open a window, the telephone rang. I pushed my heels out of my pumps, the kitchen floor cool and soothing against the balls of my feet as I padded over to answer the phone. It was Erik calling.

"Why'd you leave?" I heard people in the background and assumed he was on the pay phone at Keens.

"I was waiting over an hour." Cradling the phone between my ear and shoulder, I unzipped my dress, letting it drop off my shoulders and fall onto the floor. "If I waited any longer, someone would have had to carry me out of there."

"I'm sorry," he said, sounding genuinely apologetic. "I got pulled into a meeting with Deems and Berlin. I couldn't get away. I rushed over here as soon as I could. The bartender told me you already left."

I was inclined to believe him, but still, I was annoyed. "Oh, well," I said in a la-di-dah, couldn't-care-less sort of way.

"Ali, I really am sorry. Let's meet up now. I can come to your place."

"It's late. I'm drunk. I'm going to bed."

"Ali, please? I need to see you."

"You can see me tomorrow. Good night, Erik."

Even though I'd eaten that burger, the gin was still swimming inside my head. I reached for a bottle of aspirin, and as I was filling a glass of water from the kitchen tap, the phone rang again.

I was snippy when I answered until I realized it was Christopher calling.

"Listen," he said, "I'm in a bind and was hoping you could help me out."

"Sure. That is, if I can."

"I'm over on Park between 66th and 67th at the Armory. I've got a shoot tonight, and my assistant just canceled. Can you give me a hand? It doesn't pay much. Just $25, but I promise, I'll be forever in your debt."

I had sobered up by the time I arrived at the Park Avenue Armory, a massive but decrepit building. It was dank and eerie inside, raw space with peeling paint, the brick and stonework crumbling. It was a stark contrast to Daphne and the other glamorous models Christopher was shooting that night. There was a small entourage of makeup artists and stylists there, but nothing like the crew at J. Frederick Smith's studio for the Jax shoot. Mostly I loaded cameras, took light meter readings and brought the models coffee.

Technically, it was my first real assignment, my first paid photography job, but I told Christopher I would have done it for free, even if I'd known that we'd be shooting until dawn.

After the photo shoot at the Armory, I went home, cleaned up, changed my clothes and arrived at the office in time to bring Helen her newspapers and a cup of coffee. Judging by the number of cigarettes in her ashtray, I figured she'd already been at it for a couple hours. She set her pen down on a manuscript covered in red strikeouts with comments in the margins and reached for her copy of *The Elements of Style*.

"Do you think you could do me a favor, love?" she said, her eyes still on the pages of the book. "Will you get the comp of the July cover from Tony and schedule a meeting with Richard and Dick? I want to present it to them this afternoon."

"Of course."

I headed down to Tony's office. He was hunched over his drafting table, Nehru jacket hanging by the shoulders off the back of his chair, shirtsleeves rolled to his elbows. He looked beat as he rubbed his hands along his whiskers.

"I left the mockup on Helen's desk last night before I went home," he said.

I bounced back to Helen's office and reported the update.

"Oh, he did?" She drummed her pen against her desk. "I haven't seen it."

Together we searched her office, looking on the sofa and the coffee table and going through the stacks of papers on her desk and the credenza. I didn't see the cover, but much to my surprise, I came across my portfolio.

"Mrs. Brown?" I held it up to her.

"Oh, that," she said, distracted, still looking for the cover. "I meant to give that back to you. I found it in the wastebasket by your desk. Such a shame to throw out your lovely photos."

I wasn't sure if I was glad she'd saved it or if I was going to throw it out again anyway.

She didn't say another word about it. I set the portfolio aside and went back to helping her rummage through the file cabinet.

"Are you sure Tony said he dropped it off? Because it's definitely not here," she said.

I was about to go back down to Tony's office and double-check when Richard Berlin burst into Helen's office.

Mystery solved.

"Is this some sort of a joke? What on earth were you think-ing?" He was holding the mockup of the July cover, waving Re-nata's breasts in the air.

"How did you get that?" she chirped.

"Does it really matter?" He slapped it down on her desk. "The point is, you're not running that cover."

"Now wait a minute." Helen was dug in. Her voice was still calm and steady but I could see the determination in her eyes. "I've backed off on everything. I've let you and everyone else at Hearst dictate what I can and can't do. This cover is where I draw the line."

He bellowed back and I stood to the side trying to figure out how he'd gotten his hands on the July cover in the first place. I couldn't imagine that someone would have walked into Helen's office and taken it. Besides, only a handful of us knew she was redoing the cover, and even George wouldn't have stolen it off her desk. Admittedly, I thought of Margot, but I couldn't go around accusing her without any proof. I also thought of Erik, but there was no way he would have had any knowledge of that cover.

"But don't you see?" said Helen. "I've given in to you on *every-thing*. This is one time I'm not willing to compromise."

"I beg your pardon?" Berlin slipped a finger inside his shirt col-lar as if it was suddenly too tight.

She reached for the cover and held it up just as she would have done in the presentation she'd planned to make. "I'm sorry, but this is exactly the cover we need. This is going to catch people's eyes. This says there's a new *Cosmopolitan* on the stands."

"It's disgusting."

"It's provocative." Helen set the comp aside and reached for a cigarette, taking her time lighting it. "I believe in this cover," she said with a dramatic exhale.

"I'm warning you, you don't want to have this fight with me."

"I'm not fighting with you, Richard." Helen smiled, which only infuriated Berlin more. "Why don't we make a deal? If that cover doesn't outsell the June issue, I'll resign. I'll tear up my contract. Let's face it, you want me out anyway. Just think—you'd be off the hook. And if my July issue fails to perform, you can go ahead and fold *Cosmopolitan* just like you wanted to all along."

Berlin glared at her in such a way that I expected him to have fired back with a force that would have blown out the windows. But instead he kept his cool, which seemed more terrifying. "Is that really the way you want to play this?" he asked. "You should know that I don't respond well to ultimatums."

Helen didn't flinch. "You've left me no choice. I believe in what I'm doing with this issue and I'm willing to stake my career on it. You should be happy. You've got nothing to lose. Especially since you're so cocksure that I'm wrong."

"Fine. Have it your way." Berlin turned and walked out of her office.

I left, too, taking my portfolio with me which I dumped in my desk drawer. After I sat down, I heard a gasp and looked over to find Helen standing in the middle of her office, both hands clasping her mouth, the color already draining from her cheeks.

"Mrs. Brown?" I got up and stood in her doorway. "Are you okay?"

All that bravado was evaporating into a pool of panic. I could tell she was second-guessing herself. I was prepared for the tears to start up, but she wasn't crying. Instead she began pacing, wringing her hands, chanting, "What have I done? What have I done? What have I done?" With each step, her anxiety grew. "I think I'm going to be sick."

"Can I get you some water? A cool cloth?"

She shook her head.

"I'll go call Mr. Brown."

"No," she screeched. "I can't tell David. He left California for me. For this." She threw her arms out to the sides. "What if I lose this job? What if they really do fire me? What if David's next movie flops? What will we do? We'll have to give up our apartment."

"Please try to get ahold of yourself."

She was walking back and forth so quickly. I'd never seen her like this before.

"We'll go broke. I won't be able to send money to my mother. Or Mary."

I stepped in front of her, forcing her to stop. "You're talking about a lot of *what-ifs*. You're catastrophizing. Getting way ahead of yourself."

She hung her head, and after a moment, she allowed me to coax her over toward the sofa.

"You know in your heart that you're doing the right thing. You stood up for what you believed in."

She dropped down on the sofa, staring straight ahead, dry-eyed. "Do you really like the cover?" she asked eventually.

"I *love* that cover. It's arresting and it's going to work. People will buy it out of curiosity if nothing else. There's not another women's magazine like it on the stands. Anywhere."

She nodded. "Thank you, pussycat. I needed to hear that."

"Are you sure you don't want me to call Mr. Brown?"

She cleared her throat, shaking her head. "I can handle this myself." She nodded as if confirming it, and I swear, I saw something temper inside her. "Now," she said, "we just have to find out what little bitch in this office hates me so much that they would have shown Hearst that cover."

CHAPTER TWENTY-TWO

E ver since she gave Richard Berlin her ultimatum, Helen had been oscillating like a desk fan, going from defiant confidence to downright panic. I found lots of broken pencils scattered around, under her desk, between the seat cushions, on her credenza.

With a viper on the prowl, Helen didn't trust anyone. At times, I thought even I was under suspicion, sensing she was looking at me askance. Wanting to prove that I was on her side after the cover leak, I immediately suggested that we put a lock on her office door. And after the locksmith gave me a single key, I handed it to Helen. When I explained that only she could access her office once she'd locked the door, she insisted I have a second key made for myself. I took that as both a vote of confidence and a test, because if anything else were to go missing, she'd have only one possible suspect.

A few days after the leak, I questioned Erik. I spotted him as I was coming out of the deli on Broadway, where I'd gone to get Helen some soup for lunch, insisting that she try to eat something. They hadn't put the lid on tight enough though, and I

could see my brown paper bag growing dark and wet, beginning
to sag along the bottom.

I asked Erik if he knew anything about the cover and he was
immediately defensive. "Jesus Christ, I knew you were going to
blame me. I just knew it."

"Then tell me I'm wrong."

A man in a Hawaiian shirt was standing a few feet away,
watching us, eavesdropping. I pulled Erik to the side. "Well? Am
I wrong?"

"Ali, I swear. I didn't even see the cover until after the fact—
after Berlin confronted Helen."

The bag in my hand was beginning to drip, oily chicken broth
trickling over my fingers.

He reached for my arm. "Tell me you believe me."

"I have to go."

"Ali."

"What?"

"I didn't do it."

"Okay, all right. I believe you. I have to go."

I didn't know if I believed him or not. When I went back upstairs, I transferred the soup into a bowl, and as I was taking a tray
into Helen, I heard laughter coming from her office. *Laughter!*

"Oh, Helen," said Bobbie Ashley, sopping tears from her eyes,
"that is the funniest thing I've ever heard."

"Oh, but it's true," said Helen, laughing along.

Liz Smith, Bill Guy and Walter Meade were doubled over,
howling. I didn't know what I missed but it was a good one. I set
the tray down in front of Helen and backed away, not wanting to
interrupt the mood. With the exception of Walter Meade, it was
the first time I'd seen them genuinely appreciating Helen and
rallying around her.

Her staff was already deep into the August issue, and Helen

was going into battle on that cover, too. Hearst had determined that it would feature Sean Connery and his Bond girls, but Helen wanted to scrap Connery and keep just the girls.

When her meeting was over and the others trailed out of her office, all smiles and bright-faced, Helen grew somber. I went in to clear her tray away, not surprised that she hadn't touched her soup, chicken fat beginning to coagulate on top.

"Alice," she called to me as I was backing out of her doorway, "would you do me a favor? See if you can arrange to have a direct line put in from my telephone to David's."

She wanted to bypass the switchboard whenever she sought his counsel. I couldn't say I blamed her for being paranoid. I myself had grown mistrusting of my coworkers, who, by the way, all seemed preoccupied with the topic of the viper, too.

One day, after Helen's direct line was installed, I went to lunch with Bridget, Margot and some of the other girls. We were sitting five in a row at a luncheonette counter on 56th Street. Over platters of greasy grilled cheese sandwiches, on special for 35¢, we tried to figure out who had leaked the cover.

"Do you think it's the same person who leaked the bosom memo to *Women's Wear Daily*?" asked Margot.

"If it's not, then we have two vipers." I couldn't look at Margot when I said that, remembering that night I found her going through my desk.

"I think it's George," said Bridget.

"No." I shook my head. "George has never been shy about throwing Helen under the bus."

"She's right," said Leslie. "George would have just walked it over to Hearst with a brass band. And why stop with *Women's Wear Daily*? George would have sent that memo straight to the *Times*."

"Exactly," said Margot.

"You don't think Bobbie or Liz would betray her like that, do you?" asked Carole.

"Doubtful," I said. "I think they're actually starting to come around to Helen's way of doing things."

"I have to admit," said Leslie, "I'm starting to think she might actually be able to turn the magazine around."

"I hope you're right, but I'm not convinced," said Margot.

"Well, even if she does," said Bridget, "I doubt any of us will be getting a raise."

"I'm with Leslie," said Penny, not acknowledging Bridget's remark. "I think it's kind of exciting. I mean, yeah, she's taking a lot of risks, but that's what this magazine needs."

"Did you ever think," said Bridget, "that maybe—just maybe— Helen sent that memo to *Women's Wear Daily* herself?"

Everyone turned and looked at her.

"You know," she said in defense, "for publicity. For the magazine."

"No," we said in a chorus.

"Well, I for one," said Carole, "hope July goes through the roof. I'd like to see her prove them wrong."

I was pleased by this growing support for Helen. She needed them on her side now more than ever, and it was possible that they realized they needed her to succeed. Everybody knew that if the issue tanked, Hearst would fold the magazine and we'd all be out of work.

If anyone was already looking for a new job, it wasn't apparent to me. Despite the uncertainty, we were moving ahead, already deep into August and planning for the September and October issues. In fact, for the first time since I'd been at *Cosmo*, the entire floor was humming with a renewed sense of purpose. The typewriter covers came off earlier and earlier each morning. There was less chitchat in the kitchen, fewer personal phone calls and far fewer typos in manuscripts and memos. Whether the staff liked Helen or not, whether they agreed with her sexual politics or not, I could tell they were rooting for her.

Later that week, I was typing an advertising memo for Helen, finalizing the July ad space. We were going to press soon. The clock was ticking and Erik was hovering over my desk.

"Just meet me for a drink," he said while I typed. "C'mon. One quick drink."

"I can't."

"How about tomorrow?"

"I'm working late all week. We'll get together after July goes to press."

"Well, then, what about dinner? You have to eat, you know."

"I'm sure I'll be working through dinner," I said, my fingers continuing to type.

He was still telling me he wanted to see me even after I'd ripped the sheet from the typewriter. "Erik, can't you see I'm busy here? I have to get back to work."

"Okay, well, I'll call you later."

"Why?" I looked at him, puzzled. "What has gotten into you?"

"Nothing's gotten into me."

I knew he was unaccustomed to women saying no. It made him all the more determined, as if winning me over was needed to restore faith in his irresistible charms. I got up and pushed away from my desk, leaving him standing there. All I could think as I walked into Helen's office was that Erik Masterson was up to something.

CHAPTER TWENTY-THREE

I f I'd been putting in long hours before, it was nothing compared to those first few weeks in May. Evenings, weekends, I was at Helen's side, turning down invites to parties and movies with Trudy, an evening or two of sex with Erik. I had even given up the chance to go to a Dorothea Lange photo exhibit with Christopher. Her Depression-era street photography was on display and I'd missed it. The show had closed the next day.

I was thinking about that when the production manager handed me the July pages. No more typos, no more grammatical errors, no more tweaks to the photographs or captions. We were ready to go to press. Or so we thought.

Twenty-four hours before the presses began rolling, Helen had me deliver a full mockup to Berlin. Less than an hour after I returned, I was in Helen's office, reviewing items with her for the August issue when the four horsemen of Hearst—Berlin, Deems, Dupuy and Erik—showed up with pages in hand and a stop-the-presses urgency.

"We've got a serious problem here," said Berlin.

"Again?" Helen, sitting in her doll's chair, shook her head with an exaggerated blasé air.

"You can't go to press with this." He slapped the pages down on her desk.

"And whyever not? What's bothering you *this* time?" She was on her feet now, knuckles to her narrow hips, foot tapping with impatience. She'd gotten bolder over the past few weeks. It was as if she'd adopted a nothing-to-lose attitude and figured if she was going to kill the magazine and take all of us down with her, she might as well do it with a bang.

"You cannot go to press with that cover line." Berlin thrust his finger at the copy that read: *The New Pill That Promises to Make Women More Responsive to Men*. "Honestly, did you do this just to goad me?"

"Believe it or not, Richard, I wasn't thinking about you. At all. I was thinking about my girls. We had an agreement," she reminded him as she placed a cigarette in her holder and fired it up. "You were going to back off and let me do this my way."

"That was before you tried to pull a stunt like this."

"Do you want to sell copies of this issue or not?" But as the words left her mouth, she laughed sarcastically. "Oh, wait, of course you don't. You want me to fall flat on my face so you can get rid of me. But I'm telling you, I'm not going anywhere. That's a line that will move copies."

Surprisingly Deems, Dupuy and Erik didn't say a word. They stood back and watched Berlin and Helen battle it out. Helen was like a fencer, gracefully attacking, going in for her jabs, and twenty minutes later, Berlin was done.

Exhausted, he raised his hands and said, "I'm not asking, Helen. I'm *telling* you that cover line had better be changed before you go to press. The clock is ticking, and I insist on seeing a new line first thing tomorrow morning. If not sooner."

He turned around and left, his horsemen galloping off behind him.

After they were gone, I expected tears, but Helen stayed strong and composed. She went to her desk, picked up her direct line and telephoned David. Ten minutes later, she came out of her office with a pair of dark sunglasses propped up on her head. "If anyone asks, David and I are taking a nooner."

I contemplated reminding her that she had a one o'clock appointment but decided she needed her nooner more than she needed to meet with another photographer.

About an hour and a half later, the receptionist buzzed me, her voice squeaking through the intercom: "Alice? Mr. Scavullo is here to see Mrs. Brown. What should I tell him?"

By now I knew better than to tell anyone that Helen was taking a nooner, so I went out to the lobby and greeted her guest. I'd never met Francesco Scavullo before. He was just as striking as the covers he'd photographed for *Vogue*, *Seventeen* and *Town and Country*. He had that artsy look about him right down to the fedora cocked on an angle, eclipsing his left eye. He was very tan, his hair so dark, it was almost black, and his teeth looked capped, each one perfectly straight and a little too white.

I introduced myself as Mrs. Brown's secretary and said, "I'm terribly sorry, but something's come up. I'm afraid Mrs. Brown had to step out. I would have called and rescheduled but it just happened."

"Ah." He flashed a wicked smile and raised a knowing finger. "Maybe there's no need to reschedule at all."

"I beg your pardon?"

"A little birdie told me there might not be an August issue."

Obviously, people on the street were talking, and all I wanted to do was find Helen, wrap my arms around her frail little body and shield her from the gossip.

"Oh, surely," I said, giving off a laugh that sounded strangely like Helen's laugh, "you're not one to listen to silly rumors now, are you?" I gave him a classic Helen smile and even cooed. It was like I was impersonating her but I wasn't trying to. I just opened my mouth and she came out.

He smiled, pulled a cigarette from his breast pocket and tapped the filter end on the receptionist's desk before lighting it. "I can tell you're very solicitous of her."

"And why shouldn't I be?" I said, returning to my normal voice, returning to myself. "Mrs. Brown's a wonderful boss."

Right after I said that, Helen burst through the lobby doors. "Oh, Alice," she called to me, all smiles. "My husband is brilliant. Absolutely brilliant. Do me a favor, pussycat, type this up and get it over to Mr. Berlin right away." She handed me a scrap of paper, suddenly noticing Francesco Scavullo standing off to the side.

"Why, Frank—" She reached for his hand and brushed either side of his face with a light kiss. "I'm sorry to keep you waiting."

"No need to apologize. I was just chatting with your lovely secretary. Better be good to her," he said, using his cigarette as a pointer, "or I'll swoop in and steal her away from you."

"You try that and I'll have to kill you." She smiled. "Come, come—" She ushered him down the hall toward her office. "Step into my parlor."

I looked down at the paper she'd handed me and there was the new cover line. Or rather the old cover line with a minor tweak. The words *to Men* had been crossed out so it now read: *The New Pill That Promises to Make Women More Responsive.*

I typed up the line, walked it over to Mr. Berlin. His secretary showed me into his office, which was larger than my apartment, with a breathtaking view of Manhattan. Other than "Have a seat," he hadn't said two words to me. I sat in one of the stately wingback chairs opposite his desk. I felt like Alice in Wonderland, my body tiny as I gripped the armrests, waiting for the verdict.

He studied the line. His expression didn't change, just his eyebrows. They knitted together and relaxed, knitted together and relaxed. I didn't know which way he was leaning, and I dreaded the possibility of going back to Helen with bad news.

Berlin reached for a fancy fountain pen sticking out of his desk set and scratched something down on the paper with the new line. With his brows still drawn closely together, he picked up the phone and told his secretary to get Helen on the line. If she was still meeting with Francesco, the receptionist would have to interrupt her for the call. No one—not even Helen—kept Berlin waiting. There was already enough talk about Helen on the street; she didn't need Francesco overhearing her conversation with Berlin.

"Helen"—Berlin whipped off his eyeglasses and tossed them onto his desk blotter—"you win. I can't fight you anymore. I still think it's the wrong approach, but if you insist on digging your own grave, so be it. Get this issue to the printers."

The following Friday evening I was running late. After finishing up some correspondence for Helen and typing up the notes from her latest cover meeting for the August issue, I rushed to the train and headed for Grand Central.

I was meeting Erik for a drink at the Oyster Bar in Grand Central Station. Other than a quick *hello, how are you* in the hallway, catching each other's eye during meetings or riding a crowded elevator together between floors, this was the first time we'd seen each other in almost two weeks. By the time I arrived, I found Erik waiting for me, probably on his second drink. And of course, he was sitting next to a beautiful blonde, the only woman at the bar.

I stood back for a moment, watching Don Juan in action. My God, did he practice that head tilt in the mirror or was it just instinctive? Even the way he held his martini, fingertips teasing the stem like it was the inside of your thigh. His every move was meant to seduce. I took a few steps closer, and as soon as he saw me, he sat up straight, putting some distance between him and his drinking companion.

"Hi," I said, extending my hand to the blonde. "I'm Alice."

"Ah, Ali," he stammered. "Ali, this is—"

"Tammy," she said, shaking my hand. "Nice to meet you."

"Thanks for keeping him company," I said without a trace of malice. "I just couldn't leave the office on time."

"Place is pretty crowded," Erik said, making some vague gesture around the room. "Looks like all the tables are taken."

"That's okay." I set my pocketbook on the bar and deliberately took the empty stool next to Tammy. "Would you order me a martini? Tammy, what about you? Ready for another?"

"Tammy works for Hearst, too," Erik said, as if trying to justify something.

"Really?" I smiled and nodded. I was good. "I'm over at *Cosmo.* Where are you?"

"*Harper's Bazaar,*" she said. "I'm in editorial for now, but as I was telling Erik, what I really want to do is more on the writing side."

Erik served up a tight smile and lit a cigarette.

"A writer, huh? That's neat. Hey, I wonder if he can help you. Erik"—I leaned his way—"can you help her?" Before he answered, I focused back on Tammy. "What kind of writing?"

"Short stories and essays mostly. But poetry is my favorite. Although . . ." She paused, rolling her eyes. "I've never had my poems published. I've been working up the nerve to send them to the *Paris Review*. I'm just terrified of rejection."

I felt a stir of solidarity. It was the same for me with those photography classes. If we hadn't met under these circumstances, Tammy and I might have become friends.

"Can't seem to get his attention," Erik said, indicating the bartender, whose back was to us. Erik was fidgeting with his lighter first, then flicking his cigarette ash a bit too vigorously.

Tammy and I kept talking. "You know," I said, "there's this great poetry series down in the Village."

Her eyes perked up. "The one at the Gaslight?"

"Yes. That's the one. I've been wanting to go."

"Me, too. We should all go sometime. Erik, do you like poetry?"

"Ah, yeah, sure." His jaw was twitching, his teeth clenched.

"Well, great then," she said. "Let's all go."

I couldn't have scripted this better. I watched Erik eyeing a table across the room where a group of businessmen were paying their bill, rising from their chairs.

"Here," said Tammy, jotting her telephone number on a cocktail napkin and handing it to me.

"C'mon, Ali," Erik said, signaling the bartender for the check, "let's grab that table."

"Why don't you join us?" I asked Tammy, relieved when she backed off.

"I need to get going, but it was so nice meeting you. And call me whenever you want to go to the Gaslight."

"I will." I tucked her number inside my pocketbook.

"Ali," he said as soon as we took our seats, "she works for Hearst. What was I supposed to do, ignore her?"

"I didn't say a word, did I?"

He laid his cigarette case on the table and gave me a suspicious look. "Besides," he said, "I've been waiting here for almost an hour."

"I had some things to do back at the office."

"Like what?"

"Don't pry." I helped myself to one of his cigarettes and waited while he offered me a light.

"I'm not prying. I'm asking."

I drew down on my cigarette and exhaled toward the vaulted ceiling. "Well, that topic is not up for discussion."

The waiter came by and Erik ordered two gin martinis.

"Are you ever going to trust me?" he asked.

I gave him a sly smile. "What do you think?"

He sighed, shook his head in surrender. "Well, you'll be interested to know that I had a meeting today with Berlin and Deems. We were talking about you."

"Me? What about?"

"Relax." He reached for my hand, smoothing his thumb over my fingers. "It was all good. There's an opening at *Good Housekeeping*. It's an editorial position. The starting salary's almost double what you're making now."

"Wait—what? You're talking about an editorial position for me?"

"Yes, for you." He laughed. "They're impressed with you. I told them I think you're tops and—"

"Why? I'm not an editor."

"You'll learn. You're smart. You'll pick it up in no time."

"But I want to be a photographer, not an editor. Besides, I'm not leaving Helen."

"I know you don't want to leave her, but let's face it, if this issue tanks—"

"Don't say that. It's not going to tank. Helen's not going to fail."

The waiter came back with our drinks and we both took eager gulps.

"Ali, I'm just looking out for you."

"I appreciate that." And I did. "But I'm not interested in being an editor at *Good Housekeeping*. Tell them about Bridget—she'd kill for that job."

"Forget about Bridget. I'm talking about you. You do realize there's a strong chance that Helen *will* fail, they'll fold the magazine, and you'll be out of a job."

"I'll take my chances."

"I just wish you'd let me help you."

"You want to help me? Take me back to your place tonight."

We finished our drinks and headed to Park Avenue.

He lifted me onto the bed and began kissing my neck. He slowly started to undress me, and with each button he undid, I felt my stress and work worries dissipate.

Afterward, with the heat still radiating off my skin, I found myself in that post-coital haze. We were so good together in bed—we had such fun and passion—and it seemed that our connection should have been able to translate out in the wild. So I told him about a photography exhibit opening that weekend. "Do you want to go?"

"Why? Do you?" He reached past my shoulder for his cigarettes resting on the nightstand.

A draft swept across the room and I pulled the sheet up, over my goosefleshed skin. "Yes, that's why I brought it up."

He hesitated, made a big deal of lighting his cigarette and examining the hot ash as he exhaled. "Uh, yeah, okay, so we'll go."

"If you don't want to, just say so."

"It's just that"—he shrugged, tipping his ash—"photography's your thing, not mine."

I glanced at the clock on his nightstand, next to his Lucky

Strikes, a bottle of Bayer Aspirin and some Rolaids. It was a quarter past nine. "I should probably get going."

"Stay."

"I've got a big day tomorrow."

"Please?" he said, grabbing my hand.

"I need a good night's sleep."

He watched as I dressed, and it wasn't until I was leaving his bedroom that he said, "All right, I'll go to the exhibit with you."

Later that night Trudy answered her door holding a floral print sleeveless dress on a wooden hanger. She hung everything on wooden hangers—a result of working at Bergdorf's.

"What's wrong?" she asked. "I thought you were with Don Juan."

"I was. I didn't want to stay at his place tonight." I plopped down in a rocking chair and told her about meeting Tammy at the bar, followed by the editorial job at *Good Housekeeping*. "Me? An editor? Sometimes I wonder if Erik knows me at all."

"Well, it's not like the two of you do a lot of talking, if you catch my drift."

"Very funny." I brought my hands to my face, covering my eyes as I groaned. "I'm so confused. If we can go to dinner or go out for a drink before we have sex, why can't we go to a poetry reading or a photo exhibit? I mean, where does an affair leave off and a real relationship begin?"

"You're asking me? I haven't been on a date in six months."

"I don't know what I want. And I don't know what *he* wants, either. He's always giving me mixed signals. Am I sabotaging myself?"

"What do you mean?"

"I mean, maybe deep down I *do* want something more with him but I'm just too afraid."

Trudy gave me an incredulous look.

"Okay, all right," I conceded. "So maybe I don't want something more with him." I sighed. "But this little dance we're doing, it's just exhausting. And c'mon, we have nothing in common. I know I said I didn't want a relationship, but still, I deserve better."

"You'll get no argument from me," Trudy said as she laid the dress out on her bed.

I began rocking back and forth, the chair creaking each time I moved. Sometimes I thought of my affair with Erik like a case of the flu. Something that needed to run its course and soon he'd be out of my system for good. Helen told me once not to beat myself up about him. *"The thing about a Don Juan is that every girl has one . . . Don Juans are unavoidable. No matter how smart she is, every girl has that one man that she just can't say no to even though she knows he's no good for her."*

"I need your opinion on something," Trudy said. "Wait right there. Don't go anywhere." She dashed into the bathroom.

I rocked back and forth while I heard the squeak of her medicine cabinet opening. Trudy had a portable black-and-white TV sitting directly on the hardwood floor. The rabbit ears weren't fully extended for some reason so Johnny Carson was fuzzy with squiggly lines rolling through the *Tonight Show* set. The volume was turned down, too, barely audible.

"Why do you even have that thing on?" I asked.

"What thing?"

"Your TV."

"It keeps me company."

I couldn't really hear the monologue but stared at the screen anyway until Trudy came out of the bathroom.

"Well?" she said, squatting down so that we were eye to eye. "Can you still see them?"

"Trudy. What did you do?" I stopped rocking. She had put on a layer of heavy pancake makeup that was two shades too dark for her skin tone.

"Maybe if I go one shade lighter?"

"No. No pancake." I went back to rocking. "You look like a pumpkin."

"Thanks a lot."

"I mean, it looks like you're trying to hide something."

"That's because I am."

"You have beautiful, clear skin. That happens to have freckles. Don't cover them up."

But she wasn't hearing it. She went over to her closet, screeching hangers back and forth before taking out two dresses and laying them on the bed next to the other one.

"Are you going somewhere?" I asked.

"No. No, I'm just trying to figure out what to wear. I have a job interview."

"What?" I stopped my rocking again.

"Monday morning. I might have to go shopping for a new outfit this weekend."

"Wait a minute. Who's the interview with?"

"Believe it or not, it's at an architectural firm."

"What? Wow! Trudy, that's—"

"It's just the receptionist job," she said to temper my excitement. "But it's a foot in the door."

"I'll say. How did this happen?"

"You're not going to believe it. Last week I'm sitting in the Candy Shop, just sitting at the counter, minding my own business, reading *The Fountainhead*. And the man next to me starts asking how I like the book. We get to talking about architecture, and it turns out that he's an architect, and the next thing I know, he tells me his firm needs a receptionist."

"You never said a word. How come?"

"Because I didn't think anything would come of it. I thought it was just talk, a way for him to get my telephone number. But then they called me today to come in for an interview on Monday morning. What if they offer me the job? Should I tell them I need to think about it?"

"What's there to think about?"

She looked at me and smiled.

"And whatever you do, don't wear that pancake makeup on the interview."

CHAPTER TWENTY-FOUR

———•———

There were fewer horns honking, more taxicabs with their lights on. The lunch line at the diner on the corner wasn't snaked out the door. The elevators came faster and were less crowded. It was a Friday afternoon, the start of the Memorial Day holiday weekend, and though Monday was the official holiday, the city had already started to empty out. Most New Yorkers had fled for the Hamptons and places like Atlantic City.

Now that the July issue was on press, Helen had been promising to take a few days off, but here we were on that Friday afternoon, long after everyone else had left, and Helen was still in her office, editing a piece for August, though she knew there might not be an August issue.

"Alice? Alice, dear?" she called to me, leaning sideways in her chair as if checking to see that I was still there. "Could you do me a favor?"

"Of course." I pushed away from my desk and stood in the doorway. Swirls of smoke from her last cigarette lingered, pooling near her desk lamp.

"Would you mind picking up Gregory from the vet? Poor little guy had an ear infection. It's already four o'clock and I'm afraid I won't be able to get there before they close at five. Would you be a love and get him and take him home for me?"

"Of course." I realized just then how often I said those words to her: *Of course. Of course I'll do this, of course I'll do that.* I was there to serve and grateful that she'd given me something to do on the start of a holiday weekend, especially since Bridget had already left for Atlantic City with a man she'd just met and Trudy was in St. Louis and wouldn't be back until Monday night, just in time to start her new job.

I'd been avoiding Erik, because I honestly wasn't sure what I wanted to do about whatever it was we were doing. As a couple, we were never in sync. When I wanted something more, he didn't, and vice versa. He must have sensed me backing away because now he was doing his best to reel me back in. After turning him down for the symphony and dinner at Barbetta, he pulled out all the stops with an invitation to join him over Memorial Day weekend at his family's home in the Berkshires. On paper it sounded great—everything I'd ever wanted. Again, I questioned if I was sabotaging myself, but I hadn't even known his family had a place in the Berkshires, which seemed like something to know before going there and being introduced as . . . what? His girlfriend, the girl he was sleeping with? In the end, I couldn't do it. I lied and said I had other plans even though I knew I'd be looking at a long, lonely weekend.

The veterinarian's office was on Third Avenue between 71st and 72nd. The waiting room was crowded and noisy, a combination of barking and hissing, the jangle of collars and dog tags, the sounds of toenails clicking against the linoleum floor. It had an odd smell, too, like years of pet accidents covered up with Clorox. A tuckered-out puppy with big floppy ears lay listlessly on its side, breathing hard.

I explained that I was there to pick up Mrs. Brown's cat, and moments later the receptionist came back with a carrier that looked like a red toolbox with a wire mesh door. Gregory's big blue eyes stared at me from inside. I stuck my finger through the wire mesh and tried to reassure him that everything was okay, I was there to take him home.

Gregory wasn't happy, meowing and squealing the whole way back to the apartment. Helen's doorman, Freddie, flashed a big toothy smile. "Who you got in there?" he asked, bending so that he was eye level with the mesh gate. "Is that Samantha?"

"No, Gregory," I said.

"Well, welcome home, Mr. Gregory. And how are you today, Miss Alice?"

I'd made so many trips to Helen's home that Freddie knew me by name and always let me up to her apartment without bothering to announce me. That day he held the main door and then leaped in front of me and called for the elevator.

"You have yourself a wonderful holiday, Miss Alice."

Long ago Helen had entrusted me with a spare key on a Gucci key ring that weighed more than my wallet. When I let myself in, I jumped back and let out a yelp.

"Surprise!"

I almost dropped Gregory. I looked at David, vaguely aware of the two women behind him, my hand covering my heart, willing my pulse to simmer down. When I calmed myself, I realized the older woman had to have been Helen's mother and the one in a wheelchair was her sister, Mary.

David came up to me, glass of champagne in hand. "I'm sorry, Alice." He smiled kindly, which was always his nature. "We didn't mean to scare you. We were expecting Helen. I planned a last-minute surprise for her," David explained with a half-shoulder shrug. "Dinner tonight at Lutèce. Theater tickets for tomorrow night."

"Sounds lovely," I said.

"Lutèce." Mrs. Gurley said the name of the restaurant with disgust, as if she'd just repeated a French curse word. "Helen'll take two bites and say she's full."

I set the carrier down and opened the latch, letting Gregory loose. I noticed the bottle of Dom Perignon next to the crystal dish of caviar, and my heart sank for them, especially David. This was a wild extravagance for a man conditioned to be almost as frugal as his wife.

"Let me go back to the office and get her," I said.

"Don't bother." Mrs. Gurley had Helen's eyes, but without all the makeup and false lashes. "We should have known. All she cares about anymore is that magazine."

"You have to understand the kind of pressure she's under," said David. "It's been an uphill battle for her every step of the way. She's terrified to take her foot off the gas."

"Don't make excuses for her, David." Mrs. Gurley folded her arms, her face going sour. "I don't know why we bothered coming all this way."

"Because you miss Helen and Helen misses you. And she does, Cleo," he said when she opened her mouth to protest. "I don't understand the two of you, never have, never will. But I do know Helen loves you, and you know it, too."

"Well, I hate New York."

I felt a pang for Helen. This was her mother. *Her mother!* I wanted to like her. I wanted her to like me.

The other cat leaped into Mary's lap, giving her a start. "Oh! Oh my," she said, petting Samantha, whose back arched and rolled beneath her hand. "Don't be so hard on her, Mother. She'll be here. And remember, it's not entirely her fault. She didn't know we were coming."

"No, it's *my* fault," said David, setting his champagne down, the moment no longer warranting a celebratory drink. "Alice, I should have told you about this. Not that you could have gotten Helen out of the office any earlier."

"I can go back and get her."

"Don't waste your time," said Mrs. Gurley. "She won't listen. She doesn't even listen to her own husband."

"Just let me go talk to her," I said. "I'll get her back here. I promise."

W hen I arrived at the office, it was after six o'clock. The lobby and hallways were dark and the air conditioner was turned off so it was already stuffy inside. And eerily quiet, too. I wondered if Helen had already left.

As I turned the corner, I saw a light coming from the art department. "Hello? Anybody here?" I called out, my steps growing shorter, more tentative. "Tony? Helen?"

"Alice?" I heard Helen's heels clacking across the floor, an alarmed look on her face. "Is Gregory okay? Did something happen to him?"

"No, he's fine. He's at your apartment."

"Oh, thank God." Her hand went to her heart.

"And so is your family."

"What?"

"Your sister and mother are in town. Mr. Brown flew them in for the long weekend. It was supposed to be a surprise."

Helen's hand moved from her chest to her throat. I couldn't tell if she was pleased or not.

"They're waiting for you back at the apartment. You're all having dinner tonight. At Lutèce."

"Oh, that David. Isn't he thoughtful?" She smiled and shook her head, releasing the floral scent of her perfume. "He spoils me, you know." She turned back to the wall, studying a spread on the August flatplan.

"You have an eight o'clock reservation," I said, surprised by how irritated I sounded. I couldn't help but think about her family waiting back in the apartment, the champagne going warm, the caviar going bad.

"Eight o'clock?" She consulted her wristwatch and looked back at me from over her shoulder. "Will you be a dear and let David know I'll meet them at the restaurant." She faced front again, uncapped her red marker and began making a notation on one of the spreads.

"No. No, I won't do that."

"No?"

She turned and we exchanged an uneasy look, both of us unaccustomed to my objecting to any of her requests.

"Mrs. Brown," I said, measuring my words, knowing I should have sweetened my tone but couldn't. "Your family is waiting for you. Your husband went to a lot of trouble to do this for you, and your mother and sister came all this way just for you. It won't be a surprise anymore, but—"

"But . . ."

"Mrs. Brown"—I stepped in and gently removed the marker from her hand—"there are more important things in life than this magazine." I replaced the cap on the marker and set it on the railing below the flatplan. "It's time for you to go home. Your family is waiting for you."

I knew I'd gotten to her when she pressed her lips together in a thin line like she did whenever she was backing down, which wasn't often. Her eyes softened, and without saying a word, she nodded.

In silence, we walked through the dark, deserted hallway and went into her office. I turned on her desk lamp, sending a warm glow over the papers scattered on top. At her insistence, I packed her attaché case with manuscripts so she could do some work at home over the weekend.

"I'll telephone Mr. Brown and let him know you're on your way. And Mrs. Brown," I said as I snapped her briefcase shut, "please don't wait for the bus today. Just go ahead and take a taxicab."

I stayed in her office after she left. It was so quiet. I sat down at her desk and ran my hands along the upholstered arms of her chair, trying to imagine what thoughts ran through her mind on any given day. I looked at the clock on her credenza. It was almost seven o'clock. I wasn't sure if I was hungry or not and thought vaguely about what to do for dinner. Maybe I'd take a book and go sit in a diner. I wondered if Elaine had stayed in town, though I was sure if she had, she already had more invitations than she could possibly accept.

Without giving it too much thought, I did something I never did at work. I picked up Helen's phone and made a personal long-distance call. I gripped the receiver, listening to the shrill ringing on the line, picturing the yellow phone in the kitchen, on the counter, trilling away. It wouldn't be a long call. They never were but I wanted to hear my father's voice.

He answered on the fifth or sixth ring.

"Oh, Ali, sweetheart." There was some commotion in the background, like a blender or something going. "Are you all right? It's not eight o'clock yet."

"I'm fine. It's okay, I'm calling from work."

"And this they let you do?"

"Not exactly. I'll keep it short. I just wanted to say hello. Big plans for the weekend?" Questions were the only way to keep him talking.

"A barbecue at the Goldblats'. Faye's making her potato salad."

"That sounds nice. It's pretty quiet around here. A lot of people left the city." I felt a pang of loneliness as I looked out the window at the empty street. "I was thinking of maybe coming home for a visit next weekend," I said, having just thought of it. There were so many things I wanted to talk to him about but everything between us was so stiff over the phone. "Would that be okay?"

"You have to ask such a thing?" He laughed. "Come. I'll get tickets to the Indians game."

"How are they playing this year?"

"Ah, like hell." He laughed again. "But it's still early in the season." The blender sound in the background grew louder. "Hold on a sec, will you, Ali?" He cupped the phone and I heard muffled voices going back and forth. "Sweetheart, I'm gonna let you go before this call gets you in trouble."

I squeezed my eyes shut. I didn't want him to hang up. "Dad?"

"Yes?"

"I miss you."

"Oh, well, we miss you, too, sweetheart."

We? There was no *we*. I didn't miss Faye. Just him.

The next morning, I made myself a cup of instant coffee and sat down with the newspaper, trying to fight off the melancholy gaining on me. I had a second cup of coffee and spent twenty minutes staring out the window onto Second Avenue, envious of the clusters of people going by, laughing, off to their weekend plans. The last thing I expected just then was a telephone call from Christopher.

"Oh good. You're there," he said when I answered.

"I am. What are you doing in town? I thought you and Daphne were going to Montreal for the holiday."

"Hey," he said, skipping over my question, "you up for some great people watching today?"

An hour later, with my camera in hand, I met Christopher at the Washington Square subway station and together we boarded the next train to Coney Island.

Coney Island had been one of my mother's favorite spots, and as we strolled down Surf Avenue, we passed places like Weepy's Pool Hall and Jimmy's Luncheonette, so familiar to me from her stories. Everywhere I turned, I saw her. I pictured her riding the carousel, eyes sparkling as she whirled past the onlookers. I could see her long brown hair blowing easy as the Wonder Wheel carried her high above the park, and I imagined that devilish grin of hers as she fearlessly accepted dares to do the Parachute Jump and go on the Cyclone. She'd told me the moment she started falling in love with my father, the two of them had been walking hand in hand along the boardwalk on a starlit evening. I felt my mother all around me as I aimed her camera, taking pictures of the beach, looking like a patchwork quilt of sunbathers on their blankets, the surf filled with heads, bobbing in the water.

"Didn't I tell you this place was great for people watching?" said Christopher.

We had just passed a man wearing a woman's two-piece swimsuit.

We slipped off our shoes and headed toward the water, walking along the shoreline, the cool ocean bubbling up over our toes. Every now and then we'd stop to photograph something that caught our eye: a couple smooching under a sun umbrella, a boy giggling while his friends buried him in the sand.

"I'm glad you were home when I called," he said, his hand on his brow, shielding the sun as he studied the horizon.

"Me, too. But I thought you and Daphne were heading out of town."

"Yeah, well, Daphne got a callback," he said, eyes still focused on the water. "She's up for a commercial. They flew her out to Los Angeles. She decided to stay the weekend."

"Wow, that's great. I've never been to Los Angeles. Too bad you couldn't go with her."

"It's just that she was gonna be working the whole time anyway." He shrugged, cracked a small smile. "She's got friends out there. She said she wanted to spend time with them."

He turned toward me and something about the sunlight hitting his handsome features and the breeze blowing through his hair made me reach for my camera.

"Hey," he said, laughing. "Cut it out."

"Too late. Got it." I smiled and advanced the film.

It was getting late and we hadn't eaten all day. We stopped for a hot dog at the Nathan's stand and found a place to sit in the shade. I looked across the way, toward Stillwell Avenue, and spotted Williams Candy, remembering my mother telling me about their special jelly apples. Oh, how she would have loved a day like today, just walking around Coney Island, taking pictures.

"You okay?" he asked. "You're so quiet all of a sudden."

"Sorry." I smiled. "I was just thinking about my mom. She loved it here."

"You were thirteen when she died, right?"

I nodded.

"That's rough," he said, bringing his knees toward his chest, circling them in his arms.

I was thinking about his situation with his mother and how it was no better than mine. "Can I ask you something?"

"Sure."

"Do you miss your mom?" Before he could answer, I apologized. We'd talked about all kinds of things, including his strained relationship with his father and mine with Faye, but we'd never talked about his mother. "I'm sorry. I shouldn't have brought that up."

"No, it's okay." He shook the hair from his eyes. "I was so young when she left. I never knew her to begin with. The only thing I ever think about is *what if*? You know? What if she hadn't left? My whole life would have probably been different. You ever think about that? What if your mom was still alive?"

I clutched my chest. *Just the thought of still having her.* It was more than I could put into words. And he got that. He put his arm around me, and I rested my head on his shoulder. We sat like that, two motherless children, looking out at the ocean, watching the sun slip below the horizon.

We stayed at Coney Island for the fireworks, kids running along the beach with sparklers, everybody oohing and aahing at the flare of reds, blues and greens overhead. The grand finale was spectacular, and as a brilliant burst of colors illuminated the sky, I felt Christopher's eyes on me. I turned and the two of us held each other's gaze just a beat longer than we ever had before. I wanted to say something, but what? His eyes were so dark, so intense, you could barely see his pupils. Something had just been set in motion. I couldn't define it, I didn't know what it was, but I felt it, every bit as subtle as it was lasting. And whatever it was, it would linger with me long after I broke the spell and turned away.

CHAPTER TWENTY-FIVE

Tuesday morning arrived, and the temporary lull in the city had passed. I, along with the rest of Manhattan, was back at work. Erik called first thing, wanting to see me, and I was relieved. I needed him to snap me back to reality and keep my mind from wandering back to Coney Island, to that moment with Christopher. I'd been thinking about him too much since then and that scared me. We were friends and I didn't want to muddy that up. Besides, he still had Daphne, and for all I knew, these *feelings* were only one-sided.

Helen didn't say a word about her weekend with her sister and mother. She just told me that because Monday had been a holiday, Dr. Gerson had moved her appointment to that afternoon. "Thank God."

We were three weeks out from July hitting the newsstands, and the tension in the office was palpable. Though Helen was pushing hard on the August issue, almost everyone else was operating in limbo, knowing whatever they were working on could all be for nothing. Still, everyone was willing to put on a brave business-as-usual face for the annual Writers Guild East dinner later that week. Helen had bought a table months ago, and at the last minute, when Bobbie Ashley came down with a bout of food poisoning, she invited me to take her place.

I was ecstatic but unprepared. I rushed over to Bridget's desk and waited patiently while she finished a call with Bill Guy. She was chewing bubble gum and I could smell it on her breath when she hung up and asked what was wrong.

"Help! I'm going to the awards dinner tonight."

"You are?" Her eyes perked up as she pulled her hand away from the receiver. "You're so lucky. I've always wanted to go to that."

"Look at me," I said, hands out to my side. The dinner was at the Plaza Hotel and I'd worn a green cotton shift that day. "I can't go like this."

"Just run home and change."

"Into what? I don't have anything that's fancy enough for a dinner like this."

"Okay, don't worry." She cracked her gum as she scooted her chair away from her desk. "Come with me."

She took me by the hand and led me to the *Cosmo* Beauty Closet, although it wasn't a closet at all. It was a room, next to the mailroom and nearly twice the size. As soon as a company developed a new product or a fashion designer introduced a new line, they sent it all our way and into the Beauty Closet it went. The Beauty Closet housed floor-to-ceiling shelves filled with cosmetics, perfumes, shampoos, hair dyes and setting gels, barrettes and headbands. Stepladders reached to the top shelves, where dozens of Styrofoam heads sported wigs and cascading falls in every shade imaginable. Drawers were filled with earrings, cocktail rings, bracelets and other accessories. Belts and handbags hung off hooks on a white pegboard. The latest in shoes were lined up three rows deep on the floor. Whenever Helen needed a birthday or hostess gift, she'd send me to the Beauty Closet to pick out something.

We sorted through the clothes racks, packed with everything from casual separates to formal ball gowns. Thankfully, I found a sample size that fit though I could barely breathe after she zipped me up. It was a festive black lace sheath dress with a decorative satin bow at the waist. Bridget located a pair of silk black kitten heels and a matching clutch. She teased and pinned my hair up in a glamorous beehive that showed off the sparkling chandelier earrings we'd found.

When I arrived at the Plaza at a quarter past six, the cocktail hour was already in full swing. I searched through a long white table of place cards until I found Bobbie Ashley's name and table number done up in beautiful calligraphy. Among the other names that jumped out at me were Truman Capote, Gore Vidal, Betty Friedan and Gloria Steinem, along with editors and publishers from the big houses and magazines.

As promised, all of New York's literati were there, and with a quick sweep, my eyes had already landed on Joan Didion and Susan Sontag. I saw Helen standing in the center of the room, dressed in a Valentino buttercup yellow dress with black fishnets, which would no doubt be torn before the end of the night. A daisy-like fascinator sat atop her wig. Despite the bigger personalities in the room, Helen appeared to be the star attraction.

I stood off to the side catching snippets of conversation as one woman, surprisingly underdressed in a checkerboard shift and enormous hoop earrings the size of bracelets, was gushing over Helen. "If you ever decide to write another book," she said, "I'll be the first in line for an autographed copy. Everything you write is . . . well, it's just marvelous."

The woman she was with, wearing an unmistakable Pucci

dress, said, "All you'd have to do is ask and I'd write for your magazine in a heartbeat."

Helen said something in return that I couldn't hear, but the woman shot back with, "I'm finishing up a feature for *Vogue*. And, well, you know Diana Vreeland. Nothing's ever quite—I don't know—eccentric *enough*."

Helen was smiling, laughing, nodding, not saying much but clearly enjoying the attention.

I took to roaming about, looking for a place to land, and spotted Elaine Sloan talking to a group of men. She was very stylish in a bold print dress, her silver-white hair lying smooth and sleek upon her shoulders. Thankfully she saw me and waved me over. After introducing me to her own posse of admirers—a dashing literary agent with thick, long sideburns; one of his clients, a novelist who smoked a pipe and wore an ascot; and two handsome hangers-on—she swept me off to the side.

"I'm so pleased to see you," she said. "I didn't expect you to be here."

"Neither did I. I'm standing in for a coworker with food poisoning."

"Very strategic on her part," she said. "I loathe these dinners."

"You do? Gosh, I feel like Cinderella."

"Oh, I used to feel that way, too. In the beginning. But this circus gets old very quickly. You'll see." She sipped her drink and waved to someone across the room. "I wonder what's keeping Christopher."

"Christopher's coming?"

"I invited him. He's been so down lately, and I thought this might do him some good."

He was down? "I just saw him over the holiday. Is everything okay?"

"Oh, he'll be fine. Trust me, Daphne did him a favor. It's a blessing in disguise."

"They aren't together anymore?" *Did that explain why she'd stayed in LA for the weekend?*

"Oh, there he is now. Finally." She raised her chin.

I looked over and saw Christopher weaving through the crowd. Unlike the other men, he wasn't wearing a suit, but at the same time, unlike the woman in the checkerboard shift, he didn't seem underdressed. He wore a dark fingertip jacket with a satin collar, and dark trousers, tapered at the ankle where they met his boots. Expensive-looking boots, either new or freshly polished. As he passed through the crowd, several women turned to get a better look at him. Did he have any idea what effect he had on women? On me? I caught myself thinking about that moment between us at Coney Island, and suddenly, I was self-conscious. I felt the hairpins digging into my scalp and was reminded of how tight my dress was, how every time I inhaled, it pinched along my rib cage.

It wasn't until Christopher came over to Elaine that I realized he was with a woman. I deflated some but what did I expect? Of course he'd have a line of women waiting to take Daphne's place. I never caught the new girl's name, but she was a petite redhead with alabaster skin, pretty but not glamorous like Daphne.

When I said hello to Christopher, he gave me a big hug just like he always did. "You clean up nice," he whispered in my ear, the warmth of his breath dancing over my neck.

I didn't say anything. I was struck dumb, filled with jitters and schoolgirl nerves. His date's eyes were trained on me. I felt Elaine looking, too. We stood around making small talk, or at least *they* did. I mostly listened, too caught up in my head. A tuxedoed waiter came by holding out a silver tray of champagne and I helped myself to a glass. As I was about to take my first sip, a familiar voice called to me from behind.

"Ali? What are you doing here?"

I turned around and there was Erik. He leaned in and planted an awkward kiss on my cheek. "Oh, Erik. Erik Masterson, this is Christopher Mack and"—turning to the girl, I fumbled—"I'm sorry, this is, ah . . ."

"Meghan." She provided her name along with her hand.

"That's right. Meghan. Sorry. And this—this is Elaine Sloan. Elaine, Erik Masterson."

Elaine dipped her chin, narrowing her eyes. Immediately I could see her connecting the dots, as if to say, *This is him? Erik? The guy that's trying to sabotage Helen? What the hell are you doing with this guy?* I was embarrassed and questioning that very thing myself.

I wasn't even sure when I finished my champagne or how our little circle had broken up, but soon I found that Erik had whisked me away to the bar on the other side of the room.

He kept asking if I was okay. "You seem distracted."

"No. No, I'm fine." I was still processing Elaine's reaction to meeting him, still trying to find a place for the news about Christopher and Daphne splitting up.

Handing me another glass of champagne, Erik complimented me on my dress, my hair. He couldn't have been more attentive, acting as if I were the only woman in the room.

We continued talking right up until the lights flickered and someone chimed a bell and we began moving toward the Grand Ballroom. As we inched our way through the crowd, I spotted Christopher across the way. He was looking right at me. I smiled and turned away, ridiculously shy.

The room was filled with dozens of round tables, each with centerpieces that called out the tables: Hearst, Condé Nast, *Esquire, The New Yorker*, Random House, Doubleday, the *New York Times*, and on and on it went. The *Cosmopolitan* table was toward the rear, which Helen wasn't happy about.

"Why didn't they just put us in the kitchen? We should be up front near Hearst," she said, pouting, picking at her salad with her fingertips.

After dinner was served and before the awards ceremony began, I excused myself and went to the powder room, which was nicer than most people's living rooms: marble floors and walls, gold handles on the faucets and a uniformed attendant off to the side, waiting to disburse soft white hand towels.

On my way back to the Grand Ballroom, I nearly collided with Francesco Scavullo.

"Say, don't I know you?" He eyed me after I'd apologized.

"I'm Alice Weiss. Helen Gurley Brown's secretary."

"Ah, yes, of course. Don't you look beautiful tonight," he said, smiling.

"Don't tell anyone," I leaned in, hand to my mouth, and whispered, "but I looted the Beauty Closet."

He burst out laughing. "Your secret's safe with me."

"Hey"—I heard someone else say—"I didn't know you two knew each other."

We looked over, and my pulse quickened.

"Christopher." Francesco shook his hand and gestured to me. "So, I gather you've already met Alice, here?"

"I have. She's a budding photographer, you know."

"You don't say." Francesco turned toward me, waving his finger like I'd done something naughty. "You've been holding out on me. Why didn't you tell me that?"

"Because I'm not really a photographer. I'd like to be one, *someday*."

Another man stepped in and began talking to Francesco.

"You really do look stunning tonight," said Christopher.

I think I thanked him but couldn't be sure. We were looking at each other. It was the same look we'd shared at Coney Island.

Someone walked back into the dining room, letting a rush of applause escape through the open door. We were missing the awards ceremony but I didn't care. Something was changing between us, like something opening up, making space for something new. But at what cost? I didn't want to lose our friendship for the sake of trying something that might not work.

"So, ah," he said, "you still want to get together this Saturday like we planned?"

"Yeah. Sure. Of course."

"Okay. Good."

The dining room door opened again, letting out more applause. "Well," I said, "I should get back in there."

Christopher held the door for me, and we both stepped inside and went our separate ways.

CHAPTER TWENTY-SIX

○────────○

That Saturday, Trudy and I went for breakfast, taking our usual seats at the counter of the Candy Shop on Lex.

"I can't believe how fast the day goes there," she said, giving me all the details about her new job. "When I was at Bergdorf's, I would count the minutes till my break. Now I'm working straight through lunch and I don't even miss it. Did I tell you they're showing me how to read blueprints?"

"That's great, Trudy." I sipped my coffee and asked about Milton Steiner, one of the junior architects who'd taken a liking to Trudy. She'd already had drinks with him after work.

"He asked me out for tonight. Me, going on a Saturday night date. Oh, and did I tell you—he *likes* freckles."

I laughed. "Told you so."

"This sort of thing never happens to me. I feel like I'm dreaming. Like I'm living someone else's life. You know, when you first said I should become an architect, I thought you were, you know . . ." She brought her finger to the side of her head, making a cuckoo sign. "But now I'm thinking, why not? I could go to night school. I'm only twenty-two. I could do it."

"Of course you can do it." I smiled, thinking about my own dream and how far I'd come with my photography, how much I'd learned from Christopher.

Speaking of which, after breakfast I rushed home to get ready before meeting him. In the past, I wouldn't have made a fuss, but that day, I studied myself in the mirror while I brushed my hair and decided to change my clothes. I put on a pair of snug-fitting jeans and a blue sleeveless blouse, which I tied at the waist. After I applied some rouge and a hint of lipstick, I dabbed Emeraude behind my ears and along my wrists.

I met Christopher down in the Village and everything seemed normal. We were back to being friends, teasing each other and just knocking around for the better part of the afternoon, snapping off pictures and taking advantage of the beautiful weather.

"What now?" I asked when we ran out of film.

"You think you're ready for the darkroom?"

He'd been promising to show me how to develop my own film, but before we did that, we stopped into a café on Bleecker Street that smelled like burnt nuts. We started with coffees and segued into bourbon. I'd never had bourbon before. It made me a Chatty Cathy, and before I knew it, I was asking him about his girlfriend.

"So," I said, helping myself to his cigarette resting in the ashtray, "you and Daphne, huh? I'm sorry it didn't work out."

He squinted and rubbed his chin. "I didn't think you knew. Did Elaine tell you?"

"She mentioned it." I took a puff off his cigarette and handed it back to him. "Oh yeah, and your date at the gala was a dead giveaway."

He nodded and laughed. "Yeah, well, Elaine never really cared for Daphne. What all'd she tell you anyway?"

"No details. I mean, I don't know what went wrong."

"Well, that makes two of us," he said, taking a pull from his drink. "She called from LA and said she'd been doing a lot of thinking lately and she thought we should take some time apart." He blew out a deep sigh. "Elaine says Daphne's a user. I don't know. Maybe she's right." He rubbed his chin again. "I think I've already been replaced."

"Oh, I know how that goes."

"You, too, huh?"

I nodded, giving the ice in my glass a jiggle. "I was engaged before I moved here. He's married now to someone else." I smiled sadly, amazed that it still stung so much.

"You never told me about that. How come you never said anything?"

"Getting jilted isn't one of my favorite topics."

He nodded, raised his glass and clinked it to mine before taking a drink.

"So what makes you so sure you've been replaced?" I asked.

"There's this guy. He's been hanging around a lot. He's her agent so I'm sure he can help her acting career more than I ever could. I'm pretty sure he went out to LA with her." He pinched his cigarette between his index finger and thumb and brought it to the corner of his mouth, squinting as he inhaled. "She denies it, but I think it was going on while we were still together. And you know what the worst part is?" he said. "Now I have to find a new apartment." He cracked a sad smile and finished his drink. "So," he said in a way that indicated he was done with that topic, "that guy you were with at the gala?"

"Who? Erik?"

"You seeing him?"

"No. Not really." Maybe it was because I was sitting with Christopher, or maybe because I was just so tired of it all, but in that moment, I knew I had to end it with Erik.

Christopher cracked a small smile and took a final drag off his cigarette before grinding it out. "Well, it's getting late. I should probably let you get going."

I didn't want our time together to end and the bourbon made me bold enough to say, "Wait—I thought we were going to develop my film."

"Do you still have time? I assume you have plans for tonight. After all, it is a Saturday night."

"There's time." I excused myself and went to the phone booth in the back of the café and called Erik. He'd invited me to his place that night for cocktails and then dinner at Benihana. All that, of course, would be off once he'd heard what I had to say.

"I'm down in the Village," I told him. "I don't think I'll be able to make it uptown by seven. Can we push our plans back?"

"Till when?" he asked. "Eight?"

I glanced back at Christopher. "More like nine." I hung up and went back to the table. "Shall we?"

Christopher paid the bill, refusing to let me cover my share, and we headed to his photography studio on St. Mark's Place and First Avenue. It was a quirky little building with stained glass windows and high ceilings. It made me wonder if it had once been a church. There was no shortage of clutter—piles of books, newspapers and magazines lying about.

"Sorry the place is such a mess. I've been staying here because of, well, you know . . . ." His words ran out of steam. "C'mon," he said. "Let's get started on the photos."

We went into his darkroom, which doubled as his bathroom; trays stacked up in the tub, Lifebuoy soap and developing fluid next to a washcloth. He turned off the overhead light and talked me through exactly what he was doing, demonstrating with his hand on top of mine, but I found it hard to concentrate. The touch of his fingers went to my head along with the bourbon.

He took me through the entire process, from agitating the film to applying the stop bath and fixer chemicals, and by the time he had rinsed the photos and hung them up to dry, I couldn't have cared less about what we'd shot that day. With him standing close behind me, I could feel his breath against my neck, could feel a ripple of heat coming off him, and it terrified me. I was as fragile as spun glass. My last heartache felt suddenly raw like it had just happened. Christopher could shatter me with one kiss. If he kissed me once and went away, I would be devastated. It took all my will not to turn around because I knew I wouldn't be able to stop myself if I looked into his eyes.

"I should really be going," I said, forcing myself to take that one critical, establishing step away from him. I knew it was abrupt, but I had to get out of there.

My pulse was still racing even after I left Christopher's studio. It was getting late, already half past nine. I thought about Erik sitting in his apartment, waiting for me. I didn't even bother going home to change, because now that I knew what I had to do, I just wanted to get it over with. I jogged down the stairwell and caught the Broadway line, shoving my way inside the crowded train.

When I arrived at Erik's apartment, the doorman nodded and said good evening as if we were old friends. Using the house phone, he called Erik and announced that I was on my way up. I went over to the bank of elevators, and as I stepped into a waiting car and the doors were starting to close, I looked up and did a double take. I couldn't believe what I was seeing. It was Bridget. Sprinting through the lobby.

My stomach dropped as the elevator took off, rising, rising, floor by floor. I was shocked and wondered how long that had been going on. And how many other women he'd been sleeping with? I should have known I couldn't trust him. He'd just made it a whole lot easier for me to end it.

Erik was standing in the doorway of his apartment, directly across from the elevator. "Why aren't you dressed?"

I was still too stunned to speak.

"Do you want to stay in?" He smiled and stepped into the hallway. "Get over here. I've missed you." He reached for my arm and went to kiss me.

I pulled away. "Bridget?"

That smug look on his face vanished. The elevator doors behind me closed. "Ali, it's not what you think."

"Oh, please." I laughed bitterly and pushed the call button. "It never is, is it?"

He reached for my hand. "I can explain."

"Spare me." I yanked my hand back and called again for the elevator. "You and I are done. Good night, Erik. Good night and good-bye."

The next morning Erik was at my apartment. Someone must have left the downstairs door cracked because he was knocking, demanding I let him in, waking me from a sound sleep. It wasn't even eight o'clock yet.

"What are you doing here?" I looked at him through the sliver of an opening in the door, the chain lock pulled taut.

"I want to talk to you."

"There's nothing to talk about."

"Will you just let me in?"

"Why? No strings attached, remember? You don't owe me a thing."

"Obviously, you're upset."

"Don't flatter yourself. I expected something like this from you. Honestly, I'm more upset with Bridget." And that was true. She'd known about Erik and me. I had confided in her. She was supposed to have been my friend. I felt more betrayed by her than Erik.

"Please, just let me in. I can explain last night. It's not what you think."

His voice was loud and I didn't want to disturb the whole building. I waited for a moment and reluctantly unlatched the door. "You've got five minutes," I said, pinching my bathrobe closed.

When he came inside, we stared at each other, not saying a word. He looked bad, dark circles under his eyes, his hair unkempt, his face unshaved. He was still wearing the same clothes from the night before. It seemed as if he hadn't slept at all.

"About Bridget—"

"What about her? I honestly don't care if you're seeing her. I just wish you hadn't lied to me about it."

"I didn't lie about it. I'm not seeing her. I swear I'm not." He sat on the sofa, elbows on his knees, head in his hands. "I'm not seeing anyone but you."

I could tell he was exhausted but I refused to go weak. "Then what was she doing at your place on a Saturday night?"

"It was for work."

I laughed.

"I left some papers in Bill Guy's office and I needed to work on them over the weekend. She's his secretary. I asked her to go get them for me. I swear, that's what it was."

On a Saturday night? I didn't believe him. "How were you able to reach her on the weekend?"

"I called her at home."

"And why do you have Bridget's number?" I sounded like I cared more than I did. Yes, I was angry that he'd played me, but at the same time, I was relieved—he'd given me an easy out. But it was the Bridget thing. I was still hoping for a feasible explanation.

He sighed and dragged his hands over his face. "I took her out—once. It was a long, long time ago. Long before I ever met you. It didn't go anywhere. It's been—"

I held up my hand to silence him. "You know what—I don't care."

"Would you just come over here, please?"

I was still standing; my hand remained on the knob. "It was fun while it lasted, but I can't do this anymore. You need to go." I opened the door and gestured for him to leave.

"What? Just like that?" He looked at me in disbelief. "You're gonna throw all this away?"

"All what?"

"We're good together."

"No, we have good sex together. That was it and now it's over."

After Erik left, I threw on some clothes and went to Bridget's apartment just a few blocks away on 73rd and Third Avenue. I wanted to confront her and get it over with and not drag our personal problems into the office.

When I rang her buzzer, a groggy voice croaked through the intercom system, letting me up. It was still early, not quite nine o'clock. I passed a man on the stairwell, still buttoning his shirt, his tie looped around his neck like a scarf. The hallway was dark with dated damask patterned wallpaper, old and yellowing, unglued at the seams. Someone on her floor was cooking bacon.

"Ali, what are you doing here? What's wrong?" Bridget stood in the doorway, her bouffant deflated, mascara smeared, the belt on her bathrobe twisted.

"Can I come in?" I pushed past her without an answer. I vaguely noticed an empty bottle of Chablis, two wineglasses and a full ashtray on her coffee table. Her dress, the same one she was wearing when I saw her in Erik's lobby, was bunched up on the sofa, her patent leather pumps kicked off, one near the couch, the other halfway across the room.

"What's going on?" she asked. "Are you all right?"

"If you wanted Erik, you should have just said so."

"What?" Her eyes opened wide, the sleepy residue gone.

"If you wanted him, you should have just told me. I would have stepped aside. You didn't have to sneak around behind my back and lie about it."

"What are you talking about?"

"I saw you. I saw you at Erik's last night."

"Oh God." She shook her head and rubbed her eye with the heel of her hand. "Jesus, no. I'm not seeing Erik. I swear it, I'm not. I had a date last night. He just left here."

I thought about the man I'd passed in the stairwell. I glanced again at the wineglasses, the Chablis. "What were you doing at Erik's then?"

Her face, already pasty white, turned the color of chalk as she shook her head and dropped onto her sofa, kicking one of her pumps out of the way.

I waited, expecting her to say something. Another moment passed. "Well?"

"Ali." She tried but fell silent again and leaned forward, her bathrobe opening, exposing her bare knees. She reached for the Salems on her coffee table. The pack was empty and she crumpled it in her fist as if she were crushing walnuts.

I was still waiting for her explanation.

"Shit," she said, looking around. "I had another pack. Did you see it?"

"Bridget?"

She sprinted off to the bedroom and came back with a pack of Pall Malls.

"Why were you at Erik's?" I asked again.

She lit her cigarette, and on the exhale, she said, "This whole thing has gotten so out of control."

"What *whole thing?*"

She took another puff off her cigarette but still wouldn't look at me. "Do you remember when you first started at work?"

"Yeah?"

"Remember when Erik asked for your help? With Helen? And you said no? You wouldn't do it?"

"Yeah." A sick feeling was settling into my gut.

"Well . . ."

Oh no. This was worse than her seeing Erik behind my back. "Bridget, what did you do?"

She puffed on her Pall Mall.

"Bridget?"

"It was nothing. I swear. All I did was tell him what was going on around the office. Just stuff Helen was telling the staff—I swear that's all it was."

She still wouldn't look at me so I knew it was more than that. I recalled the times she'd hovered around my desk, reading over my shoulder. I thought about the leaks to the advertisers, about flatplans and cover art that had found its way to Deems and Berlin. Each new realization set off more alarms inside my head until there was no other conclusion to reach. "It was you, wasn't it?"

"Ali, no. C'mon."

"You leaked the memo to *Women's Wear Daily.*"

"It was a goof. I swear I didn't know Erik was going to show it to anyone outside of Hearst."

"So the memo *and* the cover leak. That was you." I paused for a moment, expecting and hoping she'd deny it. When she didn't, all I could do was ask, "Why would you do that?"

"It was Erik's idea. I swear it was. He said he'd get me promoted, get me a raise. I needed the money." Her tone seemed to suggest that the money justified her actions.

We were locked in a stare-down. She smoked her cigarette, something cold stirring behind her eyes. She didn't understand the first thing about loyalty. She was always out for herself.

"What are you going to do about it?" she asked, lighting another cigarette off the one she was about to grind out.

"I can't believe you'd do this to Helen. To all of us. Isn't it hard enough for us women to get ahead? To be taken seriously and treated with respect? Erik came to you and you just said yes? Why? For a lousy raise? A stupid promotion? How could you be so shortsighted? Really, Bridget, what would you do with all this information if you were me?"

"Well, I wouldn't think I'm so above it all. You're the one sleeping with him."

"But I never once betrayed Helen or the magazine. I kept my mouth shut."

"Maybe you should have kept your legs shut, too."

I was speechless. And hurt. She wasn't my friend. Never had been. I turned without saying another word and walked out of her apartment. I was shaking as I held on to the banister and made my way to the first floor. Bridget had leveled me with that insult, and it didn't matter that she slept around more than anyone I knew—I still felt ashamed. That *good girl* ideology was so ingrained in me.

But as the day wore on and I thought about it, I realized that I hadn't done anything wrong. Having an affair didn't make me a tramp. Sleeping with Erik without guilt or judgment had freed up something inside me. Helen had given me permission to pursue what I wanted, and as a result, I knew myself better—what I liked, what I didn't. Most important, I had discovered what I deserved.

Finding out that Bridget had betrayed me, betrayed Helen and put everybody's future in jeopardy was too much. By the time I got back to my apartment, I had turned callous toward her, just as I'd turned callous toward Erik.

I had to tell Helen what was going on. I knew it was going to cost Bridget her job and probably Erik's, too, but they'd brought this on themselves, and my loyalty was with Helen. My pet peeve was being played a fool and I resented them both all the more for having put me in the position to expose what they'd done.

I wrestled with the whole matter most of the night, and the next day as I walked into work, I was still trying to figure out how I was going to break the news to Helen.

Her office door was closed when I arrived, but she was already in. I could see the sliver of light under her door and heard voices coming from within. I was disappointed. I'd been hoping I could have just gone in and gotten it over with.

I was feeling anxious, rehearsing how I would phrase it all to her. Eventually, I went down the hall to get coffee. There were only a handful of people already in the office, but even so, I sensed something different in the air. I passed Bill Guy in the hallway, and he barely responded when I said good morning. Bobbie and Penny were in the kitchen. Neither one of them said a word as they got their coffees and left. Even Margot, who loved nothing more than to gossip, wasn't talking. I felt guilty then for being so suspicious of her all this time.

When I went back to my desk, Helen's door opened and I saw one of the building's security guards inside. The overhead light caught his badge, giving off a blinding glare. Erik Masterson was standing just to his side, with his head hung low.

Erik was pale, his hair a bit ruffled as if he'd been raking his hands through it. His eyes were empty and bleak as he paused and stared at me. I didn't know what was happening until the guard, nudging him along, said, "C'mon, let's go get your things."

Before they cleared the doorway, Helen called me into her office. Richard Berlin, Dick Deems and Walter Meade were in there, along with a second security guard, his hat resting on the coffee table.

Helen reached for a cigarette and said, "Alice, would you ask Bridget to come down here?"

I swallowed hard, my head a little dazed as I went to Bridget's desk. She had just arrived, her pocketbook still in hand. She saw the look on my face and removed her sunglasses, sliding them down her face. Her eyes were puffy, lined red, circles beneath them. She seemed to know what was coming. When I said Helen needed to see her, she brushed past me, deliberately banging into my shoulder.

Helen never told me how she found out, but I suspected that Walter Meade had something to do with it. Especially since he was the only member of her staff who'd been present for the firings. But Bridget didn't know that. Neither did Erik. They thought it was me.

CHAPTER TWENTY-SEVEN

t had been almost three weeks since Bridget and Erik were fired and aside from the initial gossip surrounding the viper, or vipers as it turned out, I was surprised by how little anyone spoke of them. The two were nothing more than footprints in the sand. Now everyone's attention had shifted to the July issue.

It was June 23rd, the day before Helen's *Cosmo* was scheduled to hit the stands. No one knew if this marked a new beginning or the scandalous end for the magazine. There was a halfhearted attempt around the office to appear normal, though everyone knew we could all be out of work soon. Margot and some other coworkers had already begun interviewing. The editors and writers were torn between looking for their next job and keeping things moving on the August issue.

Everyone at Hearst was watching us. You could almost feel the tension coming down the street from headquarters. Helen was wearing down the pile on her new carpet with all her pacing, occasionally breaking into a round of leg lifts or jogging in place. There were no tears, though. Just nervous energy.

"Why don't you go home and try to relax?" I suggested, standing in the doorway of her office. It was early, not even five o'clock yet, but almost everyone else had left, finding it too maddening to sit around, waiting to learn their fate.

"Go on," I said, hoping to assure her it was okay. "And try and eat something." The past few weeks had taken their toll on her. She'd probably dropped five pounds that she couldn't afford to lose. She nodded listlessly. I could see the sharp angles of her collarbone and sternum.

I helped her pack her briefcase, collecting the new articles she wanted to review and edit for the August and September issues. In spite of it all, she was still banking, or trying to, on the future of *Cosmopolitan*. When I snapped her briefcase shut, I looked over and saw she was tearing up.

"Mrs. Brown? Are you okay?" I hadn't seen her cry in weeks.

She shook her head and scrunched up her shoulders. "I'm so tired." She leaned against the side of her desk, as if her legs were about to give out. "I don't think I've ever been this tired in all my life. And I'm scared. Just terrified. If July is a flop, all this"—she raised her hands, indicating her office, the magazine, her editorial career—"it all goes bye-bye." She covered her mouth like she was about to scream. "Do you know that I've never failed at anything before? Not ever. I was valedictorian of my class. I don't know how to fail."

"You won't fail at this, either," I said, trying to be encouraging.

Her brow was furrowed, her eyes were misting up again and her chin began to crumble. "I wanted to do something big and important for women."

"But you already have."

She shook her head and turned out her bottom lip. "I'm not talking about my book. I'm talking about *Cosmopolitan*. Women *need* this magazine. I don't care about Betty Friedan. Or Gloria Steinem going undercover as a Playboy Bunny. Neither of them—

or anyone else who calls themselves a feminist—is talking to women the way I can. Every girl out there needs to know that she's not alone. I was alone. Even though I had my mother and my sister, I was still alone." She crossed the room and threw herself onto the sofa and collapsed into a fit of tears.

"Mrs. Brown. Please. It's going to be okay." She'd displayed so much strength lately and to see her crumble again about broke my heart. I went and sat beside her, not sure how to console her. Her whole body was shaking as she went on weeping into a throw pillow. She was saying something now, hiccuping on her every word, so I couldn't understand her. All I could think to do was rub soothing circles along her back like my mother used to do to me.

I was still rubbing her back, feeling her shoulder blades and ribs, when she turned and looked at me. She offered me a sad, faint smile as the tears ran sideways across her cheeks, heading toward her ears. "I don't want to grow old. I don't want to be just another old woman, forgotten, invisible to the rest of the world. This magazine has to succeed," she said. "It just has to. Otherwise, why am I here? Editing this magazine, bringing this information to my girls—I really believe this is why I was put here on earth."

After Helen had composed herself, I called David Brown and asked him to come pick her up. She was in no condition to get on the bus, and I knew she'd fight me if I tried putting her in a cab.

I left the building shortly after Helen, her words echoing inside my head: *This is why I was put here on earth*. It made me question why I was put here. Did I feel as passionately about my photography as she did about the magazine? I'd seen Helen go through hell, enduring all kinds of setbacks and disappointments. She'd put up with ridicule and had overcome one obstacle after another, and here I was too chicken to enroll in a photography class. I knew then that if I was going to claim my dream, I had to be as tough as Helen and I had to be willing to do whatever it took to succeed.

When I got to the corner of Broadway and 57th, a taxicab pulled up alongside me. The rear window rolled down and I saw strands of silver-white hair blowing out, caught in the wind.

"Got time for a drink? C'mon, get in."

I opened the door and scooted in next to Elaine Sloan. She smelled faintly of Vivara, cigarettes and gin. "I have a dinner appointment, but not till eight. Have you been to the St. Regis yet?"

And off we went, arriving ten minutes later at 54th and Fifth Avenue. The lobby looked like a marble palace with just enough gilded accents and crystal chandeliers to keep it on the opulent side of gaudy. I followed Elaine as she swept past the scores of hotel guests and entered the King Cole Bar.

"You see that?" She pointed to a playful painting behind the bar, stretching from one end to the other. "That's the Old King Cole mural. I just love it. Let's go sit at the bar. I want you to see it up close." Elaine was as animated as I'd ever seen her. "I'm so glad I ran into you," she said, ordering two martinis for us. "Sorry, but I just can't hold off until eight to start celebrating."

"What are you celebrating?" I didn't want to mention it but it seemed as though she'd already started before she picked me up.

"I'm finally done. Finished with *Valley of the Dolls*."

"Is it out yet?"

"No. No." She pinched open her pocketbook and pulled out her gold cigarette case and lighter, setting them on the bar. "No, the pub date isn't until February, but at least my part's finally done. There's not one word left to edit. Not that Jackie let me do much editing anyway." She laughed to herself. "No more frantic phone calls from her, no more bursting into my office unannounced. Jackie Susann is one of the toughest authors I've ever worked with. She just about wore me out."

The bartender poured our martinis with a great flourish and Elaine raised her glass to me. "I heard you saw Christopher recently," she said. "Tell me, how did he seem to you?"

"Fine." I took a sip of the best gin martini I'd ever tasted, wondering what he'd told her about that day in his darkroom.

"I worry about him. I just want him to be happy. He's like a son to me, you know." She reached over and lit a cigarette. "I'm going to tell you something. Not many people know this—I'm not even sure Christopher knows—but when I was younger—just twenty-six—I got pregnant."

"You did?" She had to have been drunk. I had no idea why she was telling me this.

"Uh-huh. I was young and scared. I wasn't ready to be anyone's mother. When I told Viv, your mother, that I found a doctor and was going to have a procedure, well, she begged me not to do it. She did everything she could to try talking me out of it. She was sure I'd regret it. But see, unlike your mother, I didn't love the baby's father."

Unlike your mother? That was an odd thing to say, but Elaine was in the middle of her story, going full force so I couldn't have interrupted her if I'd tried.

"And you know what? It turns out your mother was right. I still regret doing it." She stared into the mural and said wistfully, "If I'd kept the baby, I'd have a fifteen-year-old child now." She gazed straight ahead at the mural, her blue eyes misting up. "Your mother was right. I wish I hadn't gone through with it. The doctor—he was in New Jersey, not that that had anything to do with it. But, well, turns out he wasn't all that careful. Not that safe. I could have died."

"I'm so sorry." I didn't know what else to say, and frankly, I wasn't even sure she heard me. She just kept talking.

"After I recovered, they told me I couldn't have children." She turned and looked at me, a sad, thin smile cresting her lips. "So now you know why I'm so protective of Christopher. He's the closest thing I'll ever have to a child of my own."

Now I really didn't know what to say so I took another sip of my drink.

Elaine flicked her cigarette ash and sighed. "I probably shouldn't say this to you—of all people—but I remember when your mother found out she was pregnant, I actually asked her what she wanted to do."

Another odd thing for her to say, but at least she recognized that fact. I'd never seen Elaine quite like this before. I was certain she had to be drunk.

"Well, Viv just looked at me like I was crazy. There was never a doubt in her mind about keeping you. She never, not for a second, considered going out and doing—"

The look on my face stopped her mid-sentence. "Oh God, Ali." She reached for my hand. Her voice hung there for a moment. "I thought you knew. I'm sor—"

"Knew what?" She didn't have to spell it out. I'd always known I was born almost nine months to the date of my parents' wedding, but I never questioned it. Until now. I felt sick and took a gulp from my martini.

"Are you okay?" she asked, gesturing to the bartender for another round.

I nodded and drained the rest of my drink.

"It doesn't change a thing. You know your mother and father loved you."

I did know that, but I couldn't verbalize a thing. All I could do was nod while she kept talking.

"Oh, Ali." She shook her head. "I really thought you knew." She lit her cigarette, and I watched her whole body give way as she exhaled.

I heard a group of people entering the bar and did a quarter turn, watching them get situated at a nearby table.

A cloud of Elaine's smoke drifted toward me. She sighed and said, "I remember when Viv first met your father. It was here in New York. Right after the war. He was this good-looking sailor. Really, like a movie star, he was. He swept her off her feet. I'd never seen your mother so crazy for a fella before. It was so romantic. They had a whirlwind affair. I think it took them both by surprise." Her voice trailed off.

She wasn't telling me anything new. I'd heard the story of how my parents had met in New York City. I knew he was a sailor, and even at the age of forty-seven, my father was still a handsome man. "Go on."

"And then, well, your mother found out she was pregnant. With you. And that's when everything started to . . ." She stopped and started over. "Well, when your mother told her parents, that was it. They didn't want anything more to do with her. They disowned her. The whole family turned their back on her. Your mother didn't know where to go, what to do. Your father was from Youngstown so that's where she went. And he did the right thing by her. He married her."

left Elaine at the St. Regis, my head pounding from gin and too much new information. I kept repeating but not quite believing: *My parents had to get married because my mother got pregnant. With me. I was an accident. A mistake.* At least now I knew what that terrible thing was that my mother's father had done. He'd done that, too, because of me.

When I got home, it was warm and stuffy inside even with the windows open. Those martinis were sloshing around inside me, and I desperately needed to put something in my stomach but there wasn't much to choose from. I opted for a sleeve of saltines and a jar of peanut butter, which two crackers in proved to be the wrong choice. I switched to a bottle of orange soda, thinking in my drunkenness how they called it pop, not soda, back home in Youngstown.

Home. Youngstown . . .

This new knowledge about me and my parents carried a heavy burden. I felt responsible for changing the course of two people's lives. If it hadn't been for me, my mother would have stayed in New York, would have possibly continued her modeling career—despite what her father thought of it. She would have met another man, married him and had a different child. Maybe more than one. And what about my father? He would have come back from the war, returned to Youngstown and married some other woman, and he, too, would have had a different life with her and with a different family.

And yet, if my parents had resented me for changing their destinies, they never let on. Learning the truth about my parents didn't make me question if I'd been loved. Elaine had tried to impress that fact upon me, but it wasn't necessary. I already knew my mother and father loved me. But still, it required a mental shift, a reframing of how I thought about them, my parents. At least I didn't have to rewrite their love story. I had plenty of memories of them holding hands, stealing kisses when they thought no one was looking, slow dancing in the living room to the radio, my mother singing in his ear. They were happy as far as I could tell. So it was just a shift I had to do, by myself, for myself.

I knew at some point I would need to say something to my father, but a conversation like that was better had in person, rather than over the phone. Especially with Faye hovering in the background and him watching the clock above the stove, calculating the long-distance charges.

CHAPTER TWENTY-EIGHT

I hardly slept that night, backsliding in my thoughts and coming up plagued by the notion that I'd ruined my mother's life. My father's, too. And my dread intensified as the hour grew later. I finally surrendered and dozed off about half an hour before my alarm went off, and for a brief second, all was well. It was Thursday morning, June 24th. Our July issue was on sale. But then snippets of my conversation with Elaine came rushing back with the force of a body blow. After twenty minutes of wallowing, I peeled back the covers, and forced myself to get on with the day.

I bathed, dressed in a hurry and was out the door before seven o'clock. I stopped at the diner on the corner of 76th and Lexington and got a cup of coffee. On my way to the train station, I passed a newsstand filled with magazines and papers, cigarettes and chewing gum. I looked and looked—*McCall's, Ladies' Home Journal, Esquire, Time* and *Life*. I saw just about every magazine but *Cosmopolitan*.

It was still early, though, and it was possible that the newsstand operator hadn't set out the new magazines yet, which didn't seem very smart since he'd miss the morning commuters. There was a second newsstand near the subway stop but I didn't see *Cosmopolitan* there, either. I wondered if Erik and Bridget had managed to get in one final hurrah and did something to interfere with the distribution from the warehouse.

I was anticipating how I was going to deal with Helen that morning, envisioning her in tears while her downtrodden staff packed up their desks in search of new opportunities. I was running this exodus through my mind as I boarded the subway. All the seats were taken so I stood in the crowded car, holding on to a filthy pole. I was staring at the tops of my shoes, a pair of powder blue sling-backs that I now regretted purchasing, considering I'd probably be out of a job.

When my train began to slow, brakes screeching as it approached the 68th Street station, I looked up and a flicker of something caught my eye. There it was—Renata's perfectly seductive pout and heaving bosom. Proof that it was at least on sale. *Somewhere.* A young woman—the exact girl Helen had pictured all along—was greedily going through the pages. She was absorbed to the point that she almost missed her stop, bolting up from her seat with a start and racing for the sliding doors.

I watched as more commuters came on board and settled in. Looking down the train, breaking up the continuous wave of black-and-white newsprint, I saw a few bursts of color. It was one, two, three copies of *Cosmopolitan* in the hands of Helen's girls. When I got off at 57th Street, I looked for it at the newsstand, but again, it was nowhere to be found.

I asked the man behind the window and he shook his head. "No. All gone. No more. Sold out."

Sold out? Sold out!

Helen was already in her office, scribbling red ink all over an article Nora Ephron had delivered on *How to Start a Conversation with a Stranger* for the August issue. When I told her that the newsstand had sold all their copies, she said, "That's easy to do when they probably only ordered three to begin with."

She sounded defeated, and yet if she'd truly felt that way, why was she still editing Nora's article? Maybe it was a distraction? A last burst of hope? But as the day progressed, Helen found she couldn't concentrate. She was petrified that it was all coming to an end. I found her in her office doing isometric exercises and frantic leg lifts.

At half past eleven, she phoned David, who arrived to take her on one of their nooners. She didn't come back that day. I waited until eight o'clock but still there was no sign of her. I tried their apartment but there was no answer there, either.

walked home that night, wishing I had my camera with me to capture the last bits of sunlight streaming in through the tree-tops. It was a warm summer evening, and as I stepped over a subway grate, I was greeted by even more hot air. A thin layer of sweat collected along the back of my neck, and every now and again I'd get a strong whiff of urine and sweltering garbage. That was the thing about New York. It was either gritty ugliness or beauty and elegance. One block over, I was in another land, passing by flower boxes blooming with geraniums, the curtains caught in the breeze blowing through the open apartment windows. All the outdoor cafés were full with upbeat, happy people. I wasn't one of them.

Instead, I found myself worrying about Helen's state of mind. She must have been in a bad way if she hadn't returned to work. If she hadn't even called in for her messages. She was the one we all looked to now and we needed her to be optimistic. I felt the insides of *Cosmo* already beginning to crumble and couldn't help but wonder where that left me.

As I passed by different newsstands, I took note of the magazines, both pleased and discouraged whenever I saw Renata looking back. That morning I'd been concerned about distribution, about getting the magazine on the stands. Now all I cared about was selling copies and moving the magazine *off* the stands. I wondered how soon we'd get sales numbers. I was so distracted, I almost tumbled into a cellar doorway, wide open and looking like a bomb shelter.

Turning down 74th Street, I pulled the keys from my pocketbook just as a man reached out and tried to grab my arm. A shot of adrenaline rushed through me. I was about to scream until I turned and saw his face. It was Erik.

I didn't say anything. My heart was firing like a jackhammer. He looked terrible. His hair had no part; his eyes had dark circles beneath them. He was in a pair of blue jeans and a gray T-shirt. It was the first time I'd seen him in anything other than a suit. I got the sense that he'd been pacing back and forth, waiting for me. I was sure he blamed me for his being fired.

"Can I come up?"

I hesitated.

"Please? I need to talk to you."

Despite everything he'd done, I found myself feeling sorry for him. Neither one of us said a word as I unlocked the front door and we climbed the stairs.

"Listen," he said as he stepped inside my apartment and dropped to the sofa, his hands raking through his hair. "I've been doing a lot of thinking, and well," he sighed, not looking at me, "the thing is, I don't want to lose you."

"What? Erik—"

"Just let me get this out before I lose my nerve." Fresh beads of sweat appeared on his forehead. "I know we weren't looking for anything serious. But well—and believe me, I'm as surprised by this as anyone—but I can't stop thinking about you, Ali."

If it weren't for the look on his face, I would have thought he was joking.

"I mean it," he said. "Let's put everything that happened behind us and give this another chance."

"Erik, c'mon. This is—"

"I want to be with you. I don't want to see anyone else, and I don't want you seeing anyone else."

All I could do was shake my head. "No. We can't—"

"Is it because I'm out of work now? I've got money in the bank. Lots of money. And I'll get another job. It may not be with a magazine. I'm talking to some publishing houses. But I'll land on my feet."

"This is crazy. You only want me now because you can't have me."

"I want you because I'm falling in love with you. I'm *in* love with you. Don't you get it? I want to marry you."

I was stunned. And speechless. Helen hadn't prepared me for this. Don Juans weren't supposed to fall in love. They weren't supposed to want marriage. I took a deep breath and collected my thoughts. I sat down beside him and made him look me in the eye. "I know you're going through a hard time right now, but this"—I indicated the two of us—"is not real. You're just saying this because you can't have me and because—"

"That's not what this is about." He looked flabbergasted. "Do you know how many girls I've invited home to meet my family?" He formed an O with his hand. "Ali, I swear, I've never felt this way about a woman before."

I wanted him to stop talking. I didn't want to hear any more.

"I'm in love with you," he said again. "I want to take care of you. You won't have to work anymore. We'll get a bigger apartment, a nicer one. Hell, I'll get us a penthouse on Fifth Avenue— I can afford it. And you, you can hire any decorator you want and—"

"Erik, please, stop trying to sell me. This is not a business negotiation."

But he wasn't listening. "You don't need to do the photography stuff anymore, either."

"Please don't say anything more."

He looked at me, the hint of a smile rising up. "So, is that a yes?"

"My God"—I clasped the sides of my head—"haven't you heard anything I said?"

"What? You're saying you *don't* want to marry me?" He sounded incredulous.

"Yes. I mean *no*. I *do not* want to marry you."

"You're kidding, right? I surrender, okay? You won. You got me." He laughed in a sick defeated sort of way. "You're a woman. You're supposed to *want* to get married. That's what you *all* want." There was a long pause before he looked at me, his dark eyes hooded and confused. "Just tell me why. Why won't you marry me?"

I reached for his hands and said, as gently as I could, "Because I don't love you."

Erik looked at me with disbelief. I felt cold and heartless just sitting there, but other than offering him a glass of warm gin, because I'd forgotten to refill the ice tray, I had nothing for him.

Everyone was operating at half capacity that last week in June. Even Helen. She arrived one morning at an unprecedented half past nine, which was like showing up at noon for anyone else.

"Mr. Berlin called for you," I said when she walked in, handing her a pile of pink message slips. "I'll get your coffee. And your newspapers."

She nodded, unlocked her office door and flipped on the overhead light.

When I came back with her coffee she was just hanging up from a telephone call with Berlin. Reaching for her pocketbook, she said, "Alice, I need to step out for a bit but could you gather up the staff and have them meet me in the conference room at one o'clock? I have an announcement."

"Is everything okay?"

She said everything was fine, but there was a funny tickle in her voice and an even funnier look in her eyes. I tried but couldn't read her. She was dazed as she left her office.

All morning long, my worst fears were festering. So were everyone else's. I don't think anyone went to lunch that day, too nervous to eat. And at one o'clock everyone, including the secretaries, had crowded into the conference room. There was no sign of Helen. I hadn't seen or heard from her since she'd left the office.

People were chain-smoking, worried looks etched into their faces. No one was talking above a whisper. I sat at the conference room table with my colleagues for ten agonizing minutes before the door burst open and Helen walked in, her hands clasped behind her back. One look at her face and I knew something was up. I nervously tapped my foot, waiting along with everyone else for her to say something. *Anything.*

"I suppose you're wondering why I've asked you in here. Well . . ." She paused, and everyone in the room inhaled. "I just got our sales numbers and"—she brought her hands to the front, revealing a bottle of champagne—"I'm pleased to tell you that July has already sold more than 200,000 copies over the June issue."

The room took off when she said that. It came alive, erupting with applause and cheers, even a few misty eyes and tears.

"We did it," Helen said, her voice peaking above the celebration, while she wrestled with the cork, her thumb easing it out of the bottle. "We're on our way, pussycats!" The cork popped on cue and the roar of applause grew even louder.

While Helen made her way through the room, hugging everyone, I took over as bartender, finding a cart in the hallway filled with glasses and more bottles of Dom Pérignon. I'd never seen Helen splurge like this—on calories or the expense—but she was beaming, proud and, more than anything, relieved. I thought about that deceptively frail-looking woman I'd met three months ago who didn't even know what a flatplan was. Since then I'd watched her grow. And struggle. With herself, her staff and the good ole boys club at Hearst. I'd never witnessed, let alone been part of a fight like that. There were lessons learned along the way that I'd never forget. And I was rejoicing that in the end she'd won. We'd won. Beaten the odds.

I felt light and grounded at the same time. A few sips of champagne and my head was swimming with sparkling bubbles. I loved everyone in that room and was actually embracing George Walsh of all people when the receptionist came into the conference room and interrupted me.

"Alice," she said, tapping me on the shoulder, "I have a call for you. On line two."

"Will you take a message?" I said, sipping the last bit of my champagne.

"She said it's important."

Margot leaned over and refilled my glass. It was too noisy in the conference room so I took my champagne, went back to my desk and pressed the flashing button on my phone.

"Alice? Alice? Is that you?"

"Who is this?"

"It's Faye."

A rush of panic hit me. I set my glass down, spilling my champagne, my legs turning to rubber. There was only one reason Faye would ever call me.

"Alice, I'm sorry. It's your father—"

"What happened?" I stared helplessly at the champagne running over the papers on my desk. "Is he okay?"

She went silent for a moment. I heard a burst of laughter coming from the conference room down the hall.

"I'm sorry. He had a heart attack. It happened this morning." Her voice began to crack. "The doctors did everything they could but—"

"He's gone?"

"I'm so sorry."

CHAPTER TWENTY-NINE

◦———◦

After I hung up with Faye, I didn't remember telling Helen that my father had died, but what I did recall was that she insisted on buying me a round-trip ticket on TWA.

I hadn't shed a tear since Faye told me the news, but the hole in my heart was ever growing. After my mother died, it had been just the two of us, and my father—not knowing what to do with a thirteen-year-old daughter—took me to Derby Downs to watch the go-cart races, fishing on Lake Erie and to Cleveland Indians games. Together we learned to cook, eating fried eggs and oatmeal for dinner until we had graduated to grilled cheese sandwiches. When we couldn't stand the sight of those anymore, we experimented with my mother's meatloaf recipe. We ate dinner side by side on the sofa, plates on our laps, while we watched *Perry Mason* and *The Red Skelton Show*. But really, it didn't matter what we did, I was just relieved to be near him, grateful that he hadn't left me, too. Now he was gone and I'd never be able to talk to him again. About anything. Especially not about the reasons he and my mother got married.

I couldn't think about it, so instead I harnessed all my attention on taking my first airplane flight. Wearing my best summer shift for the event, I was nervous, zeroing in on real and imagined engine noises, turbulence and the clouds outside my window. I must have smoked half a pack of cigarettes from the time I boarded the plane until we touched down. My head felt full, my ears refusing to pop even after I'd landed at Cleveland Hopkins.

Faye was there to pick me up. The last time I'd seen her had been the day I left home. It was drizzling that morning, and as I boarded the Greyhound, I had turned to see my father's new wife holding her clutch over her head, shielding her hair from the rain while tugging on his arm, coaxing him back to the car. My father and I had shared a final finger wave before the bus driver closed the door and I moved down the narrow aisle to my seat. I remember hearing the engine rev as we eased away from the curb. My father was still standing next to his Buick, rain collecting in his hair, turning the sleeves and shoulders of his coat a shade darker. The driver's side door was open and I remember seeing Faye's hand summoning him inside.

Now she was in his Buick, waiting for me by the curb at the airport. She wore a floral scarf, tied at the nape of her neck. Her skin was pale, her eyes rimmed red and deeply sad.

"Thank you for coming," she said. And this burned me because it was as if she'd invited me and I didn't need her request to be there. He was my father. I was still his daughter. And then I realized, with a gaping hole spreading through my chest, that Faye was the only family I had left. If you could have even called her that.

As we drove through Cleveland, I noticed how living in Manhattan, even for a short while, had changed my perceptions. Cleveland, just an hour outside of Youngstown, had always been the big city for us, but compared to New York, it was tiny, slow moving, provincial.

We went straight to the funeral home—a rite of passage I'd been spared when my mother died due to my youth. It was quiet like a synagogue or a library, the floor amplifying our footsteps. We were led toward the back, into a showroom of caskets, a grotesque display of commerce. Little gold placards with catchy model names like *Serenity*, *Transitions* and *Parliament* listed each one's features—quilted satin lining, reinforced seal—and of course, the price. I couldn't have told you which model Faye and I decided on. I was in a fog, with a hazy memory of a woman with a complexion like a potato sprouting eyes, taking down information for the obituary. After that, in an equally dazed exchange, we met with the rabbi.

On the drive back to the house, Faye went the long way, deliberately avoiding—or maybe I was giving her too much credit—the very intersection where my mother had been killed. The silence in the car hung between us like a cloud. Faye and I had never been alone together, and the awkwardness mounted with each passing mile. I supposed I could have made small talk, but it was too much work.

I assumed she felt the same.

It was hard walking into the house, which bore little to no resemblance to the home I was raised in. Faye had covered up that life with new spring green wallpaper in the foyer and hallway, little floating teapots on the kitchen walls. She'd buried my mother's beautiful hardwood floors under wall-to-wall shag carpeting. The blue drapes I used to play hide and seek in were now lemon yellow with golden ties. The furniture was all different, except for my father's chair, a recliner, stationed before the TV in the family room. The seat cushions had taken on the contours of his backside and shoulders, and his scent—a combination of Old Spice and beef jerky—was woven into its nappy fabric.

I told Faye I had a headache and went upstairs to my old room at the end of the hall, which was now a sitting room with a Singer sewing machine set up in the corner and a daybed trying hard to be a sofa. It was depressing in there. Depressing everywhere. I didn't want to be in Youngstown and everything that mattered to me felt more than just a plane ride away. There was a princess phone on the side table and I thought about calling Helen to make sure she found her schedule for next week and to see if there was anything she needed. I thought about calling Trudy, too. And despite my best efforts not to even think about him, I considered calling Christopher. I wondered what he was doing at that very moment. Who he was with. Had he thought about me since that day in his darkroom?

I lay down on the daybed, trying to clear my mind, but it was no use. I knew when I caught myself thinking about Erik that I wasn't ready to deal with my father yet. Yes, I was there to lay him to rest, but as I closed my eyes, it was my mother who was everywhere. I swore I smelled the faint scent of her perfume, heard the soft murmur of her voice, like she was in the next room, talking with my father or maybe on the telephone. I remembered how she'd read to me at night, both of us squished together in my bed, under the covers, our toes touching, our heads sharing the pillow. I heard a dog barking outside and remembered the time she took in a stray, a beagle with a hurt paw. She cared for that dog, even named him Charlie, and cried three weeks later when his rightful owner came to claim him. There was a flood of other memories, too, like the times my friends weren't available so she'd grab a piece of chalk and draw a hop-scotch board on the driveway or when she would abandon what-ever she was making for dinner to sit on the kitchen floor and play jacks with me.

I heard a faint sound coming up through the floor vent—an

agonized whimpering. Faye must have been down in the kitchen. She was crying.

During the funeral, I kept thinking, *This is where a sibling or a cousin would come in handy.* Despite familiar faces—my father's golfing buddies, his clients and his coworkers at the foundry, and even some of my high school friends like Esther, whom I hadn't spoken to in over a year—I'd never felt more alone. All eyes were on me. I was on display, the poor little orphan child.

I looked down at the torn black ribbon pinned to my dress. I was seated next to Faye, and as the rabbi was speaking, I saw her tears hit her prayer book, landing on the Hebrew letters, rippling the page. I reached over and squeezed her hand. I told myself to go ahead and cry. Cry for my father, for my mother, too. But I couldn't bring myself to show even a fraction of the heartbreak wracking through my body. I was sure the onlookers found me strong and brave, or maybe callous as a stone, but even for the sake of putting on a good show, I couldn't give in to my sorrow. It ran too deep and I feared I would drown in it.

Faye wanted us to sit shiva, so the house was filled with people, there to pay their last respects. There was a woman I'd never seen before standing in the kitchen, wearing an apron with apples on the front pocket. She and the other women from the synagogue's Sisterhood—presumably Faye's friends—were milling about, preparing the food, slicing tomatoes, cucumbers and onions, carving turkey breast, corned beef and brisket. The woman in the apron spooned globs of creamed herring into a glass bowl while another woman with lipstick on her front teeth took a head count of bagels, touching each one, as if making sure they were all really there.

"Hope you're hungry," she said with a red-toothed smile.

Hungry? I couldn't have forced down a bite.

I went out to the living room and stopped, my feet unable to take another step. I felt a punch to the gut as Michael and his wife came through the front door. I hadn't expected to see him, let alone his wife, but such were the perils of a small town where everyone knew each other and felt obligated to pay shiva calls. I froze, wishing the floor would open up and swallow me whole.

Michael looked uncomfortable, even before our eyes met. The placing of his hand on my shoulder while trying to half hug, half kiss me would go down in history as one of life's most awkward moments. His wife's squeezing of my wrist—while holding her very pregnant belly—didn't go over much better.

"We're so sorry, Ali. Really, we are," Michael said.

The wife nodded emphatically, her honey-colored ringlets, like corkscrew noodles, bouncing on her shoulders. I don't remember what I said in response. All the blood was rushing through my ears. Little white stars were dancing about in my peripheral vision like right before you faint. That belly was right there—I had to say something. Had to acknowledge it.

"I see congratulations are in order. When are you due?"

"Oh, not for another five weeks." The way she said that *oh*, like she was trying to downplay it. No big deal, for fear I'd go to pieces in a fit of jealousy.

"So, New York City, huh?" Michael stuffed his hands in his pockets and did that nodding thing he sometimes did when he was nervous and didn't know what to say.

"Yeah, New York."

He looked around, still nodding, eventually asking how Faye was holding up. There was more small talk. He told me about his job at the accounting firm and that they'd bought the Mendelsohns' old house. He still got together with Aaron and the guys for poker on Friday nights.

The more he talked, the more I noticed that the angst I'd felt when I saw him and his wife was now leaving me. After we'd broken up, I'd thought about Michael often, too often. Memories, good and bad, tore so at my heart, that sometimes I could hardly breathe. Now I looked into his soft brown eyes and realized how very young and innocent we both were. How it never would have worked with us anyway. I couldn't have imagined myself married to him, still living in Youngstown.

Michael was talking now about his mother needing bunion surgery and soon it was obvious that we had nothing more to say. The pregnant wife hugged me and so did Michael.

"Again," he said, "I'm really sorry, Ali."

That was a loaded statement and I knew the *I'm sorry* was not just about my father's passing. It was also an apology for breaking my heart, but in truth, it hadn't been his fault. I'd given Michael too much power, and in the end, I think I broke my own heart, all by myself. As hard as it was getting over him, that pain and grief had forced me to start again. I'd seen and experienced more in the past few months than I had in all my years before that. Since my breakup with Michael and my leaving Youngstown, I'd had my own apartment, my first real job. I'd moved to a city where I knew no one and was making my way among the best of the best. There was a bigger world out there, and now I was part of that and I'd done it on my own. With that came confidence that no one could take from me. I hadn't realized how much I'd grown until that very moment. And it also occurred to me that it was no longer possible to deny something else that I'd been trying to push away. Since I'd been in New York, I'd discovered what it meant to really have a connection with a man. And it wasn't with Erik. It was with Christopher.

L ater that night, after the floor had been swept, the dishes had been dried and put away, the garbage taken out to the street, and the ladies from the Sisterhood were gone, it was just Faye and me. We were both exhausted and had changed out of our black dresses and into bathrobes. Actually, I had forgotten to pack one, so Faye loaned me one of hers, a soft white terry cloth that felt luxurious against my tired body. She'd made us tea with cinnamon sticks and set out a plate of *schnecken* that neither one of us would touch.

We sat at the dining room table with a box of my father's mementos, things she thought I might want to have: his Navy and Marine Corps ribbons, a sapphire pinky ring that I was surprised she hadn't wanted to keep, his diploma from Youngstown High and a wedding photo of my parents that he'd held on to, one I'd never seen before. The two of them were standing outside City Hall, arm in arm, cheeks pressed together.

A lump rose up in my throat and my voice cracked when I blurted out, "Did you know my parents had to get married?"

Faye took to stirring her tea. I thought she was avoiding the question until finally she said, "How did you find out?"

"You *did* know." I was still holding the photo.

She tapped the spoon against the lip of the cup, before gently placing it in the saucer. She looked up, her lips tightly pressed together, her nod barely perceivable.

I can't say why this bothered me—especially since I already knew it was true—but something about *her* knowing felt like a betrayal. "How long have you known?"

She cracked a reluctant smile. "About twenty-two years."

"What?"

"Alice, I think it's time we discuss a few things."

"What *things*?" I stared at the platter of *schnecken*, thinking they looked sickeningly sweet, my stomach roiling.

Faye folded and unfolded her napkin, stalling for a moment before she said, "I knew your father long before he ever met your mother."

"What?" This second *what* came out sharper, louder.

She got up from the table and busied herself at the sink. I saw her looking out the window. A light was coming from the garage next door, illuminating the basketball net. The sound of the neighbor's son dribbling the ball on the blacktop was steady as a heartbeat. With her back toward me, she said, "I bet you didn't know I grew up here in Youngstown. Born and raised. Your father and I were high school sweethearts."

"What?" There was no other word I could find.

She turned around and came back and sat at the table. "I know this is hard to hear but you asked about your parents, and well, I think you deserve to know the truth."

The truth? I clasped the side of my head. It was like something had exploded inside my skull.

"Your father and I were going to get married. But then the war came and he went off to fight. I waited for him, wrote him every day. But you see, when your father came home, he told me he'd met another woman. I thought she was in Europe—you heard about that sort of thing happening all the time. But it turned out she lived in New York City. He told me she was pregnant and that he was going to marry her. I knew he would do the right thing by her. That was just the type of man he was, and it's one of the reasons I always loved him so."

I swallowed hard. "And what about you? What happened to you after that?" Had they been carrying on in secret all these years?

"Well, naturally, I was devastated—just heartbroken, really. I couldn't bear to stay here in town with the two of them so I moved away and lived with my aunt in Columbus. Eventually I met Sid there—my first husband. He was older—twelve years older than me. But he was a good man. Kind. Very bright. An engineer. We had a nice life together. No children but still it was a good life.

"When I heard the news that your mother died, I was still a married woman. And I loved my husband, so I never contacted your father. But then about two years ago, I lost Sid. That was when your father called me." She got up from the table again and stood at the stove. The light was out next door. All was quiet, no more basketball dribbling. "Would you like another?" she asked, holding up her cup.

"So did he ever love my mother?" I knew Faye was the last person I should have asked, but there was no one else left and I needed to know.

She sat back down. "Oh, sure. Of course he loved her. It was a different kind of love than what we had—but you have to understand, your father and I were so young. Ours was an innocent love. We had no problems. Not until the war and your father met your mother. But yes, he loved her. Very much. And they both loved you. Your parents were good for each other. As different as they were—your mother, the big-city gal, him, just a small-town fellow—but still they were good together. I know he was beside himself when she died."

If ever I was going to cry, it was just then, but I blinked, clearing my tears away.

Faye got back up, went to the stove and prepared two more cups of tea. All this time, I'd had no idea about my father and her. I thought she was just another casserole-bearing widow looking to swoop in and land a husband. I felt I owed her an enormous apology, and as I was trying to compose my words, she came back to the table with two steaming cups and set them down.

"You know," she said before I could get started, "there's

something else—I don't know, maybe I shouldn't even bring it up. Your father went back and forth, trying to decide whether or not to tell you, but you're a grown woman and—"

"What is it?"

"It has to do with your mother's family." I heard the reservation in her voice.

"Her family?" I clutched my cup, too hot to hold, but still I couldn't let go.

"You see, when your mother got pregnant, it was very upsetting for her family. Her father was a prominent judge and, well, they just wouldn't stand for it. They disowned her. Just like that." She brushed one hand off the other. "Completely wrote her off. The whole family did. Your father tried to make it right with them, but they wouldn't give him the time of day. I was told your grandfather sat shiva for a week after he threw your mother out."

Something Elaine Sloan said about my mother's father being a *real shit* came rushing back to me.

Faye cleared her throat and continued with what I thought was a non sequitur. "You know I never had any children. And like you, I was an only child and my parents are both gone. I know what loneliness is. I know how important it is to have family. I realize you don't think of me as family and I understand, but—and as I said, maybe I shouldn't be telling you all this, but you're a grown woman now. I think you have a right to know."

"Know what?"

"You were always told that your mother's parents died before you were born, but . . ."

"But? But what?" I could feel my eyes growing wider, urging her to get on with it.

"Alice, sweetheart, your mother's parents . . ." She sighed. "I don't even know where to begin." She shook her head. "They didn't die. At least if they did, it wasn't before you were born.

They were alive. Presumably they still are." She reached into the box and pulled out a tattered address book. "Your grandparents live in Stamford, Connecticut. Or at least they did." She opened the address book to a page yellowed and stained with a coffee ring. "This is the last address your father had for them. I believe it's the same home your mother grew up in."

I sat there, speechless.

"I honestly don't know how they would react if you were to contact them, but I know that what happened between them was a long, long time ago. People mellow. They change. And well, I didn't want you to leave here without knowing that you're not alone. You do have a family."

And those were the words that unlocked the floodgates. Before I could stop myself, my eyes glazed over and the tears let loose. I cried so hard I couldn't catch my breath, and when Faye got up from her chair and came over to wrap her arms around me, I collapsed into her embrace and cried even harder.

"I didn't know about you and my dad," I said, bawling into her shoulder, feeling guilty for being so cold and indifferent to her all this time.

"Shssh." She held me close and collected all my heartache. "Shsssh."

I sat there blubbering, crying for my mother, for my father, and for the first time in years, I cried for myself. And when all my crying was done, and I was drained and drying my eyes, I felt a certain grace, or lightness, come over me. It was a shift that I couldn't explain, but I knew something inside me was different. I'd finally released the weight of my unshed tears.

CHAPTER THIRTY

○—————○

I took a morning flight, and when I arrived at LaGuardia one week later, I was relieved to be back in New York. It didn't exactly feel like home, but then again, I was a stray with no real place to call home anymore. Still, I relished the chaos and the bustle of Manhattan. It helped drown out all the noise inside my head.

Ever since Faye told me about her past with my father and about my mother's family, I'd been emotionally messy. Without warning, I would burst out crying. Wherever I went, clumps of damp tissues seemed to sprout up. It was as if I was making up for all those years of holding everything inside.

On the flight home, I forced myself to look onward, toward the future. I knew my father had left me a little money, and I had decided that I would use some of it to buy a new camera, a Nikon, like the one Christopher used, and a handsome leather portfolio. I was also going to finally work up the courage to take a photography class. I was ready now to put my work to the test, and surely Helen would understand if I needed to leave work on time once a week for a night class. Surely she would.

I went to the baggage claim and got my suitcase, lugging it along, inching forward in the taxicab line. As we were leaving the airport, traffic slowed to a crawl. The taxi driver switched the station on the radio and the song "You'll Never Walk Alone" came on. I'd heard that song a thousand times but never really listened to the words. When it got to the chorus and the music swelled, my eyes misted up. Through my blurred vision, I saw the signs for the turnoff to the Long Island Grand Central Parkway. Something snapped and pure impulse took over.

"Driver"—I leaned forward toward the clouded cutout window—"change of plans. I'm going to Stamford instead." I reached into my pocketbook and read off the address I'd copied out of my father's old address book.

I didn't know if this was the smartest thing I'd ever done or the stupidest. Maybe I was looking for some sort of resolution, or maybe I was a glutton, looking to punish myself. All I knew was that ever since Faye told me about my mother's parents, I'd begun thinking of myself as illegitimate. The realization that her family had been out there all along and had never once tried to find me made me feel dirty, worthless and unwanted. Unlovable.

Maybe I should have telephoned first but there was a sense of urgency, that if ever I was going to confront them, it had to be now. My cab crossed the Bronx-Whitestone Bridge stretching over the East River, the Manhattan skyline to my left. The roads were winding and tree lined, their overarching branches forming a canopy. Foliage and ravines rolled away in the distance, and out my window, I saw the tracks of the New Haven Railroad—the same train my mother used to take into the city, the very train I would be taking back into town, since this taxicab ride was going to wipe me out. The meter was ticking higher and higher, already up to $6.75.

We passed exits for New Rochelle, the New York State Thruway, past White Plains and Rye before we came to Stamford, lush and green with rolling hills. The homes were getting more majestic by the block. I knew my mother's father had been a successful judge, but never would I have imagined her growing up in such opulence.

We pulled onto Long Ridge Road and my heart began beating twice as fast. It was too late to turn back, and I hadn't a clue of what to say, what to do. The cab turned into a long curvy drive leading to a grand Victorian house that looked like it belonged on a postcard with its mansard roof, wraparound porch, all the spindles and a three-car garage.

With my suitcase in tow, I made my way up to the front door and took a deep breath before reaching for the brass knocker. It felt like I was waiting for an eternity, my palms sweating, heart racing. At last the door opened and a tall, graceful older woman with clear blue eyes, translucent skin and perfectly coiffed dark hair stood before me. Here she was, the source of my mother's beauty.

She stared at me, dumbstruck. The look on her face was one of a ghost's sighting. I'd always known I strongly resembled my mother but this confirmed it. As she looked at me, one manicured hand went to her mouth, the other to her chest.

"I'm Alice," I said. "Vivian's daughter. May I come in?"

I'm not sure if she said anything, but she stepped aside and I took that as my invitation to enter her home. As we stood in her marble foyer, beneath a spectacular chandelier, I began to take in the rest of her—the cashmere sweater, the gray wool slacks, the diamond earrings and creamy pearls about her neck. In silence, I followed her into an elegant living room with an enormous fireplace, the mantel lined with photographs. I wanted to study them, but she gestured toward the Queen Anne settee, asking if I wanted coffee or tea, which, no doubt, would have been served in fine china, on a silver tray.

With no indication of whether she was pleased or about to throw me out, she said, "What brings you here, Alison?"

"It's Alice. My mother, she called me Ali." I felt horrible correcting her but even worse that she didn't know my name to begin with.

"Well, Alice, I'm Ruth." She smiled, placing a hand over her heart, and with the first bit of warmth I'd felt from her, she said, "I suppose this makes me your grandmother."

I nodded and we both gave off the same queer-sounding laugh. The awkwardness lingered for another moment or two until she sat back and asked me about myself. I explained that I was living in New York, working for *Cosmopolitan* magazine. I told her that I'd just come from my father's funeral and how Faye had told me everything and given me her address.

"Well, I doubt she told you *everything*," she said, picking an imaginary piece of lint off her slacks. "But my goodness, you have been through a lot, haven't you?"

More silence. I was beginning to think this was a huge mistake.

"Is your husband still alive?" I asked tentatively.

"The judge? Oh, yes. He's not well, though," she said, shaking her head. "Dementia. Hardening of the arteries. He doesn't remember the accident. For the most part, I don't think he realizes that Vivian is gone." She hesitated for a moment, asking again if I wanted a cup of coffee. Another moment passed. "I'm afraid I'm at a loss here," she said. "You've caught me by surprise."

"I realize that. I'm sorry. Until an hour ago, I didn't know I was going to come here, either."

She reached up, twisted one of her diamond earrings. Everything about this encounter was strained and I was about to apologize for the intrusion and make my exit when she said, "You must think we're terrible people. I suppose you've heard what happened between your mother and her father?"

"Bits and pieces. I have a feeling there's more."

"There's always more," she said with a sad smile. "Honestly, when Viv came and told us she was pregnant, we didn't know what to do. It wasn't the sort of thing we'd ever expected to hear. I wanted to send her somewhere. There was a home in Vermont for unwed mothers, but the judge wouldn't hear of it. He was very proud. Very stubborn." She squeezed her eyes shut, the faint lines in her face suddenly growing deeper. "Oh, the yelling that went on. You can't imagine the terrible things the two of them said to each other. It was awful. People who love each other should never talk like that. He was a bear back then. Headstrong and so hard on her. When he told her to get out, I was sick inside. I tried but I couldn't reason with him. No one could. But believe me, he suffered over what he did to Vivian. Oh, how he came to regret that. And by the time he was ready to make amends, it was too late. We heard about the accident from her friend Elaine."

So Elaine knew. Of course she knew the truth. This explained some of the odd things she'd said to me, or had tried to say.

"So many times I wanted to reach out to your mother and, then, out to you, but Morris, he wouldn't allow it."

"You mean you wanted to find me?"

She looked surprised. "My goodness, you're my daughter's child. You're my blood."

Without warning, her words broke me. I sobbed when she said that. Just bawled into my hands. She reached over and gave me a delicate monogrammed handkerchief. I kept apologizing and she kept hushing me as I dried my eyes.

After another awkward, agonizing silence, she said, "I'll bet Vivian was a wonderful mother."

That ushered in another wave of tears, and through glassy eyes, I looked at the photograph on the end table. It was a grainy black-and-white of four girls, all close in age, sitting on what very well could have been the same settee we were seated on just then. "Is that her?" I asked, pointing to the one in the middle. They were all pretty girls, but my mother had a different kind of beauty. She had something magical, even back then.

Ruth picked up the photo and sat next to me. "That's her with her sisters—"

"Sisters?"

"Your aunts, I suppose. That's Laurel, Sylvia and Muriel."

Aunts? I have aunts!

"This was hard on them, too," she said. "They wanted to stay in touch with Viv—I think Laurel might have written to her once or twice, but that was it. Their father forbade it. The girls were scared of him. We all were, I suppose."

"Are they still . . ."

She nodded. "Laurel is in New York. Married with a daughter, about your age. That's her." She reached for another photograph. "That's Susan. And Sylvia"—she returned to the photo of the sisters—"she's in Greenwich. She has a daughter and two boys. And Muriel is in White Plains. Married with three boys." She smiled, got up and pointed to another photo on the mantel. "These little rascals are your other cousins."

Just then an older man with stooped shoulders, black bushy eyebrows and a full head of snow-white hair shuffled into the living room. So this was him, the beast. The almighty judge.

"Who's here? Who's"—he stopped, mouth open a good ten seconds before he spoke—"Vivian? What are you doing here?"

"I'm Alice. Ali. Vivian's daughter."

"Morris, go back in the study and sit down."

But he didn't budge. Ruth turned to me, speaking softly. "His memory goes in and out. He gets confused." She turned back to him. "Did you hear me, Morris? Go back and sit down."

But instead the judge came closer. "Vivian." He sounded be-wildered. His eyes were cloudy with cataracts.

"This is Alice," said Ruth, speaking loudly again, as if he were also hard of hearing. "This is Vivian's daughter."

"Oh, Vivian." He shook his head as his hands reached out to me, his grip surprisingly strong for someone who looked so frail. "My God," he said, pulling me in now and hugging me. "My God. My God," he said, his voice cracking.

My first instinct was to back away. I was so overwhelmed, I couldn't breathe. My arms were out to my sides, flailing. I didn't know what to do with them. "I'm not Viv—"

"Let me look at you. Oh, Vivian. Oh, my God. What took you so long? Where have you been?" He cupped my face and I looked at Ruth, pleading with my eyes, asking what to do. It seemed cruel to let him think I was his daughter but his wife wasn't stop-ping him. He still had hold of my face. "I didn't know if I'd ever see you again. I really didn't know. The whole thing got so out of hand. I don't know how it got so . . ." His voice trailed off, and just when I thought I'd lost him, he came back with, "Do you under-stand what I'm trying to say here? Do you?"

I nodded, realizing that this was a stubborn, proud man's way of apologizing and I was helping to mend a deep tear between a father and his daughter. He was crying now and so was I. By the time I'd composed myself, the judge had slipped back into a fog and I was a random stranger who'd turned up on their doorstep.

Ruth sent him back to his study and he called out in a gruff voice, "Tell whoever it is that we're not interested."

Two cups of coffee later, it was time to say good-bye to Ruth. When I asked for directions to the train station, she said, "Non-sense. You can't take the train at this hour. We'll call you a cab."

"That's just it," I said, stammering. "I, ah, I didn't bring enough—"

"Oh, Ali, why didn't you say something?" She went to a canister in her kitchen and took out two $20 bills, pressing them into my hand and hushing me when I tried to refuse. I was reminded of my father saying, *I think you dropped this.*

When the cab pulled up, the headlights shining through the big bay window where we were watching for him, she said, "I hope this isn't good-bye."

"I hope not, too."

She surprised me then, when she reached out and hugged me.

At first I was afraid to hug her back, afraid I might never let go.

Still holding me in her embrace, her floral perfume circling around me, she whispered in my ear, "Forgive us, won't you?"

I nodded, a fresh lump forming in my throat.

The taxi driver honked and I said one last good-bye.

When my cab reached the New York State Thruway, the driver paid the toll and looked at me through the rearview mirror. "Miss? I can't tell if you're laughing or crying back there. Are you okay?"

I smiled as I ran my hand across my blurring eyes. "I'm okay," I said. "I'm actually just fine."

CHAPTER THIRTY-ONE

○——————○

I was back at *Cosmo* the next day, astonished by the amount of work that had accumulated in the week I'd been gone, everything from fan mail and arranging another advertising luncheon at 21 to picking up Helen's Piaget watch from the jeweler and taking her pumps to the shoe repair.

A new girl named Thelma from a temporary service was at Bridget's desk outside Bill Guy's office. This was the third temp they'd sent since Bridget was fired. Thelma was heavyset, with rumpled brown hair like corrugated cardboard. She was friendly but not terribly resourceful, asking me where the mailroom and copy machine were, how to operate the coffeemaker and what time she should take lunch.

If I'd approached my job that way, I wouldn't have lasted a day as Helen's secretary. In fact, when Helen saw me that morning, the first thing she did was rush over, wrap her slender arms around me and say, "Alice Weiss, am I ever glad to see you." Those were the exact words she'd said the day I interviewed to be her secretary and I admit it was nice to be needed.

Later that day I was in Helen's office, going through some correspondence, when Richard Berlin, Dick Deems and Frank Dupuy showed up unexpectedly. I checked her schedule, thinking I'd missed it earlier when we'd reviewed her itinerary for the day. But Helen didn't seem thrown by the interruption.

"Boys," she said, smiling, waving them in from her spot on the sofa. "To what do I owe the pleasure of your company?"

"We need to talk about August before it goes to press," said Berlin.

"Oh, dear, what have I done this time?" She laughed. "If this is about the cover price, I'm insisting we raise it. I don't think 50¢ an issue is too much, and with our budget, 35¢ an—"

"It's not just the cover price," said Berlin. "We have some other real concerns—"

"Oh, Richard, you *always* have concerns. I think I've proven to you that I know what I'm doing."

"Well," said Berlin, "that might be up for debate."

"Excuse me?" She sat up straighter, her bare feet reaching for the floor. "What are you talking about? You know the sales numbers."

"Yes, but what if July was a lucky break?" said Deems.

"That's what we're hearing from people," said Dupuy. "That it was just a lucky break."

"Naturally, people were curious when July came out," Deems went on to explain. "They bought the magazine because they wanted to see what you were up to."

"But now," said Dupuy, "the big question is, *Will shocking us again in August work a second time?*"

"Wait a minute." Helen was on her feet, clutching a throw pillow so tightly I could see the seams straining. "Ad revenue is up. Sales are up. What more do you fellas want?"

"We've received very mixed reactions from advertisers. So—"

"So what?"

"So we've decided to change the August cover back to Sean Connery."

"What? But we already agreed—you can't put a man on the cover. You just can't. Especially not now," Helen screeched, her fingers turning white.

"It's already been finalized," said Berlin. "We're not putting another woman on the cover like the one you had for July."

"But that's the plan. We're already working on the covers for the next three months. You have to put a girl on the cover. You just have to."

"I'm sorry, but July was too risqué for our readers."

"They're not *your readers* anymore. They're *my girls*," she said with a burst of fury, ripping the pillow apart, sending a spurt of feathers into the air. "They're *my girls*," she repeated, flinging the ruptured pillow aside, "and I know what they want to read."

"If I were you," said Berlin, "I'd calm down and get back to work."

After the men walked out of her office, Helen slammed the door, stirring up the mound of feathers on the floor. "I can't believe this," she said, swatting a quill from her face. "I simply can't believe this is happening. I'm back to square one." She sat back down on the sofa and cradled her head in her hands. "Now I have to prove myself all over again."

Helen had barely recovered from that before I had to pack her up and get her to a public relations meeting across town. While she was out, I was typing up a memo to Richard Berlin when the receptionist buzzed me, putting a call through from Francesco Scavullo. I assumed he was calling to discuss the October cover shoot with Helen, which was now hanging in limbo.

"Hello, Mr. Scavullo," I said, continuing to type. "I'm afraid she's out of the office, but I expect her back in about forty-five minutes. Shall I have her call you?"

"Ah, actually, no," he said, adopting a mischievous tone, which was nothing unusual for him. Francesco Scavullo always sounded like he was up to something. "I was calling to talk to you. Do you think you could drop by my studio later today?"

I figured he had some layouts for October that he wanted me to bring back to Helen. I'd been wanting to see his studio anyway. Plus, I was thinking I could ask him for recommendations on photography classes.

"I'm here all day," he said. "You can come by anytime. You have the address, right?"

It was half past three when I went to Scavullo's studio. He lived and worked in an impressive four-story carriage house on the corner of East 58th Street and Third Avenue with a variegated brick exterior and a tympanum over the keystone doorway. He answered the door and it was the first time I'd seen him without a hat. His dark mane was combed straight back, shiny from hair tonic.

"I'll give you a tour later," he said, leading me into his studio, which occupied the entire first level. It was floor-to-ceiling white with a circular five-panel bow window that let in a wide band of sunlight. Tripods, light stands and white umbrellas were still stationed about the room, probably left there from that day's shoot. He offered me a cup of espresso and gestured toward a couple directors' chairs positioned by a bolt of muslin fabric leaning against the wall.

"So you're probably wondering why I wanted to see you, huh?"

"Let me guess. The October cover?"

"Not even close. I'm looking for an assistant, Alice. I think you'd be perfect for the job."

"Me?"

"Yes, you. I was asking around about you, and Christopher Mack says you have a good eye. He said you helped him out on a shoot at the Armory."

My first thought was Helen. "But I'm—I already have a job."

"I know. But I also know you want to be a photographer. And I've seen how you take care of Helen."

I twisted my hands in my lap. I didn't know what to say.

"But I have to tell you," he went on, "it's a terrible, thankless position that I'm offering you. And I don't know if you've heard, but I'm moody as hell." He laughed.

I was still thinking of Helen but curious enough to ask for details. "So, ah, what all would you have your assistant do?"

"Everything," His hands flapped forward as he rolled his dark eyes. "Everything shy of washing my shorts," he said, laughing again. "You'd hate most of it. You'd be sweeping floors, getting lunch, answering the phone. And the door." He cocked his head to the side as if trying to get a bead on me. "Oh, and espresso. You need to make sure I always have espresso on hand."

I tried not to show how unappealing that all sounded. I had no intention of leaving Helen anyway—especially not for that kind of work.

"I'd also have you coordinate the wardrobe deliveries, schedule the makeup artists and hairdressers. You'd be running my errands, running to the photo lab." He paused again, trying to get me to look him in the eye. "And of course," he said, changing up his tone, "there's a few other things like sitting in on pre-pro meetings with clients, setting lights, taking meter readings, and naturally, you'd be my backup shooter."

Francesco Scavullo's backup shooter? Me!

"Oh, and I'd pay you, too," he said with a charming chuckle. "How does $85 a week sound?"

I couldn't believe what I was hearing. Now his offer seemed too good to be true. *The money, a chance to do some actual shooting . . .*

He smiled, knowing he'd piqued my interest. "Alice, this is a way to get started on your own career. I was an assistant to Horst P. Horst for years, you know. He was my mentor."

Though it sounded like my dream job, I already knew I couldn't possibly leave Helen. Especially not after what had just happened earlier with Berlin and his men. Not when she was heartsick over the August cover and the controversial articles she would surely have to cut. I couldn't imagine what would happen if I left and they replaced me with someone like Thelma. As much as I wanted to work for Francesco Scavullo, I knew I couldn't desert Helen.

I should have said thanks but no thanks but what came out instead was, "Can I take some time to think about it?"

Thinking about working for Francesco Scavullo was all I did for the rest of the week, and yet I'd already made my decision. The timing was wrong. If only he'd come to me six months or a year from now, when Helen and *Cosmo* would be on solid ground, then *maybe*, just maybe, I'd consider it.

Looking back, I'm not sure why I saw myself as indispensable. It was quite arrogant of me, thinking Helen couldn't function without me. But that was my mind-set. Plus, she'd given me my start. I felt I owed it to her to stay.

It was the first Friday evening after I was back in town and I was having dinner with Elaine. She had invited me over to see how I was holding up after my father's funeral, which, given everything else going on, felt like it had happened ages ago.

Over cocktails in her living room, I told Elaine about my conversation with Faye and about meeting Ruth and the judge. I still couldn't quite bring myself to call them my grandparents.

"I hope you understand why I never said anything." Elaine opened a silver box on the coffee table, took out a cigarette and lit it. I hadn't responded to that, but it didn't stop her from elaborating. "I felt so horrible when I told you about your mother's pregnancy. I hope you understand why I didn't say anything more about her parents. I knew Viv did whatever she could to shield you from all that. I just didn't feel it was my place to tell you and I'd already said more than I should have."

I told her I understood, though I wasn't entirely sure I did. When I thought back on some of our conversations, it would have been so simple, so natural, for her to have told me the truth. But—and partly because I was so fond of Elaine and partly because I was tired of rehashing it all—I didn't make a fuss.

We thankfully moved on to other subjects and Elaine made up a fresh batch of martinis and set out a platter of cheese, rich duck pâté and slices of crusty French bread. She was telling me about her July Fourth holiday and how she'd been stranded on a friend's sailboat. "Coming about," she said with a laugh, "I couldn't wait to get back on dry land."

One thing I'd come to notice about Elaine was that a second martini always made her chatty. Now she was encouraging me to see *The Glass Menagerie*. "It's still at the Brooks Atkinson Theatre and it's just wonderful."

We talked some more and at one point she asked how work was going. I hesitated, hemmed and hawed before I finished my drink and just came out and told her about Scavullo's offer.

"Well, that's fantastic, Ali. That's just wonderful. Good for you. When are you going to start?"

"Start? Oh, no, I can't accept the job. I can't leave Helen. Not now. Did I tell you that she's back to square one with Hearst?"

"Well, I'm not surprised about that."

"But they're acting like the July issue never happened. She sold a quarter of a million copies more than their June issue. You'd think Hearst would trust her now. But they're treating her like a novice again. Challenging her on every article, every photograph, even the upcoming covers."

The covers. That made me think about Scavullo's offer again.

"Well," said Elaine, "that's what we women have to do. But don't you worry about Helen. She's a big girl. She can take care of herself."

I was sitting with that when her house phone rang. "Yes," she said. "Send him up."

My second martini was hitting me when the doorbell chimed. "To be continued." She sprang up off the sofa and headed to the foyer, saying in a coquettish voice, "Now I wonder *who* that could be?"

She came back smiling, her arm looped through Christopher's. I sat up, sober, my heart suddenly racing. He looked suntanned, his hair slightly rumpled, his eyes giving him away, for he seemed just as surprised to see me. And yet I knew it was no accident. I felt like I'd stepped into a chapter of *Great Expectations*, only the roles were reversed—I was Pip, Christopher was Estella, and Elaine was Miss Havisham, lumping us together for her own amusement, just to watch the sparks. In an instant I was filled with full-on longing and angst. I could admit it now—I wanted this man. But *how*? How could we move from being friends to something more? And was that what he wanted, or was it all on me?

Elaine strategically disappeared into the kitchen. "Be right back," she said. "Just checking on dinner." But she was gone for a long time, leaving Christopher and me alone.

"I'm sorry about your father," he said. "I tried calling but you'd already left town. I didn't even know you were back yet. You doing okay?"

"Depends on when you ask me. Right now, at this very moment, yeah, I'm doing okay."

He reached over and tucked a lock of hair behind my ear, and I could have dropped into his arms and sobbed. Instead I took another sip of my martini, feeling vulnerable. And terrified. There was no turning back for me now. Even if I didn't act on these feelings for him, they were still there. They would always be there.

There was a long, awkward silence.

"Elaine?" I called out. "Do you need help in there?"

"No. No, I'm fine," she said back. "You two visit. I'll be right out."

But she didn't come right out. And to fill the lingering silence, I told him about the job offer.

"Frank Scavullo's assistant, wow. Good for you. That's a great opportunity. When do you start?"

He sounded just like Elaine. "No, no, I'm not taking it."

"What? Are you crazy? Why not?"

I didn't know how to begin to explain my attachment to Helen, and thankfully I didn't have to, because Elaine came back out with a butcher's apron tied about her waist. She brushed her hair off her forehead with the back of her wrist and took a long sip of her martini. "Dinner is served."

She had prepared the same pasta dish she'd made for me before.

"Can I tell him about your big news?" Elaine asked.

"Scavullo?" Christopher reached for the bottle of wine and refilled all our glasses. "She told me. She also told me she's not taking it."

"Oh, I know. I think she's foolish not to take the job. Maybe you can get through to her," she said to him, talking about me as if I wasn't there. "I told her Helen would understand."

"But *you* don't understand," I said, feeling a bit tipsy from the martinis followed by the wine. "I can't just up and quit on Helen. I haven't even been there four months yet."

Elaine tossed her napkin onto her plate and opened a second bottle of Chablis.

We moved into the living room and Elaine told us about a new book she was editing along with a few new Jackie Susann stories. After we'd polished off the wine, I offered to help clean up, but Elaine, in her not so subtle way, insisted I stop clearing the dishes and suggested that Christopher walk me out and see to it that I got home okay.

"Should we get you a cab?" he asked when we stepped outside the Dakota.

"Actually, I wouldn't mind walking for a bit."

"Well, you know Elaine'll never forgive me if I don't walk with you." He smiled, that eyetooth of his killing me. "It's a nice night and I could use the walk after all that wine."

I always enjoyed Christopher's company but there was something special about being alone with him that night. We were walking down the street, the moon peeking in and out from behind the clouds. Our hands hung at our sides, fingers less than an inch apart. Every so often our shoulders and arms touched, like they had a million times before, but tonight, we were aware of the contact and quickly withdrew, like our limbs were giving off shocks.

After about twenty minutes, we grabbed a cab.

"I think you should reconsider the job offer," he said. "Opportunities like this don't come along all that often. I started as an assistant. Almost every photographer I know did. That's the best way to get your foot in the door. And this is Frank Scavullo we're talking about."

"I know, but I can't. Not now. I just can't leave Helen." I looked out the window as we pulled up to the butcher shop. "Well, here we are."

Christopher surprised me when he got out and walked me to my door. My pulse quickened, even when he said, all businesslike, "Just promise me you'll think about the job offer."

I nodded and we looked at each other for a moment that seemed to hang forever. A streetlamp overhead created a soft glow around us. My heart was pounding. This was the moment. If ever something was going to happen between us, it was now.

"Well," he said for the sake of filling the silence.

Kiss him, I told myself. *Just kiss him.*

"Well," he said again, "meter's running. I should get going." He took a half step backward, breaking the spell. As he reached for the cab door, he turned around and said, "I'm glad you're back. If you need anything, call me."

I watched him get back in the taxi and pull away. My heart was sinking fast. I'd blown it.

CHAPTER THIRTY-TWO

○———○

The next day I woke up with a hangover. My head was throbbing, my eyes burned, my stomach was queasy. I needed coffee and some greasy eggs and hash browns. I was hoping to go to the Candy Shop with Trudy but she wasn't around. My guess was that she'd stayed over at Milton's place again. So I went to the diner on my own and took my camera with me.

After breakfast my head was a little clearer, and I wandered about the Upper East Side, finding myself on Park Avenue, near Erik's building with its blue awning and the doorman in his pristine uniform with the gold epaulettes. I stood on the sidewalk for a moment, admiring the flower boxes up and down the avenue as a woman who looked like she took tea at the Waldorf strolled by with her French poodle. It was all so perfect, so glamorous, so New York. It was all that I had fantasized about back in Youngstown. But I knew the city now and I knew myself better, too. Truth was, I didn't belong on Park Avenue.

Eventually I cut over on 68th Street and went to the subway, and twenty minutes later, quite possibly by design—or the workings of my subconscious—I found myself down in the Village. It was a steamy, hot July day. Gauze-like clouds overhead did little to offer shade. The entire city was sweltering, giving off strong smells, pockets of urine and then, a block over, the scent of garlic roasting. Windows and doorways were thrown open, fans on the apartment building ledges. Bees and flies hovered over the garbage cans on the sidewalks. All the outdoor cafés were packed, people sitting under umbrellas, girls with bare arms, wearing sandals.

Since I had decided that I wasn't going to take the job with Francesco, I'd promised myself that despite whatever demands Helen made, I would still carve out time each week for picture taking in addition to taking a class.

I was down on St. Mark's Place, my camera swinging at my side from its shoulder strap. I was thinking about Christopher and the way the tips of his hair caught in his lashes. I scolded myself again for not kissing him when I'd had the chance. I kept coming back to the same place in my mind: All this emotion and intensity I felt for him couldn't have been one-sided. He had to have been feeling it, too.

As I moved faster and faster down the sidewalk, I found myself on First Avenue. I felt like the planchette on a Ouija board, an invisible force moving me to a place I'd been to only once before. I looked through the stained-glass window on the door as I rang the buzzer. I had no idea what I was going to say or do, I just knew that I wasn't willing to give up. I was drawn to this man, so drawn to him that I was willing to risk getting my heart broken.

I heard the front door buzzer sound and I stepped inside. Before I even knocked, the studio door swung open. Christopher looked stunned to see me. And why wouldn't he have been?

"Ali? What are you doing here? Is everything okay?" He was standing in the doorway, bare-chested, jeans hoisted up on his hips, the top button undone, and hair rumpled like I'd woken him from a sound sleep.

"I was just in the neighborhood. Thought maybe we'd do some shooting today? It's beautiful out."

He eyed me for a moment, not saying anything, and when he blinked, his lashes stirred the tips of his hair. He cracked a small smile and that was all the encouragement I needed. I wasn't going to let another chance pass me by. He opened his mouth to say something and that's when I leaned in and kissed him.

He took a half step back and the look on his face stopped me cold. I saw a shadow moving behind him in the doorway. My heart dropped to my stomach as the figure came into focus. It was Daphne, standing there in one of his shirts, her endlessly long legs bare and holding their ground.

bolted. I don't remember what—if anything—Christopher said or did. I ran blindly down the sidewalk, my camera bobbing at my side as I tried to distance myself from him. I sprinted past storefronts and buildings, running into intersections, dodging cars and taxis blasting their horns, drivers cursing at me. I didn't care. I kept running, pushing past all resistance inside me. I was so overwhelmed I hadn't yet felt the pain, but I knew it was chasing me, soon to catch up.

The sun was scorching down on me, and when I couldn't take the heat any longer, I ducked into a café on Greenwich Avenue, panting and sweating. I felt like my body was dragging behind me. Thankfully it was dark inside and I stood beneath the ceiling fan, windmilling on high. Someone behind the long mahogany counter called to me, asking what I wanted. I shuffled forward, swatting a fly away from my face. I ordered a glass of cheap red wine, a sickening choice on such a sweltering day, but I couldn't think of anything that was going to make me feel better. I stood, waiting for my drink, and tried to keep from thinking. I concentrated on my surroundings: the cash register, the shelves lined with coffee mugs, canisters of tea, wine bottles and pastries resting under glass domes. Gazing at the wooden staircase leading to the second floor, I had a strong sense of déjà vu. And it wasn't until I took my wine upstairs and saw the yellowing maps on the wall and the hodgepodge of antique chairs and desks that I realized I'd been there before. With Trudy. It was Caffe Dell'Artista. A couple was sitting by the window in the spot where we'd been seated that day back in March.

I took the only empty table. It was in the middle of the room. I drank two long glugs of wine, which immediately gave me heartburn. Now that I'd stopped moving, the pain was seeping in. *The one time I work up the courage to let him know how I feel, this is what happens.* It was like someone had kicked me in the gut. My chest was tight and my hangover from that morning was back in full bloom. There was so much noise inside my head. I rubbed my temples, thinking *water.* I needed water. I took another gulp of wine. Given the many tears I'd shed lately, I was surprised I wasn't crying, and perhaps I would have been if I hadn't been sitting on display in the middle of a café.

So Christopher didn't want me and that cut. Cut deep. This very feeling—the rejection—was what I'd been avoiding and protecting myself from. I'd been so terrified of *this,* certain that it would be more than I could handle. But now it seemed that the fear, the anticipation of the pain, was greater than the actual pain itself. Amazingly enough, I was still breathing. I'd been through worse, and some kernel of strength that I didn't know was inside me said I would be okay. That yes, in time, I would be fine. *This, too, shall pass.*

The couple by the window got up from their table and after a busboy cleared their dishes, I went and sat in their spot, the chair still warm from where the man had been sitting. I took another sip of wine and that moment in Christopher's doorway, just before I'd humiliated myself, came rushing back to me. I didn't want to think about it, didn't want to torture myself any more.

To distract myself, I opened the drawer filled with scraps of papers, napkins and cards. All kinds of new quotes, love letters and, yes, there, somewhere in the middle, mixed in with all the others, I found the declaration Trudy and I had made. It was on a napkin, creased in half, the ink a bit smudged here and there: *On this day, Sunday, March 28, 1965, Trudy Lewis and Alice Weiss declare that they will follow their dreams. No matter what. Miss Lewis will pursue a career as an architect and Miss Weiss will become a world-renowned photographer.*

I studied the napkin and drank more wine. It seemed like a lifetime ago that we'd made that pledge to ourselves. Trudy, who'd thought the whole thing was nonsense, was actually working now in an architectural firm. She was enrolling in night classes at The New School that fall. She was pursuing her dream.

I set the napkin aside and reached for my camera, running my fingers over the worn leather case. What was I waiting for? What was I so afraid of? Yes, the competition in New York was steep but where was my faith in myself? Was I hiding behind Helen and this absurd notion that she needed me, that she couldn't be Helen Gurley Brown without me? Christopher was gone now. I'd blown everything, including our friendship, but I still had a bigger dream out there waiting for me. I had made a new life for myself here in New York, and just maybe it was time I actually started to live it.

I looked at the declaration again before I folded the napkin and put it back in the drawer.

I finished off my wine and went downstairs to use the pay phone. While riffling through the tissue-like pages of the telephone book, I heard people calling out orders in the kitchen, the sounds of dishes clattering. I found the number, dropped a dime through the coin slot and dialed. On the fifth ring, he answered.

"Mr. Scavullo? It's me, Alice. Alice Weiss. If the offer's still good—that is, if you're still looking for a photography assistant—I want the job. I want to come work for you."

I should have been happy. I should have been out celebrating my new job. Instead, I spent that Sunday sleeping and punishing myself for kissing Christopher. And when I wasn't thinking about that, I was rehearsing what I was going to say to Helen.

When Monday morning arrived, my nerves were frayed. As I walked through the revolving door where it all began and headed for the elevator, my pulse raced. I stepped into the lobby, which looked much better—thanks to Helen's influence—than it had the first day I'd walked through those doors.

It was still early. The office was quiet, not a lot of people in yet. But Helen was there. She was standing at the edge of her desk, wearing a leopard print miniskirt and a smart bolero jacket with gold fasteners. She was straightening her fishnet stockings, one leg at a time. I didn't see a single snag or run—amazing.

I knocked on the door to get her attention. "Can I speak with you?"

When she looked at me, I sensed right away that she knew something was up. For one thing, I didn't have her morning newspapers with me but I had brought her a fresh cup of coffee.

"Sounds serious," she said, switching legs, working the fishnets up her slender thigh. "I hope everything's all right."

I nodded, forgetting everything I'd planned to say.

"Alice?" She smoothed her hands down the front of her skirt and went over to her sofa. "Come talk to me."

Her kindness wasn't making this any easier. I went and sat beside her. "I want you to know how much I appreciate everything you've done for me." My mouth had gone dry and I could barely get the words out, like they were sticking in my throat. "You took a chance on me and I'll never forget that. This job has been a once-in-a-lifetime opportunity."

"But? There is a *but* coming, isn't there?" she said, setting her coffee aside.

I nodded, feeling a rush of pressure inside my head. "I've accepted a position working for Mr. Scavullo. I'm going to be his assistant."

Helen looked at me.

I was starting to shrink into an ungrateful heap of disappointment until I saw the corners of her painted lips rise.

"This is what you really want, isn't it? To be a photographer?"

I nodded again, my eyes misting up. "I know this is a horrible time to be leaving you. I feel like I'm abandoning you and I'm so sorry."

"You shouldn't be sorry. Of course I'll miss you, but you have to do what's best for you. That's just smart business. Besides, Frank's going to be shooting a lot of covers for me. We'll still be working together."

"I want you to know that I didn't go looking for this job. He came to me."

Her smile broadened. "Oh, pussycat, I know that. Who do you think told Frank he should hire you?"

EPILOGUE

○—○

2012

read the obituary again and notice the time. It's later than I
thought so I quickly throw on some jeans and a T-shirt before
making my way to the gallery. The exhibit doesn't open until
later that night, so I'll still have time to come back home, shower
and get ready. But for now, there are some last-minute details to
iron out.

It's about a thirty-minute walk from our home on Sullivan and
Third. I probably should have taken a cab or the subway, but I
need the fresh air to clear my head. I pass by Washington Square
Park, crowded with people stretched out on the grass, others sitting on the benches, reading, feeding the pigeons. There are
skateboarders and kids playing Frisbee. Someone's dog is splash-
ing about in the fountain. A mild breeze ruffles my hair and offers
a moment's relief from the sun and heat.

With each step, I feel myself trying to comprehend that Helen
Gurley Brown is gone. It's a loss that runs deep because I owe so
much to her. If it weren't for Helen, I never would have worked
with Frank Scavullo, which I did for ten years. While I was with
him, we shot dozens upon dozens of *Cosmo* covers, so when I

went out on my own, it made sense to start off shooting fashion. I mostly worked for other magazines like *Mademoiselle* and *Glamour*. But I grew restless and started leaning more toward portraits—mostly of celebrities and musicians. I shot some *Rolling Stone* covers and album covers, too. But I found the famous, especially rock stars, exhausting, depending on how drunk and high they were. So after a few years, I abandoned studio work altogether and focused exclusively on street photography. Along the way, I hired plenty of assistants, and I'd like to think that I did for them what Helen and Frank had done for me. Given them a jumping-off point, a place to start.

When I get to the gallery on 24th Street, a whoosh of cold air blasts me, and it's only then that I realize just how hot it is outside. The owner, a handsome young man with a goatee, meets me in the center of a stark white room and kisses me on either cheek. He's very Italian and reminds me of Scavullo. He tells me he's expecting a good turnout and that we have seventy-five RSVPs for the private reception beforehand.

Together, the owner and I walk through the gallery, stopping before each photo to scrutinize the lighting, the framing, the order. We confirm details on the pricing and the editioning for the prints, and at one point he excuses himself to take a call while I go back to scrutinizing the photographs. He's carefully curated a large body of work, and I'm pleased to see that he's included *Bow Bridge in Bloom* and my personal favorite, my rain-soaked jacket hanging off the coat tree in *After the Party*.

This is not my first solo exhibit, but it is a show exclusively about my first works: *Alice Weiss, Portrait of a City 1965–1975*. I hear footsteps behind me and I turn. Even now, after children and grandchildren and so many years in between, my heart still catches at those dark eyes—which now have creases in the corners.

"I just heard about Helen," Christopher says, placing his hands on my shoulders. "You okay?"

I nod and lean my cheek against the back of his hand.

Christopher and I have been together almost forty-five years now, so as you can see, things didn't end with us that day I kissed him in his doorway. Hardly. He was still under Daphne's spell, and thanks to his mother's abandoning him, he remained there for some time, taking Daphne back, watching her walk away and still taking her back again. All his life, until me, Christopher had been drawn to women who would leave him. He felt that somehow he deserved that. After all, if his own mother could leave him behind, he must surely have been unlovable. When we did finally get together, he soaked in my love and affection, terrified that I'd take it away like the others. I may have been afraid to love, but Christopher was afraid of *being* loved. Such an obvious explanation but it took us months to work our way through it.

Helen was the one who encouraged me not to give up on him. She coached me along the way, giving me advice—some of which, as you can imagine, I chose not to follow—and Kleenex when I couldn't take it anymore. I did walk away from him at one point. Real love, I thought, shouldn't be that hard. Thankfully, it was Christopher who decided he couldn't let me go. He fought, mostly with himself, to get me back. From then on, we were both in, all the way. Three months later, we were married in Stamford, in my grandparents' backyard.

"I see I made the cut." Christopher points to the photograph of him, taken that day on Coney Island.

I crane my neck and smile at him.

"I'm sorry about Helen," he says, a strand of salt-and-pepper hair hanging down in his eyes. "It's the end of an era, isn't it?"

H ours later, following a lovely reception with toasts and flowers and posing for the press, the gallery fills with another wave of people as tuxedoed waiters circulate with trays of champagne, wine and hors d'oeuvres. I've been surrounded by the critics: Jonathan Jones from the *Guardian*, Eleanor Heartney from the *Times* and Lucy Lippard from the *Village Voice*. I'm not good at being the center of attention. I've always been more comfortable behind the scenes, hiding out behind my camera.

I feel a respite when I look across the gallery and my eyes land on the familiar faces of my children. To see my daughter and son, now grown with children of their own, reminds me of the times I bundled them up, camera bag and diaper bag in tow, and brought them with me on my shoots. Even as toddlers and young kids, they came along when I was shooting. And as a family, no matter where the four of us went, Christopher and I always had a camera or two hanging off our shoulders while we held their tiny hands. I can't tell you how many close calls we had when a camera case or telephoto lens almost clunked one of them on the head. And like my mother did for me, I have kept meticulous photo albums for my children and have started new ones for the next generation.

I glance about the room and see Elaine, who has returned from the Hamptons in time to be here. She and Christopher are off to the side, talking with Trudy and Milt, who flew in from St. Louis just for my show. They smile at me, raising their glasses, a toast in my honor.

I mentally take a step back from it all and observe the gallery walls. I see how some of the photos, especially the earliest ones from that summer of 1965, captured that pivotal time for me in New York. So new to the city, I remember wanting to photograph everything in sight. It was during my first few months that I really began to sharpen my eye and appreciate the extraordinary findings in life's everyday moments. In many ways, I was like a photograph myself, coming into focus, developing not just my art, but my life.

Across the room I see my husband and the family he gave me, but up on the walls, I see the career I gave myself. I get up every morning and do the work I love. That's a privilege and one I've never taken for granted. And if she were here now, I know exactly what Helen would say: "Oh, pussycat, you did it. You found your love, your happy pill."

I think about the women closest to me—Trudy and Elaine, here with me tonight, and my mother and, of course, Helen, with me now in a different sense. They have been my four corners, keeping me grounded and serving as my frame so I could grow and shine. And now this girl from Youngstown, Ohio, has her heart and soul on display in this fashionable Chelsea gallery, and those women in my life are the ones who truly understand what it took to get me here.

AUTHOR'S NOTE AND ACKNOWLEDGMENTS

Though Alice Weiss is a fictional character, I used her to tell the real story of Helen Gurley Brown's early and transformative days as editor in chief of *Cosmopolitan* magazine. Helen really didn't have any previous magazine or editorial experience, and several editors and staff members did quit almost immediately. She was also met with great resistance from the Hearst executives, who were conservative gatekeepers trying to tone down her message to single women. Despite this, Helen went on to establish a track record of selling over a million copies each month. Under Helen's reign, the magazine's advertising revenue more than quadrupled and helped to make Hearst what it was and still is today. Helen Gurley Brown changed the face of women's magazines and spawned countless imitators, all trying to capture that *Cosmo* magic.

But in 1997, after Helen had been editor in chief for thirty-two years, Hearst had to face the fact that Helen's message was no longer connecting with her young readers. In the 1980s, her claim that her girls were immune to AIDS because it was a homosexual disease was as out of touch as her statements a decade later that women in the workplace should be flattered by sexual attention and advances from their male colleagues. Finally, Hearst forced Helen into retirement at the age of seventy-four. As a consolation prize, they gave her the editorship of the international editions, but she knew her ride with *Cosmopolitan* was, for all intents and purposes, over.

A word about David Brown, who really was her greatest fan and biggest supporter: Not only was he very instrumental in her landing the job with Hearst, but, prior to marrying Helen, David had also been an editor at *Cosmopolitan* and knew the business inside and out. He wrote many of the cover blurbs for Helen and was always at her disposal. She did have a direct line put in that went from her office to his, and the two of them often worked on the magazine during long cab rides that they called "nooners." But what David Brown was best known for, aside from being Mr. Helen Gurley Brown, was his success as a movie producer, having brought such classics to the screen as *The Sting*, *Jaws*, *Cocoon*, *Driving Miss Daisy*, *A Few Good Men*, *Chocolat* and many others, including, of course, Helen's *Sex and the Single Girl*.

Because *Park Avenue Summer* is a work of historical *fiction*, I want to share a few places where I took some creative license for the sake of the narrative and purposes of storytelling. While it's true that Hearst had intended to fold *Cosmopolitan* and did try to rein in Helen by killing story ideas and protesting her cover line about *The New Pill That Promises to Make Women More Responsive to Men*, some scenes and incidents were embellished. Richard Berlin, Richard Deems and Frank Dupuy were Hearst executives, but Erik Masterson is purely fictional. The initial friction between Helen and the Hearst management has been well-documented; however, in the interest of plotting, I magnified the conflict, especially when it came to her relationships with Richard Berlin and Dick Deems. My research indicated that their interactions were not as contentious as I've portrayed here. It should also be noted that over time, they all became Helen's champions and supported her wholeheartedly.

Helen's famous bosom memo was indeed leaked to *Women's Wear Daily*, and she did warn her staff that there was a viper in the nest, but this incident occurred later in her career, in 1969 rather than 1965. I also have a scene where Hearst slashes her budget, which was my own plot device. However, it should be noted that from the start, Helen was given an impossibly tight operating budget of only $30,000 per issue. (A sum that hadn't been increased since the early 1940s.)

There's definitely some urban myth regarding the Jax photo shoot, which produced the provocative cover shot for the July issue. No one knows for sure who, if anyone, actually turned Renata's shirt around to expose her breasts, but regardless, no one had ever featured such a thing in a woman's magazine, let alone on the cover. While Francesco Scavullo did not shoot the famous Renata cover, he did go on to shoot *Cosmo*'s covers for three decades.

Bernard Geis Associates was the actual publisher of both *Sex and the Single Girl* and Jacqueline Susann's *Valley of the Dolls*, but Elaine Sloan is a fictional character. And yes, there really was a fire pole at the publishing house that Geis employees used to go from one floor to the next.

Helen Gurley Brown was a fascinating woman. A true trailblazer. She was famously frugal, did ride the bus and, according to Lois Cahall, always managed to run her stockings and fishnets.

If you would like to read more about her, I highly recommend the following books: *Not Pretty Enough: The Unlikely Triumph of Helen Gurley Brown* by Gerri Hirshey, *Enter Helen: The Invention of Helen Gurley Brown and the Rise of the Modern Single Woman* by Brooke Hauser, and *Bad Girls Go Everywhere: The Life of Helen Gurley Brown, the Woman Behind "Cosmopolitan" Magazine* by Jennifer Scanlon. And, of course, there's no better way to get to know Helen Gurley Brown than through her own words in *Sex and the Single Girl*, published in 1962.

This book was great fun to write, but it never would have come together without the help and generous support of many people, starting with Andy Gross, who introduced me to Lois Cahall, the woman who probably knew Helen Gurley Brown better than anyone else. My sincere thanks to Lois for vetting the manuscript and helping me paint a more accurate portrait of this iconic editor.

Also, much gratitude to Kevan Lyon, my wise and wonderful agent, who continues to take excellent care of me and my career. To Amanda Bergeron, my editor, who has amazing instincts and the patience of a saint. This was our first book together and it was a joy from beginning to end. My thanks also to the entire Berkley team at Penguin Random House, especially Claire Zion, Craig Burke, Jeanne-Marie Hudson, Fareeda Bullert, Jennifer Monroe, Danielle Keir, Roxanne Jones, Elisha Katz, Ryanne Probst, Emma Reh, Yuki Hirose and all the people behind the scenes, including Stefan Moorehead and, of course, my dear friend Brian Wilson.

I offer special thanks to Taryn Fagerness for her incredible work with foreign rights. Also to Andrea Peskind Katz, Lauren Blank Margolin, Stephanie Nelson and Colleen Oakley, who gave my manuscript early reads and provided invaluable feedback and much-needed encouragement.

Thanks as well to my trusted writing buddies, friends and colleagues: Karen Abbott, Tasha Alexander, Robin Allen, Julie Anderson, Stacey Ballis, Scott Goodwillie, Andrew Grant, Maxwell Gregory, Sara Gruen, Stephanie Hochschild, Julia Claiborne Johnson, Brenda Klem, Pamela Klinger-Horn, Lisa Kotin, Elizabeth Letts, Mindy Mailman, Kelly O'Connor McNees, Jill Niehaus Miner, Amy Sue Nathan, Marianne Nee, Mary Webber O'Malley, Javier Ramirez and Suzy Takacs.

And lastly, my gratitude and love to my amazing family: Debbie Rosen, Pam Rosen, Jerry Rosen, Andrea Rosen, Joey Perilman, Devon Rosen and, of course, my one and only, John Dul. At the end of the day it all comes down to you!

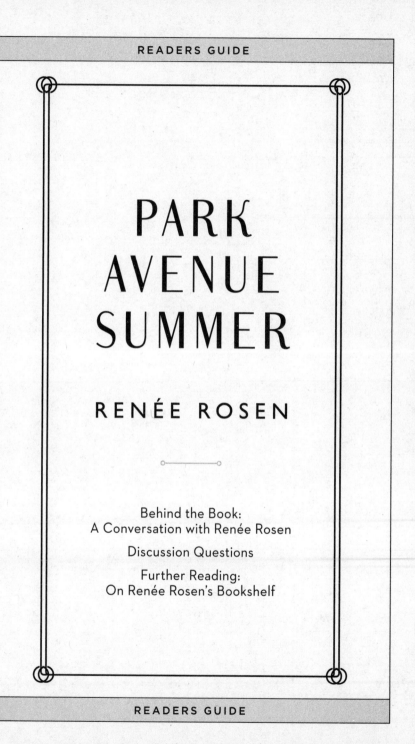

PARK AVENUE SUMMER

RENÉE ROSEN

Behind the Book:
A Conversation with Renée Rosen

Discussion Questions

Further Reading:
On Renée Rosen's Bookshelf

BEHIND THE BOOK:
A CONVERSATION WITH RENÉE ROSEN

Where did the inspiration for *Park Avenue Summer* come from?

I had been binge-watching *Mad Men* and just fell in love with New York during that time period. I knew I wanted to set a book in Manhattan in the '60s, but despite my background in advertising (prior to writing fiction), I didn't want to tread on *Mad Men*'s territory so I started thinking of other so-called "glamorous" businesses and the world of magazines came to mind.

Originally, I was thinking of creating a fictional magazine where a group of marginalized secretaries would take over a failing publication. That was the germ of the idea—but while talking with my editor, Amanda Bergeron, it dawned on us both that a great real-life story was just sitting there. We agreed to take the plunge and that the novel should be about Helen Gurley Brown and *Cosmopolitan*. I remember we were both so excited because we just knew we had hit on the right subject for this book.

You tell the story from the fictional Alice Weiss's point of view. Why did you decide to do that, rather than writing from Helen's point of view?

I actually wrestled with that decision in the very beginning, but it soon became apparent that because so much has already been written about Helen Gurley Brown, not to mention her own memoirs, to simply retell her story from her point of view would bring nothing new to readers. By writing from Alice's point of view, it allowed us to explore some new angles and show the impact that Helen Gurley Brown had on single girls. Or at least on one single girl.

How do you approach the research in your books?

Each book has come together in a way that's been totally different from the previous book(s). I never know exactly how I'll find the heart of the story, which makes the process both maddening and thrilling. Sometimes it comes out of the research, and other times it comes from the writing, in which case, then I go back and fill in the blanks with the research.

For *Park Avenue Summer*, I did a good deal of reading about Helen Gurley Brown before I started writing and talked to people who either knew Helen Gurley Brown and/or were magazine editors. I felt that I needed to have a solid understanding of the culture, the magazine industry and, most importantly, Helen Gurley Brown's journey before I could begin putting pen to paper or fingers to keyboard, as the case would be. But having said that, I continued researching, spent time in New York (as you'll see below) and added more factual details while I was drafting and polishing the manuscript.

Your previous books were set in Chicago. What was it like writing about New York, and how were you able to capture life in New York City so vividly?

After four novels set in Chicago we felt it was time to expand my backdrop, which was a great challenge for me. I did live in New York for a brief period of time, but that was long ago and despite my visits to Manhattan since then, this book required a special research trip. I needed to *observe* the city from a different perspective. It's so easy to get swept up in the energy there that you can miss all the wonderful details that are uniquely New York. I felt a little like Ali, taking hundreds of pictures of quirky things—like garbage on the curb, steam rising up from the manholes, etc.—all little details that later found their way into the book.

I also thought it was important to go to the places that Helen Gurley Brown frequented including the Russian Tea Room, the 21 Club, the Plaza and the St. Regis. It was great fun. I also paid a visit to Helen Gurley Brown's apartment building when she lived on Park Avenue.

That was Helen's world but I also needed to get a feel for the fictional Alice's world. I figured out exactly where Alice would have lived on the Upper East Side and looked at an actual apartment, which served as a reference for her efficiency in the book. I also followed the route she would have taken from her place to the *Cosmopolitan* offices on West 57th Street. I even had breakfast at the Lexington Candy Shop where Alice and Trudy always went.

Was there anything particularly exciting or unexpected that happened while you were doing the research for *Park Avenue Summer*?

I remember I was having brunch one day with Andrew Gross, who just so happened to be in Chicago. He asked what my new book was about, and as soon as I said Helen Gurley Brown, he said, "I have to put you in touch with Lois Cahall. Helen was like a second mother to her." Well, this was like hitting the research jackpot!

Lois could not have been more supportive of this book. She probably knew Helen Gurley Brown better than anyone and shared many stories, some personal photographs and even vetted the manuscript for us to make sure we had authentically captured Helen Gurley Brown. I had the opportunity to meet Lois while I was down in Palm Beach so I could thank her in person.

What's your writing process like? Do you write every day? Are you an outliner?

I do tend to write every day, but the amount of time I spend actually putting words down versus reading and researching depends on which phase of the process I'm in. Drafting a new novel is always slow going for me. I don't outline and don't know where the story is headed (beyond a few historical landmarks) or what the characters will do from scene to scene. If I can write for four hours at a stretch while I'm drafting, I consider it a good day. Once I have a working draft with a beginning, middle and end, then I go back to page one and I'll write for eight or nine hours a day. That's pretty much the pace I work at from that point on. It takes many, many rounds of revisions for me to get a manuscript to where I think it needs to be. And then, there's still much work to be done when I enter the editing phase.

When did you know you wanted to be a writer?

I knew I wanted to be a writer from the time I was a little girl. I have no idea where this notion came from, as I didn't come from a family of writers, but I have vivid memories of playing on my grandfather's typewriter (which I still have). I had notebooks of poems and short stories and plays that I wrote as a little girl. When I was in high school, I wrote a horrible first novel, which thankfully will never see the light of day. Ironically, I was a writer before I was a reader, which is not something I'd recommend! I didn't discover my love of reading until I was in my early twenties so I'm still playing catch-up ball in that department.

DISCUSSION QUESTIONS

1. Do you think Helen Gurley Brown was a feminist? How do you think her brand of feminism compared to Betty Friedan's or Gloria Steinem's?

2. What did you think of Helen's advice to Alice regarding her Don Juan? Do you agree that Don Juans are unavoidable and that every woman has that one man she can't say "no" to?

3. Speaking of Alice's Don Juan, did you understand why she got involved with Erik? Were you sympathetic to her situation or did you want her to break it off with him sooner? Or not enter into it at all?

4. Under Helen Gurley Brown's leadership, *Cosmopolitan* became a groundbreaking magazine for women and inspired many copycat publications. Were you a *Cosmo* reader? And if so, what do you remember most about that magazine? What other magazines did you read growing up?

5. Can you define today's *Cosmo* Girl? How has she evolved through the years?

6. When it comes to iconic female magazine editors, the two biggest names are probably Helen Gurley Brown and Anna Wintour. How do you think these two women are similar? How are they different?

7. In the book, Alice looks to both Helen Gurley Brown and Elaine Sloan as role models and mentors. How important do you think it was for a young woman back then to have that kind of guidance? And do you think it's still important in today's world?

8. In today's digital age we've seen the decline of physical magazines. How do you feel about publications moving from newsstands to the Internet? Do you miss reading them physically?

9. If you'd been put in Ali's position, would you have told Helen that members of the Hearst staff were sabotaging her? How do you think you would have handled that sort of predicament?

10. What prominent themes can you find in *Park Avenue Summer*? Do you think any of them are still relevant in today's world?

11. Alice, like so many people throughout history, moved to New York City to pursue her dream. Certainly, there are easier and more affordable places to live and yet Manhattan's draw proves irresistible to some. Why do you think that is?

12. How did you feel about the ending of the book and were you surprised to learn where Ali ended up?

FURTHER READING:
ON RENÉE ROSEN'S BOOKSHELF

GREAT HISTORICAL FICTION

The Alice Network by Kate Quinn
Next Year in Havana by Chanel Cleeton
A Gentleman in Moscow by Amor Towles
Manhattan Beach by Jennifer Egan
In Need of a Good Wife by Kelly O'Connor McNees
The One Man by Andrew Gross
American Princess by Stephanie Marie Thornton

MY ALL-TIME FAVORITES

It's rare that I'll reread a book. However, certain books, like the ones below, are just so special that I've gone back and reread them at least three times. Or more.

The Secret History by Donna Tartt
The Last to Go by Rand Richards Cooper
Anywhere but Here by Mona Simpson
A Home at the End of the World by Michael Cunningham
Monkeys by Susan Minot
Rules of Civility by Amor Towles

Photo by Charles Osgood Photography

Renée Rosen is the author of *Windy City Blues, White Collar Girl, What the Lady Wants* and *Dollface*, as well as the young adult novel *Every Crooked Pot*.

Ready to find
your next great read?

Let us help.

Visit prh.com/nextread

Penguin
Random
House